All Worth Their Salt:
The People of NWI
Volume III

Jeff Manes

Copyright (etc)

Copyright © 2016 by Jeff Manes
All rights reserved. No part of this publication may be reproduced, distributed, or transmitted in any form or by any means, including photocopying, recording, or other electronic or mechanical methods, without the prior written permission of the publisher, except in the case of brief quotations embodied in critical reviews and certain other noncommercial uses permitted by copyright law. For permission requests, write to the publisher, at the address below.

Publisher; Jeff Manes 219-775-3083
6742 Ramsey Road
Hebron, IN 46341

Quantity sales. Special discounts are available on quantity purchases by corporations, associations, and others. For details, contact the publisher at the address above.
Orders by U.S. trade bookstores and wholesalers. Please contact

Publisher; Jeff Manes 219-775-3083
6742 Ramsey Road
Hebron, IN 46341

Printed in the United States of America

Manes, Jeffrey, 1957-.
All worth their salt: The people of Northwest Indiana / Jeff Manes.
p. cm.
ISBN 978-0-9970047-2-4

1. Northwest Indiana – Interviews – 21st Century. 2. Indiana – Calumet Region – Interviews – 21st Century. 3. I. Title.
977.29 –dc22

Cover designed by Conservation Mike Echterling

First Edition

"I make a point to read all of Jeff Manes' interviews. Not only does he find that story that everyone has to tell, he makes his readers wish they knew them, too."

- Jim Sweeney, Izaak Walton League of America, Friends of the Kankakee

"With his Salt columns, Manes captures and documents aspects of individuals that historians rarely find in the usual resources for genealogy research. All volumes of "All Worth Their Salt: The People of NWI" provide a valuable tool for our area. These books are an asset to anyone's personal library."

- Beth Bassett, Newton County Historical Society

"With his blue-collar perspective, no-nonsense sensibility and Region wit, Jeff Manes is a consummate interviewer. Curious, persistent, and a good listener with an ear for the catchy phrase or telling insight, he turns his interactions into a shared experience among equals. What he achieves, without pomposity or artifice, is contemporary social history of the highest order – or, to quote scholar Jesse Lemisch, 'history from the bottom up.'"

- James B. Lane, professor emeritus Indiana University Northwest

"I expect Vol. III of "All Worth Their Salt: The People of NWI," to be as interesting and heartwarming as the first two volumes. Manes touches the heart of those who read his work."

- Eleanor Bailey, genealogist, historian

"I knew the first time I heard Jeff Manes read his stories that he had a unique gift, a way of transporting his audience to the heart of a story. Stories that are sometimes raw, but always truthful and passionate. He paints our most basic emotions: happiness, sadness, fear, anger and love, like an artist with a brush."

- Patty Wisniewski, executive producer of the documentary films "Everglades of the North: The Story of the Grand Kankakee Marsh" and "Shifting Sands: The Path to Sustainability"

Contents

Introduction

Chapter I: Salt of the Earth
    Rev. William Collins   2
    Jane Schreiner   5
    Mary McGee   9
    Kristy Folmer   13
    Rabbi Michael Stevens   17
    Paula DeBois   21
    Dave Gard   25
    Harold Moreland   28
    John Taylor   32
    Rosa Gamez   35
    Marcia Carlson   38
    Victor Del Toro   42
    Willie Jackson   46
    Fred Gorniak   50
    Jessica Nunemaker   53
    Kimberly Joy Harris   57
    Don & Gail Mills   60

Chapter II: Work
    Ed Sadlowski   64
    Bill Rucker   68
    R.J. Howard   72
    Butch Grimmer   76
    Dan Murchek   80
    Andrea Georgian   84
    Fred Utroske   88
    Sharon Patterson   92
    Steve Cotton   97
    Nick Petrov   101

David Wilson	105
Sharon Speichert	109
Tom Hargrove	113

Chapter III: Melting Pot
Dr. Biljan Uzelac	117
Rasi Sanuchit Smart	120
Emonn Frampton	123
Yolanta Flowers	127
Gloria Tuohy	132
Father Joseph Ivans	136

Chapter IV: History Books
Edith Sautter	140
Barney Wornhoff	144
Cullen Ben-Daniel	147
Jim Kersting	151
Dolly Millander	155
Fuzz Campbell	159
Floyd Johnson	163
Lydia Grady	166
Terry Stoner	170
Judy Kanne	173
Ed Camblin	177
Merritt Coffin	180
Dante D'Apice	183
Nick Thiery	186

Chapter V: Charaters
Chuck Hegan	190
Roby Joe	194
John Schutz	197
Tom Johnson	201
Aubrey Fullerton	205

Ralph Knapp	209
Mike Dalkilic	213
Ron Kittle	217
Neal Haskell	221
Mayre Williams	225
Brenda L. Cole	229
Pete Lange	233

Chapter VI: Caregivers & Do-Gooders

Tevin Gardner	237
Sister Brigid	241
Nell Foster	244
Larry Klein	248
Jonathan Wilson	251
Mary Joan Dickson	255
Daisy Tidwell	259
Christy Fisher	263

Chapter VII: The Arts

Ish Muhammed	267
Eric Lambert	271
Wiley Dummich	276
Trilly Cole	280
Corey Hagelburg	284
Mike Poore	288
Charlie Capek	292
Rosemary Gard	296
Dave Mueller	300

Chapter VIII: The Good Earth

Terry McCloskey	304
John Bryant	308
Mary Catterlin & Amy Lukas	311
Sandy O'Brien	315

Bud Koeppen	319
Joy Bower	322
Ed Gustafson	326
Marty Lucas	330
Jack Weinberg	334
Gina Darnell	338
Lloyd & Regina Bohl	341
Bonnie Swarner	345
George Smolka	348
Maggie Byrne	352
Thomas Frank	355
Rod Smart	359

Chapter IX: Kindred Spirits

Karen & Kelly	364
Nick Parente	368
Nanci Mazzaro Sanders	372
Rick Grevenstuk	376
Bert Pease	380
Index	383

A Note to the Reader

It was January of 2005 when the first of these human interest columns was published. More than 1,000 have been written since. Some of the folks featured in this collection are now deceased. Some have changed occupations since being interviewed. Their stories and photographs will appear as they did when first published – without updates.

– JM

All Worth Their Salt:
The People of NWI
Volume III

Introduction

Salt. The human body contains about four ounces of it. Without enough salt we perish. It was for salt that Mahatma Gandhi marched.

Around 1900, certain social leaders in New York claimed there were only 400 people worth knowing. In disagreement, author O. Henry wrote a volume he called "The Four Million." He thought everybody was worth knowing.

In more recent times, Raymond Carver, dubbed the American Chekov, spoke of the laborers and service workers who formed his submerged population: "They're my people, I could never write down to them." Ray Carver grew up on a small river town of 700 souls.

I have had the advantage of growing up along the bayous of the Kankakee River and atop the carcinogenic coke batteries abutting Lake Michigan. I'd like you to get to know your neighbor, those living, sometimes eking out a living, just across the alley or down the road. Their names don't usually appear in the newspaper. The obits, maybe. But they are all worth their salt.

Everyone has a story to tell.

– Jeff Manes

Salt of the Earth

Rev. William Collins *(April 2011)*

"And lead us not into temptation, but deliver us from evil: For thine is the kingdom, and the power, and the glory, forever. Amen."
– Matthew 6:13

Mine is not a religious column, per se, but I thought Rev. William Collins was a good fit for Easter Sunday. He is the pastor at Mt. Zion Baptist Church in Hammond.

Collins, 64, lives in Lansing, Ill., with Rose, his wife of 20 years. They have raised one daughter.

Collins grew up in Winona, Miss. He spent four years in the Air Force, then moved to Chicago in 1970.

* * *

Growing up in the South during the 1950s and '60s?

"It was typical Mississippi, you know, back in the day," he said. "The social structure between African-Americans and whites was what it was. I went through all of that. There have been some changes, but we still have a long way to go."

Hobbies?

"Fishing."

Ever fish the Kankakee River?

"Yes, its backwaters and bayous right off Indiana 10."

Rev. Collins, I grew up on Indiana 10. LaSalle Fish & Wildlife headquarters literally abutted our back yard. The walleyes are done spawning, but the pike are heating up.

"I also like to fish Wampum Lake when I get the opportunity; it's over by Thornton and Lansing Road. There's a forest preserve there. It was known for its bass and catfish."

Do you use live bait?

"Yes, with a bobber. I don't do boats; I just fish from the bank."

Let's switch gears. Did you go to Moody Bible Institute on

Chicago's North Side?

"Yes, I did."

How long have you been pastor here at Mt. Zion?

"It will be 13 years this October."

How many members in your congregation?

"Almost 300. We've seen some growth since I've been here."

Tell me more about Mt. Zion Baptist Church.

"We are the oldest African-American church in Hammond. My predecessor, Dr. A.R. Burns, was here for more than 50 years. We've developed a ministry of trying to reach the younger generation. We have quite an attractive program where we mentor spiritually as well as academically – secular training. There are some young fellas who have really gravitated toward me."

Examples?

"There are two in particular, who I call my 'grandchildren.' They are coming along; they're from a single-parent home. The mother is working and doing a great job of taking care of them. As a pastor leader, I try to give them as much encouragement and inspiration as possible."

How old are the siblings?

"Around 9 or 10. They are so enthused about being here; they live right down the street. When they see my pickup, they come in here and just sit and talk with me. I've gotten to know them and their mother real well. She trusts us with them.

"The boys have shown some growth in their behavior. There were some behavioral problems with one of them. I sat him down and I talked to him about that."

Is their mother a member of Mt. Zion?

"Yes, and the boys are involved in our programs. They're part of the children's choir and are both ushers. They love to ride in my truck; they think that's the most exciting thing, that the pastor drives a pickup.

"There are times when I've done things for the family – not that they've asked me. I'm concerned for and love their family just like I do all the members of our church."

The sign outside the church reads Matthew 6:13

"That's our theme: 'The kingdom belongs to him.' Everything we do here is related to the kingdom of God. All the things we do in this ministry fall under that concept. What we do is not of us; it's all about Christ who is our savior, our redeemer.

"Jesus is the center of everything we do here, coming up to Resurrection Sunday. We start our service with Passion Week. We have three noon day services, Tuesday through Thursday, with reflection on the work of Christ in terms of what happened to him during that week as far as His earthly life."

Sunrise Service?

"We do have Sunrise Service, but it is part of a team of churches in the community. This year, we're all meeting at New Zion. Then, at our church, we'll have what we call our Resurrection Sunday program where we put on a dramatic play."

A mutual friend of ours told me you're a great mentor.

"I'm very aggressive with my young people. I really put a lot of energy in trying to develop programs and activities that will get them to want to come to our church.

"We teach them religious concepts, but also give them other programs that help balance their lives and foster some kind of idea of what life is in the world. We have a five-day camp service in the summer."

Vacation Bible school?

"We have that also. But our camp service is in addition to vacation Bible school. We take them on trips to recreation areas throughout Illinois and Indiana where they can interact with other children. It gives them a chance to see what the world is like outside of Hammond."

* * *

In my mind's eye, I can envision Rev. Collins taking a pair of brothers for a ride in his red chevy pickup to Black Oak Bayou just off Indiana 10 near the state line. And, in my reverie, I also can picture him teaching those young fellas how to thread a nightcrawler onto a hook and prop up a cane pole with a forked twig stuck into the bank.

I believe that's something Jesus would do.

Jane Schreiner *(March 2008)*

*"I want to live,
I want to give
I've been a miner for a heart of gold."*
-Neil Young

It was in the fall of 1966 when Jane came to Valparaiso University from Waco, Texas. For many, it was the eve of an era of unrest; some were merely feelin' groovy. Jane was a theology major with her sights on becoming a deaconess.

Jane eventually married Paul Schreiner in 1971. They have raised four children. Down through the years Jane has worked as a nurse's aide, a mail carrier, and taught calligraphy. Paul is the co-owner of a construction company. The first house he built, just outside of Valparaiso, is the one he and Jane continue to live in today.

The Schreiners owned and operated the coffee house-music store Front Porch Music – a pickers paradise at 505 East Lincolnway in downtown Valpo – from 1991 until they passed the baton to the Cliffords in May of 2007. Jane remains involved. Her comforting matriarchal self still can be found behind the counter of Front Porch's basement, making coffee on open-mic and concert nights. It is in said basement where we chat on a Wednesday morning. She's drinking 100% natural Celestial Seasonings Antioxidant Green Tea made by old hippies in Boulder, Colorado.

Black coffee for me.

* * *

Talk to me deaconess.

"The reason I wanted to be a Lutheran deaconess was because I didn't have to limit myself to one thing," Jane began. "I could use my musical gifts, my artistic gifts; I could work with youth, the women of the congregation, and make calls to the sick.

"There was such a variety. That's what really attracted me. And the idea of studying theology was very appealing to me.

"I came here as a junior. The way the program worked is you did your three years of college, then you did your internship. After the internship you complete your senior year. Then you become consecrated. It's like your official seal of approval.

You are still involved with the deaconess program.

"Yes, I'm a part of the Lutheran Deaconess Association which is headquartered here in Valpo. I have had the privilege of mentoring deaconess students for the past six years. I'm not their mother, I'm not their teacher, I'm not their boss. They come to me when they want to talk. We'll have lunch or breakfast together."

Very good. Now, let's talk about this building. Probably been around awhile.

"We had a man visit us who was in his 80s; he was the grandson of the man who built this place. Front Porch also was a frat house with four apartments."

Running the show in the basement. Cool job.

"If I had the wherewithal, I could write a book. There are so many stories."

You are kind of, well, omnipresent – like Mother Nature. You are a fixture down here. You are a fly on the wall.

"Nobody knows how much I know or don't know."

But you're always willing to lend an ear to those moody artistic types touched by fire when they are ready to bare their tortured souls to you.

"I hear things that nobody else hears. Some of them call me 'Mom.' The furnace room behind the coffee bar has been known as Jane's Bonding Room.' I don't pretend to be a psychiatrist. I'll converse with people, but I don't lecture.

"I've found that the most valuable part of growing older is that little chinks of your own pride get knocked off and you pick up a lot of wisdom from other people and their experiences."

Any world-renown headliners ever make it to "The Porch"?

"Donovan Leitch played here."

They call me mellow yellow Donovan?

"Yes, he came all the way from the British Isles to attend his sister's wedding in LaPorte. We got a phone call real late one night. I thought somebody was pranking us...

"'Do you want to have Don here?'"

"I'm, like, 'Don who?'"

"'Donovan.'"

"'Oh sure, Donovan is going to play here.'"

"Come to find out he wanted a gig in a small room to help pay for expenses."

How many people can you fit in here?

"Seventy-two; we were booked immediately. People were begging us. We asked Donovan if he would consider doing a second concert. He actually ended up doing three concerts in two days."

Jane, I've always got my money's worth when attending a concert here. Whether it was Heartsfield, Eric Lambert, Tom Rosnowski – what a lyricist that guy is! Always wanted to take in that bluesman Catfish Keith who performs here every year. Does the Front Porch contact the artist?

"No, they set up their tours and usually call us. We've always been very generous. The musician gets 70% of the gate and the house takes 30%. As far as the local artists, it takes a little bit of hustle to try to fill the house -- not only by the Front Porch, but by the performer as well.

"It's not easy to get people in the door, charge a cover of $8 to $15, and audience members can't order an alcoholic drink. At a bar, they usually don't have a cover charge."

First concert?

"Harvey Reid was our first official concert, but we did have a 'bring-a-chair concert' where audience members got in free if they donated a chair. Some of those chairs are still there. The Purple Cowboys played for free that day. Our concerts usually consist of two 45-minute sets with a little break in between."

Open-mic night?

"The talent has steadily gotten better. It is rare when I'm tapping my foot waiting for someone to get their three pieces done. I do have 'taste buds;' there are some types music I like more than others. Hey, if somebody is brave enough to get up on the stage... No two open stage evenings are alike. People like you pass through and then we don't see them for a while. Then they come back."

You were always a gracious hostess. Let's face it, as a poet or story teller, I was kind of outnumbered by musicians and singers – but they were kind, too. As were the Front Porch audiences.

Jane, I remember one night – wish I had it on tape – there was a woman singing ancient Celtic tunes and playing instruments I'd never seen or heard before. There was a banjo player. There was a young genius who played the piano like Liberace. There was rock, country western, blues, bluegrass, folk, calypso...

Eclectic has been an overused term it seems, but that night was the epitome of "eclecticity." And, that, is a term not overused – because it's not a word.

"Jeff, I think of what I would have missed if it wasn't for this place. We don't go out much. I've always maintained that I am the most well-entertained woman in Northwest Indiana. That's what I want on my tombstone."

* * *

The Schreiners also operate a volunteer radio station, WVLP-LP 98.3 FM. The station is situated a few blocks from the Front Porch. The 100 watt tower is situated atop the Front Porch. For more information go to their website at WVLP.org.

Jane Schreiner: Hostess with a heart of gold.

Mary McGee *(March 2009)*

*"...Freedom's just another word
for nothin' left to lose..."*
-Kris Kristofferson

It's been a quarter-century since me and Bobby Winkel, Jay Chapman and six or eight other mill buddies of mine stood shouting within the Hammond Civic Center while pugilists Mike Landini of Calumet City (Ill.), and Hammond's Carlos Tite duked it out.

More than 5,000 fight fans filled the historic Civic Center that night; hundreds were turned away. Winkel hailed from Hegewisch (Ill.); he was rooting for Landini. Chapman lived in Highland and was a personal friend of Tite.

The Italian boy from Illinois got the nod; it was a split decision. The referee and judge who scored the fight in favor of Landini witnessed both Hoosier hysteria and hospitality as they needed a police escort when leaving the building.

Gary's Merciless Mary McGee doesn't remember any of that. She wasn't born yet. But when McGee, 22, goes toe to toe with Hanover Central grad Kristy Rose Follmar on April 25, the Civic Center will be rocking like it did in '85.

McGee and Follmar are two of the best boxers in the world who just happened to grow up about a half-hour's drive from each other.

Before they ever boxed, both of them suffered a few knockdowns. Sometimes you have to take life one kidney punch at a time. McGee and Follmar always seem to get back up.

* * *

"My grandma raised me since I was 2 weeks old," McGee began. "But I had to move from my grandmother's house because of boxing."

She didn't approve of her granddaughter boxing?

"I couldn't expect her to give up her beliefs; she's a Jehovah's Witness. I love my grandma. It was her house and her rules; she didn't want me to box. I love her because she put aside part of her life to take care of me. I could have been adopted or worse. I respect her for that."

How old were you when you began boxing?

"Fourteen."

Grandma didn't mind that you were a cheerleader at Gary Roosevelt High School.

"I tried out for the cheerleading squad my freshman year; I did maybe two or three games. I realized it weren't really for me."

You continued to box against grandmother's wishes.

"Yeah, for a year or so, I was sneaking around to go to the gym. When I became old enough to live on my own, that's what I did. I slept in my car for two months. I didn't want to look at the TV one day and see some girl boxing, and say, 'I wonder if that could have been me?'"

Your mother?

"I see her every so often. Basically, it was me and Grandma and my brothers; my mother would be in and out."

Do you see your dad?

"Not normally. I've talked to him sometimes."

Did you graduate from Roosevelt?

"No; but I made good grades while I was in school. I remember when they had us make a science project; I always wanted to do everything better than everybody else. I went and bought molding clay. I molded me a human cell. I cut out part of it and painted all the little particles that are in a cell. The teacher said, 'I've never seen anything like this.' That was nice."

Street fights?

"Yeah, I was the type of person who didn't talk too much. But if somebody said something to me that I thought I had to handle by fighting them, to shut them up, I would. When I started boxing my temper settled down a whole lot.

Does being a professional boxer pay all the bills?

"I also work for a home health care agency. I help old folks cook, clean, wash clothes, get dressed – stuff like that."

At what age did you turn pro?

"By the time I was 18. When I was first introduced to One in a

Million Inc., I was very immature, but Octavius (James) helped me mature into the sport before putting me into a professional fight. Today, I'm more ready then I've ever been. At, 22, I'm in my prime."

You're engaged.

"Yes, my fiance, Don Moore, was a boxer."

The sport of boxing is controversial in itself – you either love it or are appalled by it. It seems women's boxing might add fuel to that fire. Have you had guys tell you that you shouldn't be in the ring, that it's a man's sport?

"I haven't had any run-ins with men who were totally against women boxing, but in the beginning it was a problem getting men to teach me how to box; they didn't believe I really wanted to fight for the simple fact that I was a girl.

"I used to have to imitate other people. I'd watch tapes just to teach myself. Trainers didn't pay as much attention to me as they did the guys. But, as I progressed, then people started working with me. Nine years later, women's boxing has become a bigger thing. Women sometimes put on a better fight then the men do."

Mary, three times I've been at ringside while you plied your trade – dancing, ducking, bobbing, weaving, jabbing... When you fought Rita Figueroa, I didn't see two women boxers, I just saw two gifted athletes.

But sometimes reality smacks me in the kisser. Like when you took on that fighter from Milwaukee. I noticed something fly across the deck after you landed a solid body punch – it was one of her breast (protector) cups.

And then, in between rounds, because you had pummeled her so, I watched that woman, who I believe was announced as the grandmother of three, hang her head and literally sob from the pain.

"I basically think about painting a picture when I fight. It's all an art in boxing. It's combinations and foot movement, you know what I mean? Everything has to come together when you're in the ring boxing."

Do you think of things from your childhood that might enrage you, to help put yourself in a violent frame of mind?

"I've learned when a person gets mad, they get sloppy sometimes; they tend to get hit. You don't want to get angry; you want to do your job."

Do you consider yourself more of a body puncher or head hunter?

"I'm an all-around fighter. I determine what I'm going to do when

I'm in the ring, whether it's body punches, boxing, all-out fighting – I can do all of that."

Figueroa was tough, a head clash resulted in a no-decision. Still, Follmar will probably be the most formidable foe you've ever faced.

"You ever seen a pit bull fight? This is going to be a legal one. It's gonna be another Floyd Mayweather vs. Ricky Hatton – and I'm Floyd. Ricky was no chump, but he lost to Pretty Boy Floyd.

"Kristy has 16 wins; I have 16 wins. She got nine knockouts; I got 10. She 5-foot-8; I'm 5-foot-7. She 28 years old; I'm 22. I got more to lose."

How do you figure?

"She been beat. I got my 0."

In Follmar's eyes, she's never been beaten. I've read unbiased accounts stating that she was robbed in Mississippi the night she suffered her only defeat.

"I want to keep my belt. I want the WBC, too. She took time off and decided to come back. I been goin' at it ever since I started.

"I been waiting a long time for this. I wasn't playing that day when I walked into the gym wearing my cheerleading skirt, and said, 'I want to box.'"

* * *

The young girl who went the extra mile to mold a human cell from clay told me she wants to show everyone she is a great boxer.

Mary McGee definitely has drive and desire.

She also has her 0.

Kristy Follmar *(April 2009)*

"...Queen Mary, she's my friend
Yes, I believe I'll go see her again...
...And she aches just like a woman
But she breaks just like a little girl..."
-Bob Dylan

Tough redheads from Cedar Lake are red-hot right now. Since November, this column has featured a professional wrestler, nun, and now a prizefighter meeting the aforementioned description.

After a three-year hiatus from professional boxing, Kristina Rose Follmar, 28, recently returned to the ring. On April 25, at the Hammond Civic Center, Follmar will take on Mary McGee of Gary in a highly anticipated battle of champions.

Follmar's parents moved to Cedar Lake from Calumet City, Ill., when she was 8. Today, she lives in the Broad Ripple neighborhood of Indianapolis.

* * *

You were a three-sport athlete at Hanover Central High School.

"Yes, I ran cross country and track, and played basketball," Follmar began. "I think a lot of my desire to succeed in sports and to keep going forward with it came from the incredible coaches I had Hanover. For such a small school, we were able to compete with the big dogs and do really well."

Follmar sounds like a German name; any fightin' Irish blood running through those veins, colleen?

"My dad's mother was an O'Connor. My mother's maiden name is Feeney. I went to Ireland a couple years ago; there were Feeney signs all over the place."

Did you attend Holy Name Catholic Church while growing up in Cedar Lake?

"Yes; I don't hardly recognize Cedar Lake anymore."

I like those pastel-colored condos situated right on the lake; they help bring back the resort-look Cedar Lake must have had decades ago.

"My brother Tommy did all the electrical work for those condominiums."

Kristy, it's your call whether you want to talk about your brother or father.

"I was 14 when my dad died; Tommy was 8. The similarities between my dad and my brother are endless – obviously. My dad was the life of the party, the happiest guy. He was the best father.

"We had a sound family situation, but he made a mistake and mom busted him on it. It was just too much crashing down on him at once; he took his life. Boom – he was gone. He was a stand-up guy.

"Last September, Tommy got into a fight with his girlfriend. His funeral was unbelievable. My dad and brother were the last two people you'd figure to take themselves out. It sucks they're not around."

I doubt there were boxing lessons at the Cedar Lake Boys & Girls Club 15 years ago.

"No, but there was boxing in my garage. When Dad died, I had that Leo the lion-redhead-Irish temper thing going on. It was an awkward age for a girl anyway. I was really pissed off. I was getting into fights and verbal arguments with people.

"My mom bought me a heavy bag. I didn't know what the hell I was doing, but I went back there every day and pummeled that thing. It kind of switched from a way to vent anger to a love for it."

Was it while at Ball State University in Muncie, that you decided to hit something other than a heavy bag?

"Yeah, I ran college cross country my freshman year only. I was burned out on distance running, but I still had some competitive drive in me.

"During my first semester, I entered a tough-man competition and knocked two girls out in one night; we were the only chicks to enter. I won a trophy about six-feet tall. After about 2 1/2 years of boxing as an amateur, I turned pro in '03.

"Mark Lemerick has been training me since my first day; he's become like a father-figure to me. He's been training fighters for over 20 years; these will be Mark's first world title fights, too."

Any similarities to the film "Million Dollar Baby" starring Clint Eastwood and Hillary Swank?

"I really connected to the story of their relationship. That part got to me. I've only watched it once; it's kind of depressing. The fight scenes were pretty unrealistic. The movie came out right when I retired; everybody thought I retired because of what happened to Hillary Swank's character. No, I don't have a phobia of stools."

When I interviewed Mary, she told me the actress who delivered the cheap shot on Swank, thus paralyzing her, was the greatest woman boxer of all time in real life.

"Lucia Rijker. She could fight like a man. She more or less had to retire; she couldn't get anybody to fight her."

If you weighed 150 pounds and someone offered the right amount of money, would you fight Rijker?

"Yeah, I'd fight her."

Mary confessed that she had a few bare fist altercations. Any after-school donnybrooks for you?

"With boys, mostly. But I got nicer as I got older."

All right, Rose; I can't pull any more punches. Let's talk about your title fight with "Merciless" Mary McGee.

"People have been talking about a Kristy-Mary for a couple years. I have a lot of respect for her, considering what she's been through. We have the utmost respect for each other. By the same token, it's a sport and, when that bell rings, it's either glory or degradation; there's not a lot of room in between.

"It's really interesting, the more they promote this fight, the more it becomes a battle between Kristy and Mary or a battle of Gary vs. Cedar Lake. It's not. It's about two girls who learned to overcome adversity. About two girls who took all the shit thrown at them in their lives and turned it into something inspirational."

And after the fight?

"Regardless of the outcome, there's a bond Mary and I will share for the rest of our lives. I'm really grateful for the opportunity; I know Mary is, too. This is what we train for; it's going to be a helluva fight.

"Mary and I both have better offense than defense. I actually prefer to fight somebody like Mary as opposed to a counter puncher or an opponent that hangs on me after I get two or three shots in. Mary's going to fight back."

How's your stamina?

"I coming off a 10-round fight that went at a hectic pace. I feel confident I can go a hard 10 rounds and stand right there with her. I prefer the long-distance fights."

Mary is undefeated; you've suffered one loss.

"One controversial loss – it was my third fight; I was naive back then, thought I was invincible, had absolutely no fear of going in there with Mia St. John who was like 24-1. I felt that I beat her all four rounds; they gave her the decision. The place erupted with boos.

"After that experience, I'm never happy when I win by decision. I don't want any controversy; I train for the knockout."

Do you feel you are physically stronger at age 28 than you were five or six years ago?

"Physically, I feel like I'm in my prime. I hit a lot harder and I'm faster. I'm also a much smarter fighter."

How many more fights do you have left?

"I'll take them one at a time. I've never been cut; that's part of the decision – getting out at a certain time. There's always going to be the next best fighter; there's always going to be the next title..."

You fought in an exhibition bout last year; your brother got his hopes up that you'd come out of retirement. When you didn't, he became upset with you. After his death, you had a change of heart.

"I'm doing this for me, not Tommy. I was depressed. When I'm in training and in shape; I feel more alive. It's like somebody from above handed me this opportunity: Here, go for it; this will help you get better."

* * *

Follmar is executive director of Rock Steady Boxing Foundation, a not-for-profit group founded in Indianapolis. It helps people with Parkinson's disease have a better quality of life through exercise.

Follmar plans to marry Kyle Leis of Indianapolis, her longtime boyfriend and the father of her 2-year-old daughter, Kay O'Connor Leis. The wee lass takes after her mama; she goes by "K.O."

Rabbi Michael N. Stevens *(Sept. 2009)*

"Know before whom you are standing."
—Words written in Hebrew above the sanctuary door
at Temple Beth-El in Munster

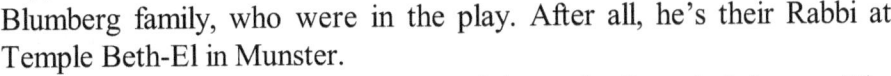

Soon after my column featuring Moanes Khawalid appeared in February, I received a nice e-mail from Michael N. Stevens regarding the article.

I don't think either one of us realized that we had already met six months before in Cedar Lake after a Paul and Angie Lowe production of "Fiddler on a Roof" at the Great Oaks After Supper Club.

Stevens was there to support members of the Blumberg family, who were in the play. After all, he's their Rabbi at Temple Beth-El in Munster.

I was there to force the Jews of Anatevka from their homes. The constable is a tough role for a liberal.

Stevens, 65, is a native of Brooklyn. He was heartbroken when his beloved Dodgers moved from Ebbets Field to Los Angeles in 1958.

Stevens has two younger brothers, one a rabbi and the other a lawyer. They are the sons of a wine and liquor wholesaler.

Stevens graduated from Haverford (Pa.) College and earned a master's degree in music composition from Hunter College of the City University of New York.

Stevens and his wife, Judy, live in Schererville; they have raised four children and now enjoy six grandchildren.

* * *

"I've also been in 'Fiddler,'" Stevens began. "I played the rabbi in the Genesius Guild production in Hammond in 1991. My great-uncle, Zvee

Scooler, who was born in the Ukrainian city of Kamenetz Podolsk in 1899, and who probably knew Sholom Aleichem, the author of the 'Tevye the Dairyman stories, was also in 'Fiddler.'

"In the original Broadway production in New York, he played the innkeeper during the entire run of the show. In the movie version, he played the rabbi. So, for my family, being in 'Fiddler' is, well, 'tradition.'"

That's interesting. Uncle Zvee must've been quite an actor.

"He was in many films including 'The Pawnbroker.'"

With Rod Steiger?

"Yes; he also was the No.1 Yiddish language radio personality in New York for over 60 years."

Your parents?

"My mother's side of the family were the ones from the Ukraine. My father's side was from Poland. Both of my grandfathers came to the United States about 1905, long before the Holocaust.

"My wife was born in Hungary; her mother and one of her aunts are Holocaust survivors. Judy's grandparents and most her aunts and uncles were killed by the Nazis. Judy lived with her parents in Budapest until the Hungarian revolution broke out in 1956."

Rabbi, I can't imagine. Can we talk a little about your love of music? You play a number of instruments.

"Yes, I currently play the piano. I played the saxophone in high school, college and in the Army band; I served for three years on the faculty of the Armed Forces School of Music in Norfolk, Va. I also am a bassoonist and play the bell lyre."

Bell lyre?

"The glockenspiel."

That big xylophone-looking beast?

"Yep, I schlepped the glockenspiel. You wear it in a holder on your belt. My high school marching band once played the pregame and halftime shows at a New York Giants football game at Yankee Stadium in mid-December.

"Despite temperatures near zero and below-zero wind chills, we weren't allowed to wear gloves while the band was performing; I remember my hands literally being stuck to the metal of the glockenspiel. But playing at a Giants' game was the highlight of the year."

Where were you ordained?

"At Hebrew Union College-Jewish Institute of Religion in 1976. I served a congregation in Montreal for five years and served in Allentown, Pa., for a year before coming to Hammond in 1987.

"We were located on Hohman Avenue, next to St. Demetrios Greek Orthodox Church. Last month, we celebrated our 10th year in this building after having been in Hammond for 85 years."

You're really outnumbered by Catholics and Protestants in this neck of woods.

"Yes, Northwest Indiana has a very small Jewish community; I would guess there are only about 3,000 Jewish people living in Lake County."

Beth-El, it's a reformed congregation, correct?

"Jeff, I would like to point out to many of your readers, that in Jewish practice, there is no 'ed' on the end of reform. Our synagogue is a reform congregation. We are not reformed like the Dutch Reformed."

Mike, bear with this not-so-genteel Gentile.

"The 'ed,' to us, would suggest we have finished our reforming, adapting, modernizing. In reform Jewish thinking, reform is a verb. It's a transformation; it's ongoing. We don't ever finish reforming. We as Jewish-Americans are continually adapting to new situations, environments and cultures."

I know there's a synagogue in the Miller neighborhood of Gary; I attended a wonderful service there. But isn't there another temple in Munster besides Beth-El?

"Actually, Munster has three synagogues. Our congregation is very progressive or liberal – more modern.

"Temple Beth-Israel is more conservative; its congregation is the result of a merger between synagogues from Hammond and Gary."

The third?

"An orthodox congregation called Chabad of Northwest Indiana. It's a Lubavitch Hasidic congregation."

My old buddy, Lawrence Ginensky, also is a native of Brooklyn. He explained to me that the term Lubavitch denotes what part of Europe a person is from.

"That is correct."

Rabbi, on a more solemn note. The High Holidays?

"In Jewish thinking, we place importance on atonement, forgiveness, repentance. The first 10 days of the year are a time of seeking forgiveness and apologizing. It is a time of promising ourselves, each other and God, to try to be better people than we were the past year.

"Rosh Hashanah is called the birthday of the world; we begin counting the years on our calendar from that. So, (Sept. 18) was the beginning of the year 5770 on the Jewish calendar."

And the 10th day of the year is the day of atonement.

"Yes, Yom Kippur is the culmination of our High Holiday Period, which is sometimes called The 10 Days of Repentance or The Days of Awe. It's a somber time because it's a time of introspection. Have I always done the right thing? Have I done what God commanded me to do? Have I always shown kindness, compassion, justice and tolerance toward other people? Have I been the best person I can be?

"We review our deeds from the past year and, as a congregation, confess our sins to God. There is a very traditional belief that God will not forgive us of any wrongdoings we've committed against him until we apologize and seek forgiveness with each other first. Only then, can we go to God and ask him for forgiveness."

* * *

According to the Jewish calendar, Sunday, doesn't begin until the sun goes down this evening. When the sun sets 24 hours later, it will be day 11 of the Jewish year, Yom Kippur will be over, and the fasts will cease.

And, come next Rosh Hashanah, on the world's 5,771st birthday, God's chosen people will strive once more to do the best they can.

And Stevens continues to lead them by example, practicing what he preaches. For the past 13 years, he has served as a guest lecturer at Purdue University Calumet in Hammond. He also teaches several classes at PUC, including, the history of the human experience as expressed in art, literature, music and philosophy, and The Bible as Literature: Old Testament.

Stevens volunteered to review Northwest Indiana Symphony Orchestra concerts; they appeared in the Post-Tribune from 1990-96. He composes numerous musical settings for Temple Beth-El's choir.

Stevens is involved with several interfaith activities, has served on the Lake County AIDS Pastoral Counseling Committee, and on the faculty of the Olin-Sang-Ruby Union Institute in Oconomowoc, Wis.

Reform is, indeed, a verb.

Paula DeBois *(Dec. 2014)*

"... Silent night, Holy night
Shepherds quake, at the sight.
Glories stream from Heaven above
Heavenly, hosts sing Hallelujah.
Christ the savior is born,
Christ the savior is born."
– Lyrics for "Silent Night,"
Joseph Mohr, author;
Franz Gruber, composer

In 1859, the Episcopal priest John Freeman Young published the English translation of "Stille Nacht (Silent Night)."

"Silent Night was sung simultaneously in French, English and German by troops during the Christmas Truce of 1914 during World War I as it was one carol that soldiers on both sides of the front line knew.

"Silent Night" has been recorded by a large number of singers through the years, including stirring renditions by Mahalia Jackson and Lena Horne.

Paula DeBois' brother Pierre dropped her off at St. Augustine's Episcopal Church in the Tolleston neighborhood of Gary for this interview. She lives about six blocks away from the church. Paula let me know up front that the interview would focus on the church and not her. But I did squeeze some personal information out of her. DeBois is an impressive woman who earned a degree in aeronautical engineering from Arizona State University.

* * *

Do you have family from Louisiana?

"Yes, New Orleans. They lived in the ward that was flooded out by Hurricane Katrina."

Tell me about your parents.

"My father was a doctor and my mother was a pharmacist. When we were burying Daddy, I thought about what a stunning building this is. I was baptized and confirmed here.

"St. Augustine's Episcopal Church is my base mark for a church. I do call it the Lena Horne of churches. She does not take a bad picture. Lena didn't take a bad picture, and St. Augustine's doesn't take a bad picture."

It is a gorgeous piece of architecture. To me, the shape of the roof resembles hands clasped in prayer.

"There's something about the design. The clerestory windows. When you enter this church and walk up those steps you are totally focused on worship and personal introspective. It takes you to that. You can't help but draw yourself to that direction."

What year was this church built?

"In 1959. This property was listed on the National Register of Historic Places by the United States Department of the Interior on Sept. 18, 2013."

Who designed this gem?

"Architect Edward Dart. He did Water Tower Place (a 758,000 square feet shopping mall and 74-story skyscraper in Chicago located along the Magnificent Mile on North Michigan Avenue). We are Dart's second church of his 26 commissioned churches that he built.

"The components of the church are very simplistic, modern architecture: cement, redwood, white oak. The altar was made from Indiana limestone. Our cross and Jesus Christ are made of bronze."

This parish goes back long before 1959.

"Our history is that we were chartered as a colored Episcopal mission in 1927. Back in the day, you were either an organized mission, meaning you were white, or you were a colored Episcopal mission.

"The 30 congregants who chartered back in '27 were not welcomed to worship at Christ Church in downtown Gary due to segregation. As Martin Luther King said – and it still holds in 2014 – the most segregated hour in the United States is the hour on Sunday. I'm paraphrasing, you can look it up. The colored Episcopalians were coming to Christ Church at 2 p.m. That's not church time."

Whereas the white members of Christ Church worshiped at 8 a.m. or 10 a.m.

"Correct. Our original congregants re-purposed an Italian-Catholic Church in Midtown (neighborhood of Gary) at 19th and Adams. It was vacated and pretty rickety from what I was told. We had Benedictine monks out of Valparaiso who serviced us.

"Anna Washington was one of those 30 original congregants. I believe she expired just before this building was completed. She named the church after her alma mater in North Carolina. I believe she was an educator by trade. St. Augustine of Hippo was one of the saints of African descent and the son of St. Monica.

"Anna's great-grandson, Charles Graves, recently preached the homily here. He grew up in Baltimore and is studying at Yale University."

Give me some more history of this particular church.

"We originally held 340 people in this building. The maximum congregation occurred in 1969 under Father Hood. He was young and working on his doctorate at the University of Chicago. He was almost like a pied piper. Father Hood would go on to New York and work under Desmond Tutu. Dr. Robert E. Hood was just kickin' it."

Bear with me, the "preacher" of an Episcopalian church is deemed a priest, correct?

"Yes. If it's a man, we call him Father. If it's a woman, we call her Mother. One of the benchmarks of the Episcopal religion is that they have women who are confirmed. I think we've had 12 American presidents who were Episcopal. Our priests can marry. We are so close to the Catholic religion that they will take our priests. The men, not the women."

The Episcopal Church seems to be a liberal one.

"We're known for that."

* * *

St. Augustine's Episcopal Church has also been known for having a congregation comprised of many prominent professionals through the years, including Henrietta Bell Wells who was an educator, social worker and the wife of Wallace Wells, St Augustine's first rector. The character Samantha Booke in the 2007 movie "The Great Debaters" was loosely based on Henrietta Bell Wells.

Educator Quentin Smith also was a member of St. Augustine's. Mr.

Smith was one of the last of the Tuskegee Airmen during World War II.

And let us not forget the daughter of a doctor and a pharmacist who earned a degree in aeronautical engineering. The impressive woman who worked tirelessly to see that her beloved house of worship would be placed on the National Register of Historic Places.

Amen.

Dave Gard *(May 2011)*

"I guess I just miss my friend."
– From the film, "The Shawshank Redemption" and the novella "Rita Hayworth and the Shawshank Redemption" by Stephen King

Dave Gard, 57, grew up in the 4800 block of Baring Avenue of East Chicago. He has lived in Lowell about 30 years.

Dave and Debbie Gard raised three sons. During the 1980s, I car-pooled to and from the steel mill with Dave. Also, during the 1980s, Debbie baby-sat my twin daughters.

Gard is a town councilman from Lowell's 5th ward

* * *

You never knew your father.

"No, Dad was 29 when he died," Gard said. "They didn't know anything about the heart in 1955; it was the moon. They gave him a bottle of nitroglycerin pills and six months to live; he died 5 1/2 months later. I was 18 months old."

Did your mother remarry?

"No, we moved in with my maternal grandparents."

Wasn't your mother born with four kidneys?

"Yes, something like one in a 100 million – some bizarre number. In 1961, they did a real groundbreaking surgery to take two out, reposition two, and do all the necessary 'plumbing.' Five months after that enormous surgery, she took all of us – along with the dog – to California, camping along the way. We never knew the agony she was in the entire time. We never knew it."

What did your grandfather do for a living?

"He worked 46 years for (the) Sinclair (refinery) which then became Atlantic Richfield. He was a pipe fitter who did plumbing on the side and I was his helper. I've threaded more feet of pipe with a hand threader than most people have ever seen in their lives: 'Here Davie, cut this and thread it.'"

Your brother?

"He passed away three months shy of his 40th birthday from pancreatic and liver cancer as a direct result of Agent Orange. He was 5 years older than me. I also have an older sister."

Dave, you've always been mechanically inclined, but you've also got an artsy side. You sang and played the saxophone in a band while living in East Chicago.

"It's funny you mention that. I hadn't seen any of the guys from the rock band in like 35 years, and one day, I got a friend request from our drummer on facebook. So, I responded and, the next thing you know, the lead guitar player and both bass players, the keyboard player and another singer who also played sax all showed up.

"Now we're practicing and plan to have a reunion concert in July."

Where?

"At Sopranos in Griffith."

You met Debbie because of the band.

"She lived across the alley from where we practiced. She actually liked the bass player and not me. But he liked really heavy-set women and she wasn't.

"We were on one of our iced-tea breaks and I looked out the window and she was sitting on the porch with her girlfriend. I said: 'You see that girl sitting over there? I'm going to marry that girl some day.' The bass player said, 'No you're not, she likes me.' I said, 'You don't even like her, she's not heavy enough.' Three weeks later, we were talking about when we'd get married."

How old were you during the band era?

"I actually started in the band in seventh grade. I had to paint on a mascara moustache so we could play in the clubs."

What was the name of the band?

"Jacob Grimm."

Some of your favorite bands during the 1970s?

"Steely Dan, Mott the Hoople, Traffic, and I was always a big fan of Styx because they were coming up on the South Side of Chicago the same time we were. They got the gold mine and we got the shaft. We played with those guys; we played with almost all the Chicago bands at one time or another."

You attended Illiana Christian High School in Lansing, Ill.

"Yes, my teachers would spell my name Gaard, assuming I was Dutch."

Reading?

"I basically read to clear my mind. Now, I pretty much read when I travel. If I fly from here to California, I'll finish a 600-page paperback on the way there and another one on the way back."

Favorite Stephen King novel?

"'The Stand,' without a doubt; I've read it a dozen times."

Favorite movie?

"'The Shawshank Redemption.' I'm absolutely powerless to change the channel when it comes on the TV – no matter where it starts. I cannot change the channel. I know every line."

When did you hire in at Inland Steel Co.?

"My first tour of duty in the mill began in 1973. I worked until 1976; then Debbie and I moved to Iowa where I pursued a career in life insurance sales. In '81, I hired back in the mills and worked there until about '89. I was laid off for so long, after two years, I just quit."

How long were you at Inland's No. 3 Coke Plant?

"About 2 1/2 years before it shut down."

Dave, that place was a pistol.

"We froze and fried. Everything was outside; we were like cavemen. All winter, we'd stand in front of 2,000-degree ovens with sweat running down our faces and coal fines sticking to our necks and, at the same time, have icicles hanging from our backsides. And we used to feel bad for the guys who worked in the sintering plant; that place was crazy."

What do you do for a living now?

"For the last 20 years, I've been working for United Services out of Griffith. I'm a certified restorer; we help people whose homes have been damaged by water, fire, flood... . We estimate and negotiate settlements with the insurance company, then actually do the restoration work of the structures. I'm also doing some national sales training in our industry."

* * *

Dave Gard is a religious man. He told me his faith is what gets him through rough times. He doesn't know how people can live without faith.

You see, Dave lives alone now. He's not only a guy who lost his father and brother at young ages, he also lost his best friend, the mother of his children. Debbie died of ovarian cancer on Oct. 31, 2006.

They were married 35 years.

Harold Moreland *(April 2014)*

Used car salesman: Guarantee? We guarantee it to be an automobile. ...Got anything to trade?"
Pa Joad: "Got a pair of mules I'll trade."
Used car salesman: Mules! Hey, Joe, hear this? This guy wants to trade mules. Didn't nobody tell you this is the machine age?"
– John Steinbeck, from "The Grapes of Wrath"

Harold Moreland is the sole proprietor of H&R Auto Sales located at 2450 W. Ridge Road in Gary. Besides being a used car salesman, he's an auctioneer and avid duck hunter.

Moreland, 77, also is a widower who lives in Crown Point. He and his deceased wife had two sons, one of which died of leukemia when he was 10.

* * *

"You ask the questions and I'll answer 'em," Moreland began.
How long have you lived in Crown Point?
"Since 1959."
You weren't born in Northwest Indiana.
"I was raised in Hillsboro, Ill."
How do you spell that?
"Don't ask me. Hillsboro is in between Springfield and St. Louis."
Tell me about your childhood in Hillsboro.
"I quit school when I was in the fourth grade. My sister quit in the fifth. A horse had throwed my daddy out of a wagon and broke his back. So we had to do the farmin' and stuff.

"Helluva thing sittin' behind four horses on a two-bottom plow with them tootin' in your face all day long. My sister did the discing with two horses. Believe me, you ate whatever you could get your hands on."
Was your father paralyzed for life?

"No. But my dad was blind in one eye and deaf. Me and him was walkin' down the street one day and he stopped and started squinting his good eye.

"Daddy takes out across the street there in Hillsboro. Old Model T's and Model A's hittin' each other in the ass to keep from runnin' over him. Daddy turned this guy around and he busted him. I mean he laid it on 'em."

What happened next?

"A cop was standin' about a half-block away. He ran to the scene and asked my father: 'What's the matter, George?' Daddy said: 'Nobody calls me a deaf, dumb son of a bitch.'"

Your father read the man's lips from across the street.

"He could do that. The guy tried to deny it, but the man he was talkin' to was honest and said exactly what he'd said. The guy my daddy punched had money. Some people like that look down on folks who are down-and-out. We're just peons to them.

"We lost the farm. But dad got him an old dump truck and would get jobs cleanin' other people's ashes. Back then, you burned wood and coal. I'll say this, my daddy was a hard worker."

Hard times.

"There was six of us kids. We lived in a two-room house. My mother's brother died. His wife was no good. She was gonna give the kids away. Mother took my three cousins in. That made nine kids in a two-room house. For a week, the boys had to sleep on the floor around the pot-bellied stove and the girls got the bed.. The next week, we'd switch. It wasn't no joy, but my parents took care of us."

When did you move to Northwest Indiana?

"When I turned 17, I came up here to work at Youngstown Sheet & Tube. One year of that place was enough for this country boy.

"I went to Clark Oil & Refinery sellin' gas and cigarettes on Calumet Avenue. I was makin' more money than I was in the mill – Teamsters Union. I was with Clark about nine years. I ended up on 15th Avenue and Clark Road by Tarrytown (neighborhood of Gary). I knew every colored man in Tarrytown."

Other occupations?

"I was in the pile drivers union out of Chicago and only lacked three months for a pension. Like a dummy, I quit."

How long have you been operating H&R Auto Sales?

"About 33 years."

How many vehicles do you have on the lot?

"Hell, I don't know. Count the keys hangin' on the wall. Looks like 14. I got a car out there that's a '91."

You're not particular as far as the make.

"I'll sell anything I think I can make a dollar on. I go down around Pontiac, (Ill.) – all the little farm towns. I buy all the stuff the new car dealers don't want to mess with."

Employees?

"Run the place by myself. I sell most of my cars around tax time."

Oddities that might have occurred on the lot over the years?

"Been held up one time in 33 years. I shot at 'em and missed 'em."

With a pistol or shotgun?

"A .357 magnum with hollow points. If I'd a had my scatter gun, I'd a probably got 'em."

Haggling?

"I just had a guy today who didn't want to pay me my price so I told him goodbye. I told 'em he could have that real nice little hotrod out there for 1,800 bucks, plus tax. He said: 'All I got is $1,800.' I told him no. It was a '94 Eagle Talon. They don't make 'em like that no more."

What do you drive?

"That Dodge truck with a hemi in it. You can be driving 50 (mph) in it and you hit the passing gear and yer doin' a hundred before you can bat an eye. Do you know anything about duck huntin'?"

I shot a pair of white-winged scoters the other day on the Kankakee River.

"What was you using?"

A Nikon.

"Semi-automatic?"

Digital.

"You know how I started out? I went to Willow Slough with a guy named Donnie Woods – helluva duck caller. We took one boat for me and him and another boat loaded with decoys. I bet we put out 100 decoys. There was a blind there that nobody wanted."

And?

"Here come a hen mallard. Donnie called her in and she was about to land into those decoys. I come up ready to unload on her, but Donnie said: 'No, no, no. Leave her sit there. Here came more ducks. Donnie went: 'Quack! Quack!' Then Donnie said: 'Now!' We limited out in an hour-and-a-half."

On being an auctioneer?

"Self-taught. I just picked it up. I did dinners for Lake County Fish & Game, Waterfowl USA and Ducks Unlimited."

Harold, can you make that music for me?

"I got 20. Anybody gimme 30? I got 30. Anybody gimme me 40? I got 40, who'll gimme a 50 dollar bill? Fifty, 50, 50.... Sold!"

* * *

From the dusty fields of Hillsboro to a used car lot in the Steel City, Harold Moreland has led a hardscrabble, but colorful life.

John Taylor *(July 2011)*

"You always say, 'I'll quit when I start to slide,' and then one morning you wake up and you've done slid."
– *"Sugar" Ray Robinson, member of the International Boxing Hall of Fame*

John Taylor, a former pugilist, has coached or trained aspiring boxers for decades through the Gary Police Athletic League youth program at North Gleason Pavilion.

Taylor, 80, lives in Gary's Midtown neighborhood. He and his wife, now deceased, raised four children, one of whom graduated from West Point where he ascended from lieutenant to full colonel. Taylor's son also had an office in the Pentagon and is a friend of Colon Powell, former chairman of the Joint Chiefs of Staff and the first African-American secretary of state in United States history.

* * *

"My mother was a sharecropper in Tennessee; we came to Gary when I was about 12," Taylor began. "I was an only child."

Your mother raised you during the Great Depression.

"Oh, yeah. Then we came up here and things weren't much better."

High school?

"I went to Froebel, we paid book fees just like everybody else, but blacks couldn't swim in the pool and they couldn't play in the band. That's the way is was; nobody bucked the system."

You were in the service during the Korean War.

"Yes, I was drafted by the Army, but chose the Marines. I traveled all over the world with the boxing team. I started out boxing at 132 (pounds) and went all the way up to 145 (pounds)."

John, the welterweights always have been my favorites.

"Yeah, man – ("Sugar") Ray Robinson."

What did you do after your four-year stint with the Marine Corps?

"I stayed out in California and boxed. I was discovered by actor Jose Ferrer; Rosemary Clooney's husband. Jose asked me to turn professional and hired ex-featherweight champion of world Chalky Wright to be my trainer.

"I fought under the name of Tommy Chalk. Here's some of Chalky's greatest accomplishments taped to the wall."

Sept. 11, 1941, Wright beat Joey Archibald by knockout in the 11th round to win the world championship.... It also says Wright drowned in his bathtub.

"After Chalky passed, they hired Eddie Fletch to be my trainer. I stayed with him for about a year and then he told me to go home and get a job. It set me back for awhile. And home, it wasn't nothin' but the mill. I seen guys comin' out of the mill lookin' pretty tough."

Where did you find work?

"The Budd Plant; I worked there 30 years and retired. Then, I hired onto the Gary Police Department and eventually retired from there after about 20 years."

You were one of the founders of the Gary P.A.L. youth boxing program.

"Yeah, we started out at the Hudson-Campbell Fitness Center right behind City Hall."

You've trained scores of young boys and girls for decades. Name a few standouts.

"Angel Manfredy, John Lark, Merciless Mary Magee... I think we've had seven amateur state champions come out of here."

John, the last time I was here, I saw Angel; he wasn't doing too well.

"He stayed too long. I begged him not to fight (Floyd) Mayweather (Jr.). Floyd stopped him in the second round and then everybody started stoppin' him."

This building also has seen its better days.

"This building is 70 years old, maybe more than that. It has a flat roof. When it rains.... In the back of this place was a swimming pool for blacks. In this area, where we have the ring set up was office space; this is where you could buy your ticket to go swimming. That field over there was a golf course; Joe Louis played golf out there; now look at it."

Joe Louis would have a tough time putting in that weed patch. Did you ever meet the "Brown Bomber" or see him fight?

"The only time I'd get to see Joe Louis was on the newsreels at the theater. At times, we didn't even have a radio."

When you were boxing, did you have any trouble with southpaws?

"Naw, I'd shoot a lot of right hands at 'em; I teach the same thing to my fighters."

Are you looking for a new building?

"Yeah, they were kind enough to let us use their facility at the Radisson (Hotel) in Merrillville for awhile, but I don't like all that loud, disco music going on there. I don't have no records playin'. You come here to box. And I tell 'em, 'Pull your pants up; I don't wanna look at your drawers.'"

You're old school, John. through this program, you've given a lot of kids something constructive to do, rather than getting in trouble.

"Training young boxers is a fulltime job, but its not just training; sometimes, you got to step out in the streets. I can't save everybody, but there are kids I can help. I'm available; it's up to them.

"This is my way of preachin'; this is my sermon. These kids need something now, not tomorrow – today. They are the future voters, the future mayors, future pastors; give 'em a chance.

"All these kids aren't bad, some of them might turn bad. But some preachers and politicians turn bad, too."

* * *

P.A.L. is a not-for-profit group, and Taylor always has volunteered his services. It would be nice if P.A.L. could receive some kind of grant to get the roof fixed at North Gleason Pavilion. The place has "done slid."

At age 80, John Taylor could use a hand. There has to be a one-two punch somewhere willing to help – for the kids' sake.

Give 'em a chance

Rosa Gamez *(May 2011)*

"A mother is a person who, seeing there are only four pieces of pie for five people, promptly announces she never did care for pie."
Tenneva Jordan (author and mother)

If Rosa Gamez baked a solitary pie for dessert in the past half-century, it would've been sliced into very thin wedges; she is the mother of nine.

Rosa, 77, has been married to Jesse Gamez for 60 years, the last 22 of them on Hemlock Street in East Chicago. They are members of St. Patrick Catholic Church in East Chicago.

* * *

"I was born in Wautoma, Wis., but raised in Milwaukee," Gamez began. "I moved here in 1949 when I was 16."

Did your father get a job in the steel mill?

"No, I moved here by myself. My mother died when I was 9. My father worked nights where they make the beer. I believe he was a janitor. The social workers didn't want my seven siblings and me to be alone."

What happened?

"We were put in St. Rosa's Orphanage. I remember getting to see my mother one time after she was hospitalized. I remember that."

What was wrong with her?

"Stomach cancer, plus she was a diabetic. My father would come see us every Sunday at St. Rosa's. He would tell us we were going to get to come home.

"Then, one day, he came to see us and said we weren't going to get to come home. My sisters and I were crying and crying and asked him, 'Why not?' Papa said, 'Your mother has gone to heaven.' I think she was 42 when she died."

Of the five sisters, were you one of the oldest or youngest?

"I was the third one; my two older sisters are twins. One of the twins moved to this area and got married. When I turned 16, she got me out of the orphanage. I took care of her two kids until I got a job at the five-and-dime on Main Street. When I was 18, I married Jesse."

Rosa, how were you treated at the orphanage?

"It was all right; I had to braid four girls' hair every morning before I could eat breakfast."

Let's fast forward to Northwest Indiana. Have you always lived on Hemlock?

"No, we lived on both Fir Street and Parrish Avenue for a while; we also lived in the Black Oak neighborhood of Gary for about 12 years. Then, we moved here. Some of my children graduated from Horace Mann (High School) and some from East Chicago Washington (High School)."

How many of your children were boys and how many girls?

"I had four boys and five girls. But now I only have four girls. One of my daughters died in a fire; she was 37. She had twin daughters."

Did you have any difficult births?

"Yes, with my daughter who passed away. I had a kidney infection and almost died."

Oldest and youngest children?

"I have a daughter who is going to be 60 and a daughter who is 40. I had two girls, two boys, two girls, two boys each of them about a year or so apart and the last one was about five years younger than the eighth one."

As my deceased Irish-born friend, John J. Brandley, used to say, "Sweet Mother of Jesus!" As a parent, were you strict or doting? Or, were you strict and doting?

"They say I was strict."

What is easier to raise, boys or girls?

"I think the girls were easier. The boys like to get into mischief. One of my boys was in the Marines and one was in the Navy."

Do your kids visit you?

"Yes; one of my daughters just left before you got here; she stops by every day. Another one of my daughters lives with me; she takes care of me. I've been covering up my left arm with this comforter; it has been paralyzed for 20 years – I had a stroke. My left leg isn't much better."

Were you a good cook?

"Jesse and the kids said I was. After the stroke, I can't cook much anymore. I can still make rice. I try to wash some of the dishes and vacuum."

Woman of the house, you put on the pots for 50 years. That's plenty. Did you teach your kids how to cook?

"I tried to, like when I'd make tortillas; a couple of them caught on."

Fond memories of your children?

"In kindergarten, each one of them made their little hand prints in the clay. I've kept them all."

* * *

Jesse Gamez worked production at Inland Steel's Plant 1 Galvanizing Department for 44 years. They weren't the Rockefellers. But Rosa made sure her children's hand-me-down clothing was clean and their hair was combed or braided before they caught the school bus.

Mama Gamez learned how to do things like that at an orphanage in Milwaukee that bore her name.

In her children's eyes, she's East Chicago's St. Rosa.

Marcia Carlson *(Dec. 2005)*

"A wise woman puts a grain of sugar into everything she says to a man, and takes a grain of salt with everything he says to her."
-Helen Rowland

It was a beautiful morning and I was drinking coffee with a beautiful woman by the name of Marcia Carlson. Marcia has lived in Lowell all of her 73 years. She is a widow now, but she and husband Butch raised four children.

Marcia is a member of the Gleaners and also Three Creeks Historical Society. Her mantra has always been: "If you have a job to do, you do it. You don't take breaks and fiddle around."

* * *

So, Marcia, your maiden name was Bolt?

"Yes; my father opened up a butcher shop in Lowell in 1932. Being in the midst of the Depression, he figured he had nowhere to go but up. After a while, he added groceries.

"He actually raised two families. His mother died giving birth to twins. My father became responsible for four younger siblings because his father died a few years later. My Uncle Bob ran Garden City after my dad retired."

Although I grew up in Sumava and Lake Village, my parents often grocery shopped at Garden City long before it became Costas. I remember my mother commenting about how the man who owned the place had a reputation for hiring people with disabilities.

"My father and uncle were very compassionate men. You mentioned Sumava; my earliest memory of Sumava is of Mr. Lukes bringing his delicious freshly baked bread to my dad's store."

You must be talking about Jimmy Lukes' father. That's going back a ways.

"I go a long way back."

Venus Lukes. We used to live above their bakery when I was a little shaver.

"Jeff, I don't know how you find these people. I read them all. And I think to myself: 'Isn't that interesting, all these people in our community who have so much history.' Venus is an amazing woman."

To me, she looks the same as she did 40 years ago. Both of you have remained so slim and trim.

"I'm lucky. Because I sure do like my sugar."

Are you of Irish descent?

"Yes, and Scotch, too. My father's family settled in the Virginia area many generations ago. My maternal great-grandfather came to the United States from Ireland during the potato famine."

You have tickets for a concert series in Munster and also attend the Memorial Opera House in Valparaiso. Marcia, have you read about that Norman Rockwell exhibit that's showing at the Center for Visual and Performing Arts in Munster?

"I saw it in Phoenix and just loved it. I grew up with that. The Saturday Evening Post came to our house every week. We're so related to Rockwell's drawings."

I've got that big book with all of his –

"So do I."

Are you retired?

"Since '95. I was clerk treasurer. One of the neat things I did was marry people. I have no idea how many people I married. I married women who'd be trailing behind there soon-to-be husbands with curlers in their hair, and there were big formal affairs too, where we'd have to practice beforehand.

"When I first went into office they had just gotten rid of justices of the peace. Some of those poor kids would come in without a dime in their pocket and want to pay me. I couldn't take their money. One couple got married in a video arcade; that was a noisy one.

"One wedding took place at Evergreen Park. The bride and groom were flower children – barefooted flower children. I remember one particular bridegroom who was having a real hard time. His eyes would go up and he'd start to go down. They'd grab him and take him out the door. That happened three times. Boy, did I shorten that ceremony up. My daughter was the first person I married. I also have married my sister, grandson, and granddaughter."

Political affiliation?

"I'm a democrat. And I'll be democrat until the day I die. I'm not an extremist. But you have to protect the poor people. You have to protect the people who can't protect themselves. The working man had nothing years ago. He didn't own his home. He didn't have money. He had scrip that could only be spent at the company store. When he got hurt, he was out the door. When he died, his family was out. They had absolutely nothing. They were totally dependent on the man who had the money. The democrats helped change some of those things. I'm a champion of the underdog.

"Now welfare, I'm all in favor of any kind of help, but you have to work for it. You shouldn't be sitting at home. I'd pay people's water bills at City Hall, but they'd pick up trash along the highway to pay for their bill.

"Times have changed in Lowell. While I was clerk there were times when all five of us were democrats, but even when there was a mix from each party – once the election was over – politics were forgotten. It was all about what was best for the town of Lowell. I was the only person who was there every day. The men had other jobs, other commitments. I was the person who knew what was going on. It really was a neat job."

Do you miss it?

"Do I miss it? No! You had a million deadlines. You had to know all the laws. When the state laws changed each year, it wasn't the councilmen who sat down and read all that junk. It was me. I'd say, 'Hey, we've got to change this, we've got to do this, we have to pass an ordinance now, we can't do this anymore.' And I kept the money well-invested. At one time, I was getting 20 percent interest on our money!"

Sounds like you were running the show, kiddo.

"Don't put that in, but I was."

You have my word on it.

"They'd come into my office and if I had something I thought was beneficial, I'd hint: 'At the meeting, maybe you should suggest this...'"

You were probably somewhat unheralded or unsung.

"I never minded that. The good councilmen over the years were the ones who came into my office, sat down, and asked me every morning: 'What's going on Marcia?' Bill Dunn was one of them. He always had his pulse on what was going on in this town."

You're leaving us for a while.

"Yes, I go to Georgia all winter and stay with my daughter. I was going to Arizona every winter until Butch passed away in 2001. There's too much ice around here. I walk two miles, five days a week. I've been saving my newspapers so I can fill up the refrigerator before I leave. It won't use as much electricity that way."

Hootman!

"I am frugal. We were raised that way. You didn't buy something to throw it away in a year. I remember the first television I had to throw away. I thought, 'You've got to be kidding, that beautiful oak cabinet, and we're just supposed to throw it away?'"

* * *

As I left her home, I thought about this intelligent, liberated, hard working, redhead, who enjoys the fine arts, history and likes crossword puzzles. A compassionate democrat born on the first day of spring, a beauty who makes a great cup of coffee and is frugal, too.

It suddenly occurred to me. She's the woman of my dreams! If we had only met sooner.

Better late than never.

Victor Del Toro *(Dec. 2007)*

*"...runnin' against the wind
runnin' against the wind
watch the young man run..."*
-Bob Seger

Victor Del Toro. What a great name for a kid who could churn up a cross country course or blaze around a track ahead of the pack.

We meet at the East Chicago Library on Columbus Drive. He arrives atop a yellow "crotch rocket" and is wearing green scrubs. I admonish him for not wearing a helmet, but realize the kid needs speed.

Del Toro, 20, holds most of the distance records at East Chicago Central.

Before we take a seat to begin the interview, he asks me about the photograph, letter, and medal on display at the library. I tell him that Lance Cpl. Emilio A. De La Garza, Jr grew up here in East Chicago, worked in the steel mill for a year, and then left it all out on the course about four miles south of Da Nang, Vietnam. I explain to young Del Toro that they don't come any bigger than the Congressional Medal of Honor.

* * *

"I was born in Mexico City, Mexico," begins Del Toro. "I came to the United States with my mother when I was 6. We lived in an apartment here on Columbus Drive. Once my mother got her legal status she petitioned for my father to move here. They bought a house near Bishop Noll (Institute) on 148th Street. My dad designs jewelry; he got a job right away.

"I think it was my eighth-grade year, the Olympics were going on. I was watching the women's marathon. I watched the whole thing. I told my mom: 'I want to do that. I want to be a runner.' My mother ran distance in Mexico from the time she was like 12 years old."

"The unfortunate thing is that there is no middle school program in East Chicago for track and field or cross country. I went out for the soccer team my freshman year. Two races before the sectional the cross country coach approached the soccer coach. Francisco Gomez and I joined the cross country team for extra conditioning. My first race was either at Rensselaer or Lowell. I ran like (18 minutes, 20 seconds). I took ninth place. I ran in basketball shoes that were a size too big.

"Other kids were walking around with big medals; my medal was real little. I felt ashamed because I didn't take first place."

I remember, Victor. I was there. I overheard your heartfelt apology to your coach. I thought to myself, "I want that kid on my team."

"There's a lot of talent at East Chicago Central – so much potential. There were guys on the soccer team who could keep up with me. We could have been a great cross country team, but soccer was their life. Hey, soccer is a great sport; I love it. I played both sports as a freshman and sophomore."

"My maternal grandparents retired in Mexico, but my mom was able to get them visas, so they moved here. Eventually, my parents moved to Michigan. I stayed with my grandparents here in E.C., but my grandmother became fed up. It wasn't like Mexico, where everybody knew everybody.

"She was like: 'My neighbors won't even say hi to me. They don't even want to come over and eat dinner on Fridays. I want to go back. I miss mi compadres y comadres.' My grandfather said, 'Adios; I'll stay with my grandson.'"

"Then, he started missing my grandmother. When I turned 16, he went to Mexico to try to bring her back. He never came back.

"My mom didn't want me staying in East Chicago by myself, so she pulled me up to Michigan. It was the winter of my sophomore year – Romeo High School. I didn't like it. It was so different. I grew up with kids who were more open. It was a whole different culture. Hey, East Chicago Central is a different culture than Lake Central or Munster."

"At Romeo High, it was mostly Italians. Most of their dads were in the Teamsters Union or had their own companies and stuff – a bunch of rich kids. I'm not lyin' to you; they were driving new cars to school. I'm used to not having everything I wanted; I still have the car that I bought – a '92.

"It wasn't that they were Italian or white; to me, it was like the high school from the movies. If you didn't belong to a certain clique, you weren't accepted at all. A lot of them thought I was Italian. They'd say: 'What part of Italy did your family come from? I've never heard the name Del Toro before. Is that southern Italy?'

"I was like, 'No, man, my parents are like straight up from Mexico City.'

"I begged my mom for weeks on end to go back to E.C. She talked to my coach, Willie Askew; she told him, 'He better keep his grades up and he better go to college after he graduates. By track season I was back. This is my home. I love Northwest Indiana.

"Throughout high school, I worked at Meyers Castle (in Dyer). They asked me if I wanted to be a host or valet driver. I didn't want no cushy host job. I saw this nice little hill that the drivers had to go up to get to the cars. I figured I could get my workout and still make money while doing it.

"I was parking cars left and right. I made $110 the first night. The boss said, 'Man, you're fast.'

"The other workers would walk up the hill. I tried to tell them, 'I'm going to be taking all your tips if you keep walking.'

"When I was senior, I got sick during the winter. When you're on your own – going to school, running, working – you really don't have time to cook for yourself. I wasn't eating that good."

"When I first got out of high school, I got a running scholarship to a college in Louisiana near New Orleans. They gave me the whole shebang. I got down there the week before (Hurricane) Katrina hit. My mom told me to get my butt back up here as soon as she heard. I was disappointed when I had to leave Louisiana and move back to Michigan. I lost my track scholarship. I love running."

"I considered being an emergency room nurse; I like helping people. I received physical therapy at St. Margaret Mercy (Healthcare Centers) in Hammond because I messed up my knee playing rugby. They healed me. They were real cool. I thought, 'Man, this is what I want to do – become a physical therapist.' And I will. I work at St Margaret's as a rehabilitation aide right now.

"I'm also working on my bachelor's at Indiana University Northwest and training with Coach Taylor – club status. Next year Coach Taylor hopes to have the full-out NAIA (cross Country) team. Hopefully, if my times meet his criteria, I'll run for him. I've been training real hard. I feel like a runner again; I'm getting back in shape.

"If there was a middle school program, E.C. Central would be stacked. There is money in this town; we have a casino. They could do it.

"I'm hoping when I graduate from college, I can bring something back to this city – start a running program.

"Some of these kids aren't the best of kids, but I'd like to try it. I think they just need a little understanding. Some of them don't have the perfect home lives. There's a lot of single moms trying real hard to raise them. These kids don't have direction."

* * *

Victor Del Toro has never run from anything – always toward something.

Mentor this next generation growing up in East Chicago, mi hijo. Do this thing for them. Run alongside them.

Like the wind.

Willie Jackson *(Nov. 2014)*

"No one ever talks about the moment you found out that you were white. Or the moment you found out that you were black. That's a profound revelation. The minute you find that out, something happens. You have to renegotiate everything."
– Toni Morrison

Willie Jackson, 63, lives in a beautiful townhouse in Hobart with Beverly, his wife of 32 years. They have raised five children. All five are college graduates.

Willie and I worked together at Inland Steel Co.'s (ArcelorMittal) No. 2 Coke Plant for many years.

* * *

"I grew up on the Small Farm (neighborhood of Gary) between 25th Avenue, south over the Expressway (Interstate 80-94) – Clark Road to Chase Street," Jackson began. "We moved from up Gary way. I enjoyed the Small Farm. There were no paved streets or sewer systems. We had septic tanks and the whole deal. It was a place to run around and grow up. You know, just have a good time as a kid. We played from sunup to sundown.

"About the time we moved out there, there was the Kangaroo Gangs up in Gary. I don't know if you ever heard of those. They were getting pretty big. I was glad to get away from all that."

You went to Calumet High School.

"A 1969 graduate."

It's mostly kids from the Black Oak neighborhood of Gary who attend Calumet High School.

"We were bussed. I should have gone to (Gary) Roosevelt (High School). My wife went to 'Velt."

Willie, you remember Rich Maynard from the coke plant. That tough hillbilly grew up in Black Oak and went to Calumet High School. He also owned the Friendly Tap in Black Oak for a while. I once asked him if the joint was really as rowdy as people said it was. Maynard told me: "Jeff, it was so rough that I had to check people at the door for weapons. And if they didn't have one, I'd issue them one."

"Maynard, he was a piece of work. Once I got to junior high school there was racial issues, you know. This is like in '64. There was a restaurant across from the high school on Ridge Road called the M&E. We couldn't go there. But by the time I graduated high school, that was pretty much over. Playin' basketball for Calumet, gettin' to know all the guys.."

Was the basketball team a mix of black and white kids?

"Yeah, oh yeah."

Some good things can come out of sports.

"I played basketball all four years in high school. We were 18-3 my senior year. I was a guard, sixth man. Loved every minute of it.

"Chris Traicoff was our coach. Tough. Tough! But he was a fair guy. Trust me. He would take us back to the Small Farm and drop us off after practice. Coach Traicoff lived on 47th Avenue. He had a beautiful home. Coach would have picnics for us. He was a nice guy, but on the court and in practice – forget it."

Old school.

"You got it. I continued to play ball in leagues until I was 48, then I had the hip replacement. I always said I wanted to play against or with my sons, and I had that opportunity quite a bit. I'm a golfer these days."

Let's switch gears. The mill?

"I got hired at Youngstown Sheet & Tube in '74. I worked in the open hearth for a year and then they laid me off for a year. I remember working the afternoon shift at Youngstown when a guy got killed. I knew him. That really affected me.

"In '76, I got hired by Inland. I went straight to the coke plant. You know how that went."

The blacks were usually sent to the carcinogenic coke batteries. Management figured the coke plant was no place for a white man.

"I was on the battery top for maybe six months before I got a mechanical apprenticeship."

Better than a production job on the battery, but it was still the filthy coke plant. By the end of the shift, we were all black.

"You read the articles in the paper about how steel workers don't deserve their pay and that type of thing. I disagree with that. There's not a lot of jobs where day in and day out you don't know if you're going make it back home or whether or not you're gonna lose a limb or a finger."

Were you working the day shift when Loerra and Newman were killed in the '90s?

"I was there."

I thought all of East Chicago and Whiting was going to be blown off the map.

"Before I retired from the 80-inch Hot Strip, a girl got caught up in a slab yard coupling. She died. There was a young guy, about 35, who worked with me for two days. He was supposed to double over from midnights to days and work with me on the third day. I come into the shop, 'Where's he at?' He got killed that night."

What happened?

"He was crushed to death. But you know the one that really hurt me the most was when Ron Robinson was killed."

March 16, 2001.

"That really bothered me. Ron and I were good, good friends. I talked to him that morning... I ..couldn't... ."

It's all right brother. I've shed a few tears, too.

"I couldn't believe it. I didn't know Norm. I'm sure it was just as hard on his family and friends. Ron knew my mama. He'd bring her deer sausage. I knew his kids. I wonder how they're doing."

Ronnie and Angela are doing fine.

"Jeff, it wasn't just the fatalities that happened within the mill. It was the cancer. Kunnie, Weasel, O'Connor... Willie Holland had to retire because of the cancer. He's gone now, too.

"For years, we didn't wear respirators. Guys would heat up their lunches wrapped in aluminum foil on the coke oven doors with that yellow toxic gas just floating around their food. We washed our tools with benzene. I'm glad I got out in one piece."

I'm glad you did too, my friend. How long have you lived in Barrington Ridge Townhomes?

"Twelve years. For the past seven years, Beverly was the president of the Barrington Ridge Townhomes Association. She has recently taken a sabbatical. I help put the four fountains in and take them out every year. I change the lights at the mail stations and shovel snow from them as well.

I also did the piping for the pond after it burst. We have clean-ups here.

"About five minutes away is the Maria Reiner Center. I go there at least three times a week. It's for people 50 and older. They have all kinds of activities. I do the tread mills, lift weights, shoot baskets and play chess. Me and Beverly took Spanish lessons there. We did Zumba, too. It costs $25 a year for seniors who are residents."

* * *

The coke plant workers at Inland were pretty much the red-haired step children of the mill. But we were a band of brothers and sisters. Willie Jackson was an easy going kind of guy with a wry sense of humor, he was a damn good mechanic, and the best of the lot. Never met a person who has known Willie and not liked him. He has done well for himself and I wish him the best in retirement.

Believe me, he earned it.

Fred Gorniak *(March 2013)*

"My happiness grows in direct proportion to my acceptance."
– Michael J. Fox

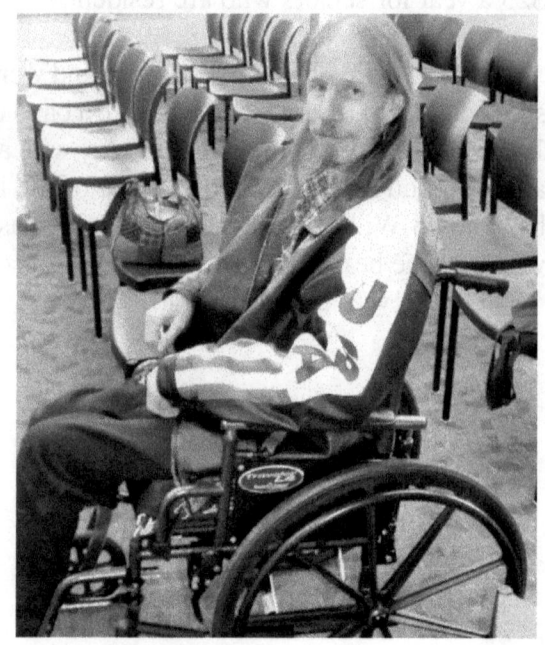

Fred Gorniak, 50, spent the first 30 years of his life in South Chicago. For the past 20 years, he has lived in Lake Village.

Gorniak used to play the drums and worked as a millwright, but not any more. Because of multiple sclerosis and throat cancer, he can no longer walk or talk.

Gorniak wrote his replies to me on an erasable board. It's not the first I've conducted an interview in such a way.

* * *

Growing up around 93rd Street in Chicago?

"I remember rolling down the railroad hill in an empty refrigerator box with my buddies," he said.

Did you fish Wolf Lake as a kid?

"Oh, yeah. I fished Wolf Lake, Calumet Park and Powderhorn."

Did you catch a few channel cats?

"We caught everything."

Several years ago, I interviewed a musician named Eric Lambert who grew up near where you did, he's probably a few years older than you. I believe Eric attended Mendel Catholic High School.

"That name sounds very familiar. I'm Catholic, but I don't brag about it."

Is Gorniak a Polish name?

"Yes. My father worked a meat cutter, in heating and air conditioning, and was a steel worker who ended up in the millwrights. My mother's maiden name is McGregor. After retiring as a nurse practitioner, she became a lawyer. Mom is my power of attorney because I can't speak."

Life after George Washington High?

"I got into the Chicago Millwrights, Local 1693. I did that for about 17 years."

Did you enjoy being a union millwright?

"I loved my job. I worked on a lot of conveyor belts in steel mills and coal mines. I also spent a lot of time at Dresden Generating Station in Grundy County."

The first privately financed nuclear power plant built in the United States. I've boated right by it. The plant is near the confluence of the Kankakee and Des Plaines rivers, which forms the Illinois River.

"That's right."

How old were you when got into the millwrights?

"I was 18."

Did you serve an apprenticeship?

"No, I bought a card. One day, I couldn't spell millwright and the next day, I was one."

When did you realize you had multiple sclerosis?

"I started feeling it when I was 20; the doctors didn't know what I had until I was about 26. Thank God for MRIs."

How long were you able to work?

"Until I was about 38."

Have you ever been married?

"No, I've lived on my own since I was 20."

Can you use a walker?

"Not since 2010. After my throat surgery, I laid in bed for almost three months. The muscles in my legs went flat like a tire. If you don't use it, you lose it.

Your inability to speak?

"In 2010, I suffered from Stage 3 throat cancer. But I won't let things bother me; I deal with it. Hey, I can drive; my car has hand controls."

You have a good attitude.

"I try to keep a positive outlook and stay happy. I always remember someone out there has it a lot worse than me. My doctor asked me, 'Why are you so happy?' I said, 'Why not?'"

* * *

After having to put down his wrenches because of his disease, Gorniak attended culinary school from 1998 to 2001. He told me lamb is his speciality and continues to cook for small parties and weddings. At Thanksgiving, he prepares turkeys for his friends.

In 2007, as a participant in Skydive Boogie for M.S., Gorniak jumped from 14,000 feet. On his board, he wrote down for me: "It was a RUSH!!"

And, then, Freddie Gorniak smiled.

Jessica Nunemaker *(Aug. 2013)*

"Well I was born in a small town
Prob'ly die in a small town
Oh, those small-communities"
– John Mellencamp

To my knowledge, Jessica Nunemaker never has been crowned Miss Indiana, but she is Ms. Little Indiana. She is the owner of *littleindiana.com*, a PBS host, and a small town explorer. Her television show is *"little* Indiana: Where to Stay, Play and Eat in Small Towns Across Indiana."

Nunemaker, 33, is married to Jeremy, they live in Rensselaer and are raising two sons, ages 8 and 3.

* * *

"I lived in Chicago Heights, Ill. until I finished kindergarten," Nunemaker began. "I remember going to story hour at the library in Chicago Heights. Then my parents moved to Demotte."

Maiden name?

"Holobowski.

Did you attend Kankakee Valley High School?

"Yes. I really liked theater when I was in high school."

When you left DeMotte, where did you go?

"Indianapolis. I attended the University of Indianapolis. I made better grades in college than I did in high school, but I dropped out after a year because of financial reasons.

"I've always loved writing. In college, a professor told me I had a nice turn of phrase."

You're left-handed.

"How did you know that?"

53

Your likes, dislikes, what you're good at, what you're not good at. Nine of 10 times I can tell if someone is a southpaw. Do you dislike math and are you directionally challenged?

"You got it. It's funny, my husband and our oldest son also are left-handed. Our poor youngest has to watch everything being done backwards."

Is Indianapolis where you met your husband?

"Actually, we met at Ball St. (University), even though neither of us went to Ball St. We had mutual friends there. We just started talking. I had never given out my phone number to a guy in my life, but for some reason, I gave it to Jeremy. He told me within an hour of meeting him, 'I'm going to marry you some day.'"

Yeah, I used to use that one back in the day.

"Turns out it he was right, but he also joined the Navy two weeks after we were married. 9-11 had just happened; I guess he was feeling patriotic. We moved to Charleston, S.C.; then we were transferred to Seattle. After two years, we moved to Rensselaer. Housing was outrageous in Seattle."

The birth of "little Indiana"?

"One evening during our first December in Rensselaer we started hearing sirens – lots of sirens. My husband decided to see if there was something he could do."

What was it, a bad fire?

"Jeremy returned almost immediately and said: 'Grab your coats, you're not going to believe this, but there's a huge Christmas parade going on out in the street.'

"We had no idea they do that every year. It got me thinking, if we didn't know about the parade, how many other people didn't know?"

When did you get your own website and start blogging?

"I registered the name in January of '09, but the site didn't go live until September. It took me a while to find my groove, but I eventually decided if a town is 15,000 people or less, I'll go there.

"I've been to more than 100 small towns now. I just went over the 50,000 reader mark and have more than 4,400 facebook fans. We were taking a tour of a college the other day and a man tapped me on the shoulder and asked me: 'Are you *little* Indiana?' The group I was with let out a collective gasp as if I were a celebrity."

You're getting there.

"My mom knows who you are. She reads your column all the time."

Did she mispronounce my last name as if were spelled "Mainz"?

"Yes."

I've been called Mainz my entire life.

"That's like Nunemaker or Holobowski. There's a book that tells you how to look up the background of your name. So if you have a name that's strange or difficult to pronounce and want to go by a stage name that has the same meaning as your real name, you can change it. I looked up my name hoping it would translate into something like Hall or Jones."

And?

"Castrater of pigs."

Getting back to little Indiana. How did you get from having your own website and blogging to television?

"In June of last year, I got an e-mail from a woman who said she was a PBS producer. She had been following my blog and thought it would be a great segment."

What station airs your program?

"WTIU out of Bloomington. I give her a list of places and usually do a big chunk at a time. Like, I've done 11 one right after the other and then I write a script for each one. I'll include the information I want the videographer to capture.

"Right now, PBS has no budget. They would love to give me my own show, but there's no money. I do an introduction in front of the camera and they also do a fade away with my voice-over at the end. They're are trying to find a sponsor for me."

Tell me more.

"I focus on businesses a lot. If you go to a small town, what would you want to know about it? Where are you going to eat? Is there somewhere to stay?"

How long is each segment?

"About three or four minutes. Slowly but surely, my scripts are getting a little longer. My dream is to have a 30-minute show. There is so much cool stuff to write about in these small towns.

"We've been to places that don't even show up when you Google them. People think they have to travel out of state or overseas for neat things to see and do. Small town travel is memorable and affordable; it's an experience."

Name a few neat places or events you written about.

"Oh, my. Everything from exploring caves to eating duck."

Mallard?

"That was in a town of 142 – Perkinsville. The restaurant is called Bonge's Tavern. We were looking for the place and couldn't find it with the GPS. Finally, we see this little sign with an arrow way up high on a telephone pole that said, 'Bonge's Tavern.'

"It was so packed, we had a two-hour wait. It's a bedroom community and the only business in town. The guy had been a chef in some very exclusive places. Now, it's a father-daughter chef team. The restaurant used to be a general store more than 100 year ago."

Very cool.

"Everyone knows there's going to be a wait, so they tailgate in the parking lot. They even have a port-a-pottie out there."

Where is Perkinsville?

"North of Noblesville."

Another interesting little Indiana haunt or tidbit?

"Rensselaer should not be called Rensselaer. It should be named Yeoman. Back in the day, a man named Yeoman had a land claim in this area although he didn't have it registered officially. Well, this guy from New York – Van Rensselaer – comes to this area.

"It was horrible weather conditions so Yeoman invited Van Rensselaer to spend the winter in his cabin."

Hoosier hospitality.

"That spring, Van Rensselaer went to the courthouse and purchased the property. He had Yeoman kicked out his cabin and off the land."

Stinkin' New Yorker. Probably a Yankee fan.

* * *

Nunemaker told me that she would go for car rides with her dad when she was a girl. She said he would always frequent or at least point out all the mom-and-pop restaurants and shops, saying: "Those are the salt-of-the-earth people right there."

Good for Mr. Holobowski.

And, today, it's quite obvious the apple of daddy's eye didn't fall far from the tree.

Kimberly Joy Harris *(April 2014)*

"Go, tell it on the mountain..."
– African-American spiritual song

Kimberly Joy Harris has worked for Enbridge Pipeline Co. the past 17 years. She supervises corrosion control for more than 40,000 miles of pipeline in the United States and Canada.

Harris has a bachelor's degree in electronics engineering, several master's degrees, and is less than six months from earning her PhD.

Harris has traveled to Mexico, Spain, Columbia, Peru, Brazil and Oman. She is fluent in Spanish and Portugese and is working on French.

Harris is part Cherokee Indian, runs five miles a day, and has volunteered her services for the Emergency Services Disaster Agency in South Holland, Ill. for the past six years.

Our interview took place in Schererville after I'd sat in on her "energy4everyone" presentation, part of an Enbridge Employee Volunteer Assignment.

Kim Harris is a whirlwind.

* * *

You live in South Holland with your husband Keith Brock.

"At times; I'm on the road a lot," she said. "I grew up in Englewood (a community in Chicago) and spent my high school years in Beverly (another Chicago community)."

I know Beverly is a blue-collar and historic neighborhood, tell me about Englewood.

"We still have a family home there; my folks are originally from Yazoo City, Miss. Back then, Englewood was a very close-knit neighborhood. We had what we called block clubs. You took care of your blocks; you had the rules. Rule No. 1 was you can't play loud music – this was the '70s. You couldn't wash your car in front of the house. No littering and that kind of stuff."

Englewood today?

"It has changed a lot in the last five to seven years. When I grew up in Englewood, everybody was family. Today, a lot of the homes are boarded up and vacant. There is a lot of subsidized housing. Most of the people don't care about their neighborhood or care about their grass or flowers – things that we grew up with. You didn't walk on people's grass. That was a big no-no.

"The people who live in Englewood today come from an environment where they didn't even have grass. That's what has kind of ruined Englewood and other communities."

I've been told you cook Thanksgiving dinner for a lot of people.

"Yes, we have a little bit of everything. There's fish – I'm really big on fish. There's chicken, pot roast, ham, turkey, green bean casserole, black-eyed peas, greens, macaroni and cheese... ."

How does a city girl become an expert on pipe corrosion?

"By accident. My first love has always been electronics. That was my first desire when I went to college. But my last year in high school, I was into computer science because that was the next thing. Right?

"When I finished high school, Devry University came to my house and met with my parents – I had scholarships. We were about to sign on the dotted line and I looked in their book and saw electronic engineering. I said: 'This is what I want to do.' The councilor said: 'Are you sure? There aren't many women in electronic engineering.' I didn't even think about that; it didn't matter."

Good for you.

"I wasn't out of college two weeks and I started with Enron (Corp.) in the liquids division. Enron was a great company. They had some greedy people there, but the company itself was awesome. I was with Enron for nine years."

How did that turn out?

"I lost everything."

Tell me about energy4everyone and your trip to Peru last fall.

"I volunteered in Peru for about 30 days. Our vision is to help empower people and communities to improve their own lives by providing energy to everyone. We installed solar systems for the people living in the Andes Mountains. Energy poverty affects over 2 billion people worldwide."

The mountain people living in huts?

"Home is where the heart is. In my mind, I didn't see what I consider poverty. I've seen poverty in my travels. Poverty is not having means for clean water or being able to grow food. The Peruvians grow their own food. They have fresh stream water. They were always smiling and are extremely friendly people."

Kim, maybe I playing devil's advocate here, but during your presentation you stated that those folks slept on dried cow pies, ate guinea pigs, and made a dollar a day.

"What do you need a dollar for? Maybe for medical reasons. When I cut my finger in the mountains, we couldn't get it to stop bleeding for two days. One of the locals used cactus juice to stop the bleeding. None of us Americans could do that.

"My parents lived in the country outside of Yazoo City, Miss. They didn't have power. They had an outhouse. They also fished and always had a huge garden. They had each other."

We don't want to downplay what Enbridge volunteers are doing.

"The quality of life is better because of what we are doing. The kids can study after dark now and the moms can mend clothes after the sun goes down. They can listen to music now."

Back to the United States. You've set up your own scholarship.

"Of course. You have to give back. It's a scholarship that I give out to young engineers."

It's for females only.

"I've opened it up; you can't be biased. It's called Engineering New Minds. It's in my mom's and grandma's names. Students have to apply for it and have to put in so many hours of volunteering. You have to have a 4.0 (grade point average) or close."

You're a very spiritual person.

"Yes. I'm a Baptist, but whatever country I'm in, if they have a church, I'm going in. My faith is the greatest part of my life and the essence of how I live. I start and end each day in prayer."

* * *

Most of her accolades and accomplishments came from a mutual friend of ours. She wouldn't even let me take her photograph. She is one of the most humble human beings I've ever met.

Kimberly Joy Harris is salt of the earth.

Don and Gail Mills *(July, 2014)*

"Eventually, all things merge into one, and a river runs through it. The river was cut by the world's great flood and runs over rocks from the basement of time. On some of those rocks are timeless raindrops. Under the rocks are the words, and some of the words are theirs. I am haunted by waters."
– Norman Maclean

For nearly 40 years, Don and Gail Mills have lived along Ramsey Road on the southern bank of the Kankakee River. They have a Hebron mailing address yet live in Jasper County. You see, at one time, before their time, the land where their house is located was Porter County. But that was before man altered the course of the river.

Don, 61, and Gail, 59, grew up in Griffith. They have raised four adult children: Wendy, Andy, Jamie and Alex. All four graduated from Kankakee Valley High School.

Don is a member of Steelworkers Local 1014 at U.S. Steel in Gary, and Gail cleans houses.

* * *

When did you two start going steady?

Gail: "We met each other in April of '69. We've been together ever since. I was almost 15."

Don: "I'd ride my Stingray bicycle to her house. Plus, she worked at Stan's grocery store at the intersection of Colfax and Miller and I'd see her there, too."

Don probably was the star athlete and you the ever-smiling bouncy cheerleader at Griffith High.

Gail: "No, we were nerds."

This place on Ramsey Road?

Don: "I was spending my weekends here by the time I was 8. I can remember my dad driving here all the way from Griffith and not passing a car. True story."

Gail: "We moved here when Wendy was six months old back in the spring of '76. I've always been an outdoor person. Before we were married, we'd come down here. Don's uncle owned this little summer shack. It had a motorcycle in it and Playboy magazines. That was it. But it did have a real cool fireplace. I always wanted a fireplace and I always wanted to live on water. We moved in."

Don: "Gail used to put butter dishes on the ceiling to catch the rain. It had a flat, leaky roof."

Gail: "I used to make toast in the living room. There was only one outlet. It was pretty bare bones for a long time. It took a month to get a phone. It was kind of scary out here at first. My dad bought us a dog."

Don: "We used to go tubing a lot. We'd take a plastic barrel, wrap an inner tube around it, and put a keg of beer inside it. The keg would float along with us. We'd just hit the tapper and pour ourselves a beer while tubing in the river."

Colorful characters living on Ramsey Road through the years?

Don: "Vestie built the two shacks upstream from us. They were never meant to be lived in year-around."

Vestie?

Don: "Vestie Reder. His real name was Sylvester. My dad and uncles had places here before Vestie. Tex and Maury lived in the trailer on the very end. Maury, the husband, was something. I don't know if anybody has ever done this, but he built a snowmobile track on the back of a Mercury outboard so he could get to the bar at Baum's Bridge through the bayou when the water level was real low. Tex was a good old gal."

Flooding?

Gail: "Jamie was born during the flood of '82. She was about three days old when we brought her home from the hospital. We had to park at Doc Johnson's near the four corners, put her and the other two kids in a boat, and then row another half-mile up Ramsey Road to our home."

Don: "That was the worst flood since we've been here. The river broke out at 231."

Gail: "But that's how we really got to know our neighbors. We sandbagged together. Everybody helped each other out."

Don: "Marti's would stay open all the time during a flood. You could go in there and have a beer and a sandwich."

Let's fast forward. Your yard is landscaped beautifully. You both really keep the place nice.

Don: "We've put a lot of work into the place. Gail would be right in there with us mixing concrete when we poured the stairs to the river"

Gail: "It has been a longtime labor of love."

Final thoughts about life on the Kankakee?

Don: "I think it was a lot better for our kids growing up on the river than in town or in a city. I don't know that I would've wanted to live anywhere else but here. It's like we're camping every day. We have a fire every night. You can relax. It's like you're vacationing every day."

Gail: "People have to pay to do what we do every day. We can watch our TV out here, play darts on summer nights under the stars, go for pontoon rides or just watch the river flow. It's so peaceful. I never take it for granted. It's always good to come home. It makes me want to cry... ."

* * *

Being as I live about 100 feet upstream from the Mills, in one of the shacks Vestie Reder built, I've sat in on more than a few of their campfires.

As far as the interview goes, all I did was record their riparian and hauntingly beautiful tale. The words are theirs.

And, yes, all things do eventually merge into one.

And for Don and Gail Mills, the Kankakee River runs through it.

WORK

Ed Sadlowski *(May 2011)*

"The time will come when our silence will be more powerful than the voices you strangle today."
– August Spies

August Spies spoke those words moments before he and three others were hanged.

Spies was one of the speakers at a labor rally that took place at Haymarket Square in Chicago on Tuesday, May 4, 1886. Civilians and police officers lost their lives that day in what would be known as the Haymarket Massacre.

In honor of May Day, I've opted to interview former USW District 31 Director Ed Sadlowski.

Sadlowski, 73, is married to Marlene. They have raised four children and are currently staying in St. John with one of their daughters.

* * *

"I was born and raised in South Chicago," Sadlowski began. "I moved to the East Side after we were married a couple of years. My wife was originally from the East Side. We met at Bowen High School."

Tell me about South Chicago during the 1940s and '50s.

"It was a very vibrant community. U.S. Steel's Southworks, fabrication shops, a big commercial district, men's stores, pool rooms, bars, furniture stores.... I was born on the second floor of a house that was located at 93rd Street and Commercial Avenue."

May Day?

"One of the things that spurred how the world celebrates May Day happened in Chicago in 1886. I said the rest of the world, not the United States.

"In the United States, instead of it being a worker's day, the powers that be chose to make May Day a festival with children playing around maypoles. Even worse, they sometimes called it Law Day. That was a psychological effect of erasing any semblance of the workers' day. And, after about two or three generations, it's done just that.

"There's a great tribute to those guys who were unjustly hung because of the Haymarket affair at the Waldheim Cemetery in the western suburbs of Chicago, right off the expressway."

I'd like to see that.

"You've got a date; I'll make it my business to be your tour guide. This May Day there will be a tremendous amount of festivities going on."

When did you hire in at U.S. Steel in Chicago?

"I quit school when I was 17 and joined the Army. When I got out of the Army, I went to U.S. Steel in 1956. After I was there four or five years, I ran for union steward and won. After that, I became a griever. Then I became president of Local 65 and I eventually ran for district director in 1973."

That would have been District 31, which included Chicago metropolitan-area locals and Northwest Indiana locals. Wasn't that the election that got ugly?

"Yes, it was. There were 250 local unions in the district with 150,000 (total) members. It was the biggest Steelworkers district in America. The vote was tampered with; they cheated me out of about 5,000 votes. I supposedly lost by 1,500 votes.

"It became very obvious that there had been hanky panky. I filed a protest; naturally, the protests were turned down by the executive board."

What then?

"I took that protest to the Department of Labor, which, from a philosophical sense, was one of the hardest things I ever did. I love the union; it's my life's blood. My grandfather, my father, and here I find myself in a situation suing the union. I didn't like that at all, but I had no alternative."

What happened in federal court?

"It was agreed to rerun the election. I was looking for the government to step in and recount the ballots, but it was so tainted by that stage, who knew? The opposing caucus had the ballots in their possession the entire time.

"We had a new election that was held for three consecutive days; it was manned by the Department of Labor. There were more than 300 federal agents on hand at different job sites. They counted the votes at the Federal Building."

What was the outcome?

"We won 40,000 to 20,000."

You also ran for International President of the USW in 1977.

"Yes, we put a slate together with five candidates from different parts of the country."

Your opponent?

"Lloyd McBride. It was a knockdown, drag out battle; I lost that one. Labor leaders have to be held to a higher standard than most, and should be. Unfortunately, that doesn't always hold true.

"Workers have an obligation themselves. Not just to be fed and bottle-fed by unions, but to create unions that are going to stand up and be counted. They have to be in the guiding role in doing that. The working stiff, he has to participate, make suggestions and be the watchdog. He has to know contracts, he has to understand working conditions, and most importantly, he has to understand what side he is on.

"Joe Block or Judge Gary hired you for one specific reason – to make money off of your labor. If you didn't contribute to their welfare, they wouldn't have hired you.

"When the squeeze is put on by the legislature and the governor of Wisconsin, thousands of people rallied around that. I was up in Madison and have never seen a crowd like that – 200,000 people. Just think if you would have had every working stiff on that street in Wisconsin. That governor would've been running for the hills.

"The same in Indianapolis. What the Indiana Democrats did was commendable; I hope the working men and women don't forget those guys who stood up for them by walking out. But at the same time, the workers have an obligation to stand up for themselves."

Eddie, can you imagine working in the mill in the early 1900s?

"I have a piece that was written in 1907; it appeared in Everybody magazine. It was a leading magazine at the time, a progressive magazine, not the muckraking type of writing that existed during the turn of that century. This particular piece was written by William Hard; it's entitled 'Making Steel and Killing Men.' It's a masterpiece in the sense of description of what went on in the steel mills."

You're quite the history buff.

"Yeah, I helped found the Illinois Labor Historical Society more than 40 years ago We should learn from history, but we don't. It's the banks that have caused all of these problems that we see around us today. The politician does whatever the bank tells him to do. Nothing has changed in this country in that respect."

I got to meet Studs Terkel, thanks to you.

"Terkel and I were in a movie together; it starred Jane Fonda."

The Dollmaker?

"That's it. I played Bender, an organizer on a soapbox."

Typecast again.

"Terkel played a cab driver. The director told Studs, 'Once Ms. Fonda gets in the cab, I need you to drive toward that telephone pole about 100 yards away and then stop.'"

Yeah?

"Terkel told him, 'I can't do that; I've never driven a car in my life.' Everybody on the set was laughing. The director eventually rounded up four kids to push the cab while Terkel steered."

Yeah?

"Studs crashed into the fuckin' pole."

My hero.

* * *

Ed Sadlowski is one of the most articulate, intelligent men I've met.

And he's old school.

Bill Rucker *(Oct. 2007)*

*"...and the sons of pullman porters
and the sons of engineers
ride their fathers' magic carpets
made of steel..."*
- Steve Goodman, *"City of New Orleans"*

I arrive at Maple Grove Greenhouse and the home of Bill Rucker on a Sunday night. Years ago we worked side by side at the Gary Farmers' Market. The Ruckers opened up Maple Grove two years after moving to Lowell. They have been in business 19 years. Tonight, we'll sit together in his pickup – and his train. Rucker also is a locomotive engineer.

Bill and his wife, Marie, have raised two adult children. Sarah is a medical coder who works at St Margaret Mercy Healthcare Centers in Hammond. Andy is a lieutenant aboard the USS Miami, a fast-attack submarine, operated somewhere in the Persian Gulf.

We head west, across U.S. 41, then north.

* * *

"I was oldest of eight children," Rucker begins. "Basically, the whole south side of Indianapolis was a German-Catholic ghetto. There's actually a memorial at the corner of Bluff Road and Hanna Avenue honoring all the German gardeners."

German gardeners?

"They operated truck farms. Part of the extension of having a truck garden was to have greenhouse. Initially the greenhouse was used to grow the transplants for the field, but people who had vegetable gardens needed transplants – an industry was born."

"I attended Cathedral High School in downtown Indianapolis – The

Fighting Irish," chuckles the big German. "I'll have 30 years with Amtrak next October. I started out as carman welder at Beech Grove maintenance shops. Beech Grove was the entire country's railroad passenger car maintenance facility. It was originally 'the big four shops' owned by the New York Central.

"In 1979, Amtrak took over the shops. I've been with Amtrak ever since."

So you work for the feds?

"Amtrak is an arm of the Federal Railroad Administration which is the Department of Transportation. We're like two steps removed from being a government unit."

You guys don't pay into social security, right?

"Any railroad employee pays into railroad retirement as opposed to social security. Railroad retirement was the first government-sponsored pension plan that existed in this country; it dates back to 1869."

We drive by the Pullman neighborhood... Were the old pullman porters gone by the time you hired in?

"I worked with some of them. The pullman porters became employees with the emergence of the Amtrak Act of 1970. They were actually the first Amtrak takeover of employees, along with the coach attendants, dining car stewards and the station ticket agents. Amtrak needed them."

They were mostly African-American guys, weren't they?

"At the beginning, the workforce consisted of African Americans, yes – all male. A lot of these men continued to work for Amtrak because that was their life – riding the rails and serving the customer.

"They were the first line of customer service. There were different classes, you had coach attendants who basically tended to the people who were riding in the coach class. You also had the sleeping car attendants; they were the actual remnants of the old pullman porters. Pullman cars were all sleeping cars. In the modern era, each sleeping compartment had its own restroom. It was considered the first-class travel."

We drive past US Cellular Field; mercifully the Sox had played their final game of the season a few hours before. Our destination is the southwest side, 37th and Kedzie, 51 miles from Maple Grove...

Union?

"I belong to The Brotherhood of Locomotive Engineers. That's in the transportation division of the International Brotherhood of Teamsters.

The BLE was one of the very first organized labor groups in the United States. It was originally formed in Jackson, Mich., prior to the Civil War. We provided a model for the modern labor movement.

"The railroad's heyday, as far as passenger service was concerned, was from its conception in 1828 until the early 1950s. The advent of passenger aviation pretty much sealed the fate of the railroad. But there will always be people who don't like to fly. The biggest thing we have over airplanes is we stop at places they don't. Amtrak services more than 600 cities that have no aviation transport. We operate 72 trains a day out of Chicago – 162 trains nationwide"

"Out of Chicago, I've worked as far south as Carbondale,(Ill.), as far west as Galesburg, (Ill.),as far north as Grand Rapids, (Mich.). and as far east as Pittsburgh. The route to St. Louis basically cuts the state of Illinois at a diagonal. The train actually travels underneath the arch. Pittsburgh was 11 hours and 14 different stops – Hammond, South Bend, Elkhart, Toledo, Cleveland...."

What do you do once you get to Pittsburgh?

"The railroad provides us with away-from-home accommodations, which usually is the cheapest hotel they can find."

We arrive at Brighton Park Maintenance Facility...

"Once you leave the station it's the conductor, assistant conductor, fireman, and the engineer's responsibility to ensure the safe operation of the train. Locally, we're able to do 79 miles per hour. In some parts of Michigan, 100 mph. Between Washington D.C. and Boston (the Northeast Corridor),125 mph. People don't realize that a passenger train traveling at 79 mph will occupy a 35-foot-wide crossing in exactly 1.2 seconds. Some people can't wait that long. The train always wins."

Have you ever...?

"I've never personally been involved in a fatality with a human being. I hit a cow just south of Joliet along the Southern Pacific.

"I'm on what is considered a transfer job now. We transfer the repaired and rebuilt cars from the Brighton Park Maintenance facility to the 14th Street yard in downtown Chicago."

"We'll be riding in 519. She's used as a switch engine now. This locomotive is a 16-cylinder diesel engine that powers a 600-volt DC generator. It generates approximately 3200 HP. It's a four-axle locomotive geared for passenger speed; it can obtain 110 mph. In the last fifteen years she's probably accrued four million to five million miles."

* * *

Rucker's task this night is to take four Superliner double-deckers to the yard and bring back seven cars for repairs. His brakeman gives him signals with a switch lantern.

The Canadian National is on the set of track we need to use. Can't do nothin' till she moves. When he gets the green light, Rucker tells the dispatcher, "We're headin' for the yard."

He follows the track; there's no steering wheel on a locomotive. It's an 8 1/2-mile journey each way. As Sunday turns into Monday and September becomes October, we pass by Chinatown, Canal Street, Lawrence Fisheries, the Chicago River, Pilsen, Connie's Pizzeria, Bridgeport, and then the South Loop into the yard. We go underneath the U.S. Postal Service and beside an illuminated Sears Tower.

In the tunnel, Union Station.

We head back. Much to my surprise, "Big, Bad Bill" becomes "Sweet William" now. He delivers his seven cars and, like a latter-day Burls Ives, "The L & N Don't Stop Here Anymore"... .

"When I was a curly-headed baby
My daddy sat me down upon his knee
He said, 'Boy you go to school and learn your letters
Don't you be a dirty (railroader) like me... ."

R. J. Howard *(July 2011)*

"Horrifying Vegetarians Since 1995"
– Boss Hawg's Barbeque & Catering, Topeka, Kan.

DeMotte had suffered quite a storm a few days before I interviewed R. J. Howard. Scores of trees were down from what some folks refer to as a 110 mph microburst.

But the main tool of Howard's trade, his smoker, remained standing behind his place of business, Bub's BBQ.

Howard, 39, is single; he grew up in North Judson but has lived in Demotte since he opened up his business last December.

* * *

"I started Bub's in North Judson from May through November of last year," Howard began. "The volume of business is much greater here in DeMotte.

"In North Judson, I tried to compete with the Subways and the Burger Kings but couldn't. Those places were still full during lunch periods and mine was not. Over here, it's a completely different story."

R.J., I like the mom-and-pop places.

"Absolutely; I've always supported those kind of establishments, and now that I am one, I'm even more adamant about supporting the local businesses. Sure, I could buy something cheaper at Walmart, but I'll stop at Fase's Water to buy my salt for my water softener because they are customers of mine."

Ever been married?

"Twice. This is my life now; Bub's is my life."

College?

"I went to Ball State University for two years, but didn't graduate.

At that point in my life I was young and stupid and had no idea what I wanted to do."

Why did you go to college?

"Photojournalism. It wasn't until I was 37 that I found what I wanted to do – here it is."

Who taught you how to cook?

"My mother's side of the family; her maiden name is Griffo. I also got their looks, thank God. I'm half-Italian and half-hillbilly. Back in the day, a large portion of North Judson's population was made up of Italian immigrants. We were always a very close-knit group."

When I interviewed Starke County attorney Marty Lucas he also told me that.

"Marty was a regular when I had Bub's in North Judson; he's a great supporter of his community.

"I'm the only person who does the cooking here. Like my mother, I don't measure anything, but my recipes are consistently the same."

Why the name Bub's BBQ?

"Bub was my nickname growing up. My father still calls me Bub. I thought Bub's BBQ was kinda catchy.

"People still manage to mess it up; I get Bob's BBQ or Bubba's BBQ a lot. I'm particular about that; I correct them. It's funny, I'm starting to get a little recognition lately. I was in Valparaiso the other day and a guy and his wife were walking out of Starbuck's and he said, 'Hey, honey, it's Bub.'"

Do you advertise?

"Yes, in a local newspaper and on Indiana 105, the country radio station out of Valparaiso."

You've surely dealt with my buddy Mac MacLeod the disc jockey.

"Mac writes all my commercials. I do my own voicing. Mac's a great guy.

Word of mouth is good, too.

"Yes, I get customers from Hammond, Dyer, Crown Point, Lowell, Lafayette... . People will drive 45 minutes to an hour to eat my food. I am humbled beyond belief by that. I'll ask customers how they heard about me and often they'll say something like, 'A guy I work with up in the mill said it's the best BBQ he's ever had.'"

Other than those picnic tables outside, it's all carry out. Ever think of expanding?

"My standard line to folks when they ask about permanent seating is, 'As long as people keep walking through that door, I will put seats in this place.' I'd like nothing more than to knock down some walls and put some tables and chairs in here."

You only make so much food each day.

"Correct. I'm proud to say everything on my menu is homemade. Nothing is canned, processed or prepackaged. All the recipes are my recipes. I don't make a whole lot every day because I want to maintain the quality of the product.

"I've had situations where people have come in to order my ribs and I'll pull a rack of ribs out and maybe they've been in the warmer too long and they're overcooked or something. I won't serve them; I'm that particular about the quality of my food. When we first started six months ago, I was running out of food every day. I'm tracking it better now."

Bub, your mother and Grandma Griffo taught you how make a mean marinara. When or where did you master barbequing?

"I lived outside of Kansas City (Kan.), for a couple of years; that's where I learned my style. I went to a lot of the places you don't go to at night because they were in dangerous neighborhoods. But they were some of best places you could go to for BBQ. I learned a lot from those places."

What's your most popular item?

"Pulled pork. Full and half racks of ribs are good sellers. I have people tell me they are the best ribs they've ever had. I won't sell them if they're not falling off the bone.

"I like to think I've introduced beef brisket to this part of the world. Local customers would ask if brisket was anything like pulled pork. I'd say, 'No, but it's one of the best things you'll ever eat in your life.' I'd give them a sample and they'd say, 'I'll take that.'"

Bub, I can't help but chuckle. Leave it to an Italian to get the Dutchmen of DeMotte to buy soul food. It's not a sin, to get sauce on the chin.

"Another unique item that we do is Bub's homemade potato chips. Some people get irritated because we don't serve French fries."

What do you tell them?

"McDonald's is right up the road if you want fries."

No. 14 on the menu looks like it would fill a hearty appetite.

"Big Bub's Combo: four ribs, one-quarter pound pork, one-quarter pound brisket and a half chicken which includes bread, pickles and two sides. It'll feed two people for 20 bucks."

What side dishes do you serve?

"Bourbon-fried apples, cole slaw, potato salad, cowboy beans, green beans or Bub's chips."

Do you cater?

"Yes, I (recently catered) a wedding in Lafayette for 125 guests."

They say for a small business owner to survive, you have to be a human dynamo.

"When I first started here, I was working 18 to 20 hours a day. I'm down to 16- and 18-hour days right now."

Who's this young lady?

"Kelly Dykstra; she's director of global expansion. Kelly will graduate from Kankakee Valley High School in a few days. She's a great worker."

* * *

R.J. Howard's unique menu is a reflection of himself. He doesn't serve Mountain Dew or Pepsi, but he does carry Filbert's Old Fashioned Soda. It's a family-run business out of Chicago that's been around for a long time.

I have a feeling Bub's BBQ will be around a while, too.

Butch Grimmer *(April 2013)*

"Opportunity is missed by most people because it is dressed in overalls and looks like work."
– Thomas Alva Edison

Until about two years ago, Butch Grimmer, 60, lived in the town where he grew up – Schererville. Today, he lives in Morgan Township with his wife Joan so they can be closer to their daughter's family.

Grimmer attended St. Michael School in Schererville and graduated from Bishop Noll Institute.

Like his father before him, Grimmer owns and operates Grimmer's Service Inc., located just west of the U.S. 30 & 41. Brian Grimmer – one of Butch and Joan's four adult children – has chosen to stay in the family business.

Butch balked at the thought of being interviewed, saying he wouldn't be of interest to anyone and that I was barking up the wrong tree. I finally coaxed him into it. Past experience has proven it's usually humble folks like him who have the best stories to tell.

* * *

"During the 1870s, Peter Michael Grimmer left the Alsace-Lorraine region at the age of 22; he eventually ended up in Illinois," Grimmer began. "This document – written in French – lists the texture of his skin, the color of his hair and the size of his nose."

Your father, Norbert Grimmer, started the business?

"Yes, Dad came back from World War II and hired in at U.S. Steel. He worked there for a very short period of time. He said, 'Well, I survived the war, why would I want to spend the rest of my life in the mill or possibly get killed in the mill?'

"So, he started his little business in the same location we're at right now. He purchased 2.8 acres for $700. I'm sure he was up many nights trying to figure out how he was ever going to pay it off."

Was Norbert Grimmer always the sole proprietor?

"For less than a year, it started out as Grimmer-Bonney Auto. Mr. Bonney was a bomber pilot during World War II. After the war, with the rebuilding of Germany, they were looking for American pilots who could deliver the supplies. Bonney decided that's what he would do."

This place has been known as Grimmer's before I was ever born. I'd never heard of the short-lived partnership. Butch, I can't help but think of one of my favorite George Carlin lines.

"What's that?"

Have you ever walked into Sears and wondered whatever happened to Roebuck? Enough levity. Early memories of the place when your dad had a booming towing business and had gas pumps here.

"I was taking car parts apart at this station when I was 5. When I was 6 or 7, I came home from school and Dad said we had to change the price of gasoline. I asked him, 'To what?' He said, 'To 30.9 (cents per gallon.) '

"I knew my dad was an intelligent person, but at that moment, I was thinking he was crazy. I didn't believe there would ever be a day when someone would come to Grimmer's and pay 30 cents for a gallon of fuel."

Outrageous!

"Growing up in the town of Schererville was great. I was so fortunate to grow up next to Roscoe and Gladys Protsman. They were both longtime teachers who grew some of the best strawberries you ever ate.

"The Protsmans had identical twin grandsons who lived in Fort Wayne. Their names were Peter and David. Because of me, they became great successes."

How's that?

"When they were 6 or 7 and I was a couple years older, I told them how stupid they were. We didn't have air conditioning back then, so the kitchen window was open and my mother heard me. Mom took me in the house and explained why I shouldn't call anyone stupid."

And?

"Life went on, and probably 30 years later, I found out that the twins probably weren't as stupid as I thought they were."

Did they go on to invent a longer lasting light bulb?

"No, but their photography has graced the covers of Newsweek, Time, Look and Life magazines about 150 times.

"They've shot the massacre around Tiananmen Square, the fall of the Berlin Wall, the end of Apartheid in South Africa and the genocide in Rwanda, just to name a few assignments. In 1990, David won a Pulitzer Prize."

Wow, man. You're talking about Peter and David Turnley. They were featured on "60 Minutes" several years ago.

"That's right. And I've never called anyone stupid since that summer day in Schererville."

Changes at Grimmer's through the years?

"A lot has gone on over the years. In this photo, you can see what our building looked like in the '50s. That's Dad next to what I believe is a '56 Chevy. Those are our Phillip's 66 gas pumps. We were a distributor of Frank Phillip's Petroleum Co. products for at least 40 years."

Then what?

"In the '60s, we went with a new style of building with these slanted windows you see in this photo. Looking at this picture reminds me of a real crazy time of my life."

Probably a lot of sex, drugs and rock-n-roll, huh?

"I usually got the detail of cleaning the bathrooms, being the young man I was. As you would shut the door of the restroom, there would be a sign that read: 'This certified restroom, No.1776, is kept hygienically clean for your comfort and protection with daily disinfection with Lysol. If you find any untidiness or any supplies missing, please let me know so that I may correct them immediately.' Signed, Norbert Grimmer.

"I can't remember my own Social Security number or my wife's birth date, but I remember every stinking word of that sign because I looked at it three times a day for at least 10 years."

Butch, you're killin' me.

"Everything was available at Grimmer's in those days, not like today's specialized field."

Explain, please.

"We got out of the gasoline and towing business about 15 years ago. We pretty well stay in the areas of exhaust, tires, brakes, starters, alternators – repairs such as that. We typically like to get the customer in and out in half a day or less.

"We also have the Pennzoil 10-minute quick lube. In our heyday, we've had as many as 400 cars per week come through here. We pride ourselves knowing that we've changed the oil in more than a half-million cars in 67 years. Believe me, Butch Grimmer sat in on the greater majority of those."

Is Grimmer's one of the oldest businesses in the Dyer, Schererville and St. John area?

"Probably second-oldest. Teibel's Restaurant was here at least 10 years before us. We are very close with the Teibel family."

This area has really grown up since the 1960s.

"When I was a kid, there was a stop-and-go light at 41 & 30. Heading south, the next one was in Kentland."

Your son, Brian?

"Brian is the manager and pretty well takes care of everything now. I'm just here today to deal with the IRS and clean the restrooms."

* * *

All three generations of Grimmers have been known to work their share of 20-hour days in the last 67 years.

And any longtime customer will attest that when a Grimmer lifts up the hood of a car, there's a ton of experience staring at that starter.

Dan Murchek *(Sept. 2010)*

"We want our tax dollars to provide a hand up for the millions of working people who live on Main Street and not a handout to a privileged band of overpaid corporate executives."
– John Sweeney, former president of the AFL-CIO

Dan Murchek is president of Lake County Police Association, Local 72, and president of the Northwest Indiana Federation of Labor, AFL-CIO, CLC.

Murchek, 49, lives in Schererville and has been married to Alisa for 18 years. Dan's 25 year-old son, David, also is following a career path in law enforcement.

* * *

"My family is originally from East Chicago, but I grew up in the Hessville neighborhood of Hammond and graduated from Morton High School in '79," Murchek began. "Basically, if you weren't going away to college, you got a job up in the mills and bought yourself a Firebird or Camaro. And you either married a girl from the neighborhood or possibly expanded and married a girl from Highland or Gavit."

Steel workers who hired into the mill in '79 didn't fare to well.

"You're right. By the time I graduated; they really weren't hiring; they were starting to lay guys off."

Who hired you?

"Goldblatt's; I became a Local 142 Teamster. We were the guys who delivered all the appliances and furniture. I was making good money. Then, they started downsizing and subcontracting our jobs out."

Were the truck drivers who took over your jobs non-union?

"Yes, we were gradually getting phased out by seniority; being a new employee, I was one of the first to go. So, I got a job at St. Margaret

Hospital) in their security department; I worked there for a few years. That got me interested in police work. I started applying at different police departments once I turned 21, but I didn't have any connections. I'd get on the list, but nothing would ever happen.

"Finally, I got hired in Porter County by the town of Hebron as a full-time officer. Because I was very young looking, the town of Hebron lent me to the Porter County Drug Unit."

You became a narc.

"Yes, I worked undercover as a senior transfer student. I'd attend classes, make friends and buy drugs around the school. I was pretty good at it.

"After about a year-and-a-half, I took a job with the Dyer Police Department."

How long were you with the Dyer PD?

"A little over nine years; I left Dyer to take a job on the (Lake County) Sheriff's Department. It was a cut in pay, but I wanted to go to a much bigger department so I could expand my career in police work. I have 15 years with the county."

Your current position with Lake County Sheriff's Department?

"I'm a sergeant and a patrol supervisor on midnights. Working straight nights, we're in Gary on a regular basis. Gary cops are underpaid and way undermanned. I believe all cops are underpaid – firemen and teachers, too."

You lost your partner 13 years ago.

"Yes; on April 30, 1997 when I was working in our gangs crime unit; it's a date I won't forget. We got in a chase; the assailant jumped out of his car. I released Ajax to apprehend him. The bad guy shot and killed my dog at close range. That's when we got in a gun battle. Ajax saved my life."

Lake County Police Union?

"We're the only union police department in Northwest Indiana, maybe, in the entire state – Terre Haute might be part of a regular AFL-CIO union."

How long have you been president of Local 72?

"For six years, now."

Tell me about Northwest Indiana Federation of Labor.

"We – Lake and Porter Counties -- belong to what we call the Central Labor Council, the NWI Federation of Labor. We report to the state AFL-CIO in Indianapolis, who then reports to Washington D.C., where the national and international offices are located.

"The federation is made up of about 62 affiliate locals; we're like an umbrella organization. I represent labor in general to provide good working jobs for our community."

How many union members, from their respective locals, are part of the NWI Federation of Labor?

"About 52,000."

What do some of those workers do for a living?

"You name it: boilermakers, bricklayers, ironworkers, steel workers, teachers, firefighters, police officers, postal workers, Teamsters, carpenters, health-care workers, operating engineers.... Newspaper Guild #34014 is part of our Central Labor Council. The Post-Tribune is the only union newspaper in Northwest Indiana."

Sounds like NWI Federation of Labor is as diverse as the peoples who live here. I like that.

"Jeff, I can't say enough about the executive boards of the NWI Federation of Labor and Local 72. That goes for local labor leaders and business agents, too. I get a lot of information from them; they're a great learning tool. Jim Robinson of the USW and Dave Fagen from the Operator Engineers are both a wealth of knowledge. Guys like that have laid the groundwork for a lot of us. And somebody laid the groundwork for guys like Robinson and Fagen."

Unionism in a nutshell?

"Unions protect the employee and the employer, too; it's a two-way street. We know our rights and management knows its rights. Everybody knows what the rules are. The contract spells out the dos and don'ts. Unions level the playing field for the employee. Union jobs are traditionally well-paying jobs with medical benefits for middle-class American families.

"Unions also have been very adaptable over the years. Significant concessions have been made by many union members across the country. But we also feel that when the company's bottom line is good, those profits should be shared with those workers who helped make that bottom line like that. We want the companies to succeed."

You support projects such as making the Cline Avenue extension operable again.

"We should rebuild that bridge with steel made in NWI and using

NWI tradesman to do it. You wouldn't have to ship the material very far, would you? There were workers who paid the ultimate price building that bridge over our steel mills. It's a vital link that needs to be reopened."

Labor Day?

"Labor Day is a day to recognize the people who made some great sacrifices for us. Some gave their lives. People need to take a minute and think about what Labor has done for the communities of NWI."

Can it be a struggle?

"Jeff, working the night shift as a cop, I've been beat up and shot at a few times. During the daytime, I sometimes deal with hostile negotiation situations or stand on picket lines. It seems everybody is coming after you at times. You gotta have big shoulders and be able to take the heat, I guess."

* * *

Murchek is in contract talks representing Lake County police officers. The rank and file has faith in him; he has run unopposed or been reelected to six consecutive one-year terms as Local 72 president.

Night and day, Dan Murchek has taken the heat.

Andrea Georgion *(May 2014)*

"...When the moon hits your eye like a big pizza pie, that's amore..."
– As performed by former steelworker Dino Crocetti (Dean Martin)

Along with her husband James Chaddock, Andrea Georgion sells homemade, wood-fired, flatbread pizzas out of a 1952 Studebaker truck. The name of their business – I love this – is The Rolling Stonebaker.

Georgion, 29, grew up in Valparaiso and played soccer for Valparaiso High School. After graduation, she took culinary classes at the French Pastry School in Chicago.

Gregorian and Chaddock live in a brick house that was built in the 1920s. It's located on U.S. 12 in Beverly Shores. They have a son, Oliver, 4, who is into dinosaurs and ninjas.

* * *

What kind of name is Georgion?

"Greek," she said. "I'm Greek, Italian and a little bit of Polish."

No wonder you're quite the gourmet.

"My mother owns an Italian restaurant in Valparaiso named Pestos. I grew up working there. I used to own Cafe 444 on Lake Street in Miller (a community of Gary). When I was much younger, we spent a lot of time at an Italian hall, I believe it was in Merrillville. I remember my 'Nana' and all her sisters filling cannolis and making pastries. I think that's where I got my first passion for food – being around that. My paternal grandmother is full-blooded Greek. She was always baking and cooking – the smells. I really enjoyed that."

Where is your husband from?

"Beverly Shores. He grew up catching the school bus at the corner where we park the pizza truck."

Tell me more about this traveling pizza operation.

"We started the business in 2010. We didn't really have a business plan. We figured we could take the truck to weekend festivals. Something where we could make a few bucks, but not a fulltime commitment. That didn't work out so well. We don't have the ability to make 2,000 pizzas in an hour at large festivals. Plus, there are so many other variables like weather.

"At the end of that initial season, we were working the In Water Boat Show in Michigan City and got to talking to some residents of Beverly Shores. They asked why we didn't park the truck along U.S. 12 in Beverly Shores."

You took them up on the idea.

"It completely changed our business from carnival food vendor to roadside pizza. We grow the majority of our ingredients in the front yard."

How many tomato plants did you raise last year?

"More than 200. We do cherry tomatoes, heirloom Earl of Edgecombe tomatoes, we do a purple tomato called The Black Prince. There is nothing like a fresh, homegrown tomato."

What else do you grow?

"Spinach, kale, peppers, eggplant, all of our own basil.... Last year, for a couple of weeks, we were able to offer morel mushrooms that we'd gathered in the woods. It's a very basic pizza: light garlic, morels and mozzarella."

My tastebuds are in ecstasy just imagining it. Best selling pie?

"The Purple Pig. It starts with barbecue sauce, our own smoked pulled pork, mozzarella, provolone, and is topped with a purple slaw when it comes out of the oven. The slaw is dressed with a sweet balsamic reduction making it similar to a Carolina-style slaw. We were really excited in 2011 when Food Network Magazine did a feature called '50 States-50 Pizzas' and the Purple Pig was named best pizza in Indiana."

Would I like to pig out on a Purple Pig right now.

"We recently experimented with porter beer from Hunter's Brewing and created the Drunkin'Shroom pizza which was a huge fan favorite. It has a silky porter sauce made with baby bella mushrooms."

Hiccup.

"From Journeyman in Three Oaks, we used farm-fresh peaches and made a whiskey peach barbecue sauce for a special pizza with bacon, wood-roasted peaches, caramelized leeks and mozzarella cheese."

You're killin' me. Explain the on-site making of the pizzas?

"First of all, our crust is very thin. I think our customers appreciate that. They can eat a pizza, continue with their day, and not feel bloated."

Andrea, several years ago, I was in Italy for a couple weeks. I didn't see a pizza crust more than an 1/8th-inch thick.

The oven mounted inside the Studebaker?

"The oven is wood-fired. We use mostly red oak and we chop it ourselves – have to keep the muscles strong."

How hot do you keep the oven?

"About 700 degrees. The pizzas are made fresh to order and are ready in 90 seconds."

Are there specific times when customers can expect The Rolling Stonebaker to be set up for business?

"We try to be at our corner location five days a week from spring until about Thanksgiving. We have two '49 Studebakers and the '52. We don't operate the trucks in snow due to the salt. Most of the parts on the Studebakers are original.

"More people are entertaining the idea of booking us for their catering needs so it's getting more difficult to be at our corner location on U.S. 12."

Is it like a to-go thing only?

"Oh, no. We have picnic tables set up. Sometimes we offer desserts. There's also a liquor store next door if you want to have a cold beer with your pizza. And it's right across from the campgrounds, so we get a lot of visitors who are on vacation. It's working out great. Indiana Dunes Tourism has done a fabulous job promoting us."

A typical pizza catering?

"Whatever the customer would like. We customize as much as possible."

Expansion?

"We just purchased 'Pumps on 12'. It's an old gas station that was a restaurant for quite some time. It has been shut down for six or eight years. Our plan is to park the truck under the carport and serve pizza into the restaurant from the truck. We had to gut the place. We're hoping to have everything ready to go by early winter. It's ironic; Jim's first job was at 'Pumps on 12.'"

Beverly Shores?

"Jim and I really enjoy living in heart of Dunes Country. Beverly Shores is a little hidden treasure town. Our relationship together formed here, our son was born here, and our business has started here. It's a special thing to be able to feed our friends and neighbors at the corner where our pizza truck parks."

* * *

What an interesting couple. Jim was out of town the day of my interview with Andrea, but I've been told by several people he is an extremely talented musician who plays about a dozen instruments and has played bass for legendary bluesman Buddy Guy.

Morel and mozzarella pizza with a hint of garlic... That's amore.

Fred Utroske *(Nov. 2010)*

"Any jackass can kick down a barn, but it takes a good carpenter to build one."
– Sam Rayburn

Fred Utroske, 70, still doesn't need glasses and looks like he's in his early 50s. He has been married to Julie for 23 years; they have a Hanna phone number and a Union Mills mailing address. Both are members of the Sierra Club.

Julie is a tremendous artist and Fred is the most incredible woodworker I've ever met. Photographs of some of the doors and staircases he has created blew me away.

Our interview took place at the LaPorte County Historical Society Museum. Utroske often works there.

* * *

High school?

"Hanna; there were about 100 kids in grades 1 through 12. Today, those kids would go to LaCrosse High School. I'm the oldest of five kids; when I was 15, we got running water."

Been self-employed your entire life?

"No, I worked for a general contractor out of LaCrosse for about five years. After that, I was an apprentice sailboat builder. That's where I learned woodworking skills like steam bending. Then, I built prefab homes in Merrillville for about 15 years, but I always did woodworking jobs on the side.

"I've had my business license since 1962. I've been completely self-employed since 1976. I have about seven customers who keep me as busy as I want to be."

Is Julie originally from the Hanna-Union Mills area?

"No, she's from Rolling Meadows (Ill.); a stone's throw from Arlington Park racetrack.

"Julie and I went hunting together in Montana 24 years ago; we got along so well, the next year we got married in Montana by an Indian judge. Julie told the judge, 'We want it short and sweet.' The judge asked, 'How short and sweet?' She repeated, 'Short and sweet.' He said, 'You're married; that's as short as I can make it.' We went antelope hunting for our honeymoon."

Sounds like you two are birds of feather.

"Yeah, we grind our own flour and corn meal and eat wild game. We raise our own vegetables, too. We never once went out to eat in a restaurant this year. Some people say we're eccentric or artistic recluses."

Fred, I'd take that as a compliment. How much property do you own?

"We live on 11 acres, but also own 32 acres near Wheatfield. One of our hobbies is rescuing native wild plants. We're thinking about putting part of our property back into prairie. State botanists and a representative from JFNew have helped us identify 214 species of native plants on our land."

That's great; it seems more and more people with acreage are getting away from planting traditional Kentucky bluegrass or red fescue.

"Another one of our hobbies is training dogs. River, our black Lab, is going on 14. She's a Delta dog; meaning she could go into nursing homes and schools. River also got second place in the National Labrador Retriever Obedience trials. Julie did most of the training. We had to put our Doberman down. Red was a 90-pound therapy dog, too. He was the No. 1 (United Kennel Club) dog in the United States. Everybody loved Red."

Fred, this historical museum in LaPorte is one of the best I've ever been in. And you had a lot to do with it, hanging antique flying machines from the ceilings and mounting huge store fronts onto the walls.

"(American Automobile Association) ranks this place very high. I really feel privileged to know Dr. Pete."

You refer to LaPorte native, Dr. Peter Kesling. Didn't he invent retainers or braces for people's teeth?

"Dr. Kesling has about 60 patents."

Fred, I've watched Ken Burns' documentary entitled, "Horatio's

Drive: America's First Road Trip." Tell me about the Winton touring car that was the first automobile to drive across the country in 1903. And then tell me about the Winton on display here at the museum that did the same 100 years later in 2003.

"Winton Motor Carriage Company was located in Cleveland; the car was a 20-horsepower, two-cylinder, with a wooden body and wooden fenders. The original price was $2,500.

"The car that was driven from San Francisco to New York City by Dr. Horatio Nelson Jackson in 1903 is in the Smithsonian (Institution)."

How was the 2003 model created?

"I was hunting in Montana when Dr. Pete's secretary called me saying they found a (Winton) frame that had a serial number on it in a smelting plant in Bozeman, Mont. Somebody was smart enough to realize the frame was worth more than the price it would bring as melted-down scrap."

Then what?

"I made a frame out of wood, put it on top of my truck cap and brought it back to LaPorte County where we basically built the car."

Did Kesling help you?

"Oh, yeah. He's a very hands-on kind of guy. We had the help of a full time mechanic; I did the woodwork on the car. We borrowed a motor from a guy in California, had a patternmaker make a mold, cast it and make the engine."

And Mr. and Mrs. Kesling reenacted the road trip that Jackson took a century before.

"Yes, they did. It took Dr. Jackson 64 days; Dr. Pete did it in 40."

Tell me about the Door Prairie round barn that's standing right next door from where we're sitting.

"It's actually a nine-sided barn that was built in 1882."

Was it moved to this location?

"No, Marion Ridgway was the original owner. He was a horse man; the barn was built for horses. The P.C. Kesling Foundation owns the barn today. The property has been placed on the National Register of Historic Places by the United States Department of the Interior."

I love to hear stories of old buildings being saved; tell me more.

"Everything has to be made the way it was back in the 1880s. Even the cornerstones are the same cornerstones it sat on."

Was the barn in bad shape when you began the project?

"Yes, it was in disrepair. The city of LaPorte and the Historical Society couldn't afford to fix it up. So, Dr. Pete and his wife bought the barn and got a roof put on it. Since that time, I've raised it up, put a foundation under it, new timbers, siding – we've preserved it. I love working on it."

How long have you been working on the nine-sided barn?

"Off and on for about 25 years, at least. And all that time, I've only found one bent nail. The original carpenters were really good carpenters."

Ever plan on retiring?

"No, I love my work."

* * *

For Fred Utroske, working from the cornerstones to the cupola of the rustic and historic structure has been a quarter-century labor of love.

Kudos to the likes of Utroske and Kesling for opting to raise rather than raze the 1882 Door Prairie nine-sided barn.

Sharon Patterson *(March 2009)*

"Neither snow nor rain nor heat nor gloom of night stays these couriers from the swift completion of their appointed rounds."
-Herodotus

I never had met Sharon Patterson, 41, before interviewing her Saturday, Feb. 28.

She told me her youngest son, Ryan, 14, was an undefeated wrestler this year for Lowell Middle School.

Coincidentally, while we talked, Crown Point High School's wrestling team, including Patterson's 215-pound nephew and my 119-pound nephew, were vying for the team state championship in Indianapolis. They defeated Roncalli, Cathedral and Perry Meridian high schools one right after another. The young men rolled up their sleeves and performed the task at hand. The Bulldogs reached their ultimate goal, but had done the work all season.

And why not? Many are the sons of electricians, pipe fitters, Teamsters, steel workers and heavy-equipment operators.

Patterson is petite and sweet. She also is the president of National Association of Letter Carriers, Local 1624. When I pulled into the driveway of her Lowell duplex, I noticed a vehicle wearing an Obama-Biden bumper sticker. Another bumper sticker explained, "W. Stands for Weasel."

Her license plate stated that she supported our troops.

Patterson is the mother of four children; all but Ryan have left the nest. She has resided in Lowell for 14 years, but as a young girl, lived on the South Side of Chicago, just a Bill Melton home run from old Comiskey

Park in an Irish-American enclave called Canaryville. Her family moved to suburban Oak Lawn, Ill., in the mid-'70s.

* * *

"I had taken the post office test while living in Illinois," Patterson began. "Six months after moving to Indiana, they called me. Ryan was seven months old when I started. I figured it would be no problem to transfer; I delivered mail in Joliet (Ill.) for three years while living in Lowell."

That's a long commute.

"I was driving at least an hour each way, working 10-and 12-hour days. They gave me a walking route in the projects; there were gangs. It was interesting..."

Then what?

"I finally got in at Crown Point."

Although you're local president, you're not stationed at a union hall; you're still a full-time letter carrier.

"Yes; I sub on the same five routes all the time. My job title is carrier technician; it pays more money because it's considered a higher skill, knowing all five routes.

"Our normal shift is 7 a.m. to 3 p.m., but it's not like we're out there for eight hours delivering mail. We have to sort our mail before we go out."

How many addresses on an average route?

"I'd say a minimum of 500."

Do people who are stuck indoors behind a desk ever remind you how lucky you are to have a job where you can get a nice tan plus a little exercise without going to the gym?

"Jeff, I had never worked outdoors before. I hired in the summer of '95, the year all those people in Chicago died during that incredible heat wave. Still, I can take the heat better than the cold."

Slipping on ice is probably a leading cause of lost-time accidents.

"Yeah, we can't see what's underneath the snow. Extensions cords used for Christmas decorations can be dangerous, especially when your hands are full of mail."

Cave canem.

"Excuse me?"

Beware of the dog.

"I've only been bitten once – by a blind Shih Tsu named Mr.

Higgins. He snuck up behind me and got me on the calf – barely broke the skin."

Junk mail. I mean, Sharon, it just keeps coming. Day after day. It's enough to make a person "go postal," perhaps?

"We don't call it junk mail; we call it bread-and-butter mail – it keeps us working.

Postage stamps are going up again.

"Yes, in May, to 44 cents. But where else can you send something for that price? You can't drive your car from Lowell to Crown Point for 44 cents. My mother lives in Arizona; it's just as cheap to mail a birthday card to Tucson as it is Chicago.

"The economy is hurting us. People aren't getting the advertisements they used to. More people are paying their bills online."

More people are reading their newspapers online, too. Sharon, some gas stations charge more for a squirt of air than it costs to buy a newspaper.

"Jeff, I like to hold the paper, fold the paper, come back to it later. I need to cut things out of it; I don't want to read my newspaper on a computer screen. But that's just me."

Are you from a pro-union background?

"Yes; I'm not full-blooded Irish-American; my maternal grandfather emigrated from Spain – he worked at U.S. Steel as a blacksmith. My father worked for the phone company and was a union steward for the International Brotherhood of Electrical Workers. He brought me to the picket line when I was 18 months old. My brother lives in Crown Point; he's a member of the operating engineers, Local 150."

Did you become involved with your union right away?

"As soon as I transferred to Indiana, I got more active. I'm in my third, two-year term as local president. I also was vice president for a term.

"I was a Teamster before working for the U.S. Postal Service, so I was amazed when I was told it was optional whether or not I joined the union. I signed up right away, of course."

The NALC is an open shop compared to, say, a Steelworker from Local 1010 working in a closed shop where everyone but supervision has union dues taken out of their paychecks.

"Yes, nationwide, all of our members work in open shops."

And some choose not to join the union?

"Yes, but they receive all the benefits of being in the union without paying dues. I serve and represent the nonunion employees the same as I do my dues paying members. Who knows? Maybe I can sway them over."

You work strictly out the Crown Point post office, but your local also includes the letter carriers from the Lowell post office. I have some good friends who deliver mail in Lowell. What percentage of the Lowell letter carriers are union?

"All of them."

Crown Point?

"Most of them."

Can you go on strike?

"Not legally; there was a wildcat strike in 1970."

What is a hot topic right now regarding the NALC"

"There was talk the postmaster general, Jack Potter, was going to try to institute 5-day delivery to save money. It wouldn't save money. That's the only edge we have on the competitor, that we deliver for the same price six days a week. Our union will lobby to make sure six-day delivery continues."

You mentioned competitors.

"UPS (United Postal Service) and FedEx."

Are they unionized?

"UPS workers are teamsters; FedEx employees are nonunion."

Do you get paid a decent monthly stipend for being local president?

"I don't get paid a nickel for being union president. For me, it's a passion. I'm also vice-president of the Northwest Federation of Labor for public employees – police officers, letter carriers..."

"When I retire, I'd like to be a union organizer. I have a certificate in Labor Studies from Indiana University Northwest in '06."

Sharon, those Labor Studies almost were discontinued a few years back.

"I know; I made phone calls to help make sure they weren't."

* * *

The wildcat strike that began on St. Patrick's Day of 1970 began with postal workers from New York's Branch 36. Branches from Boston, Philadelphia, Detroit, Cleveland, Pittsburgh and Chicago were some of those to follow suit.

In an effort to break the strike, President Richard M. Nixon sent thousands of Army and National Guard personnel into New York to deliver mail. They were ineffective.

Branch 36 was the first to go out and the last to go back. Once its members returned, negotiations began around the clock. By April 2, a contract was agreed upon.

Sharon Patterson is currently doing her part to help bring awareness to the
the Employee Free Choice Act, which would make it easier to unionize work places.

Steve Cotton *(June, 2014)*

Rooster Cogburn (played by John Wayne): *"I mean to kill you in one minute, Ned. Or see you hanged in Fort Smith at Judge Parker's convenience. Which'll it be?"*

Lucky Ned Pepper (Robert Duvall): *"I call that bold talk for a one-eyed fat man."*

Cogburn: *"Fill your hands, you son of a bitch!"*

– From the movie "True Grit."

Little Stevie Cotton was only 9 when his father took the family to the Y&W drive-in theater in Merrillville to see "True Grit." The youngster was riveted to the mammoth screen as "The Duke" put reins in his teeth, and with guns a-blazin', charged four bad guys.

The youthful Cotton had no way of knowing that years later he and his brother Mike would own their own outdoor movie theater – the 49'er Drive-in Theatre in Valparaiso.

Cotton, 54, lives in Valparaiso with his wife, Phyliss.

* * *

"I went to River Forest High School in New Chicago," Cotton began."It was pretty much a Polish community back then. My dad worked at U.S. Steel. That house in New Chicago was the first house and the last house he ever bought.

"New Chicago was a great community for us. You knew everybody. I graduated with about 90 other kids. It was a blue-collar neighborhood."

Any other childhood memories?

"I remember Dad coming home from the mill and telling Mom: 'Pack up the kids, were goin' to the drive-in movies.' We'd have our jammies on. It was great."

Part of Americana nearly gone. What did you do for a living before you and your brother bought the 49'er?

"We owned Mike & Steve's Auto Repair in Valparaiso for about 12 years. It was next to Hannon's Drive-In Root Beer Stand at Ind. 2 & U.S. 30."

Great location.

"Walgreens felt the same way. After several attempts, they eventually bought out our place and Hannon's. Mike and I were still young and the buyout wasn't enough to retire on. That's about the time a friend of mine asked me if I was aware that the 49-er was for sale.

"The first year, we didn't do anything to the place. The second year, we gutted it. Everything was from '56, which was cool, but it wasn't efficient. The concession stand was way too small, for one thing."

Give me some history on the 49'er.

"We're the third owners. It was built in 1956 and was known as Shauer's Drive-In Theatre. Then the Shauer family sold to Bruce Shinabarger in 1985. Mike and I bought it from Bruce in 2000. Here's a newspaper ad from when the theater first opened on May 3, 1956. The first feature was 'The Seven Little Foys' starring Bob Hope. The second feature that night was Walt Disney's 'The Vanishing Prairie.'"

Wow, the ad says admission for adults was 65 cents including tax. Ticket prices today?

"For $8 an adult can see two movies. For kids 5 through 11 it's $4. Kids under 5 get in free. We try to keep it affordable."

Steve, it's $8 for a beer at a ballgame. And you and your brother don't charge to park. If you don't mind me asking, how much did you have to pay for the remake of "Godzilla"?

"Everything is percentages. There is no flat rate for a movie; 60 percent of what you take in goes back to the studio. That's why the concession stand is so important to us."

One of your all-time favorite movies?

"I love Westerns. They just don't make good Westerns anymore. My all-time favorite Western with John Wayne would have to be 'True Grit.' That was 'The Duke's' only Academy Award, by the way."

When are you open?

"We do Friday, Saturday and Sunday in the spring and fall. When the kids get out of school in the summer, we're open seven nights a week. We've opened as early as March and closed for the season as late as the end of October."

What's a "full house" at the 49-er entail?

"A little more than 600 cars. There have been a few times when I've had to turn cars away."

Drive-in theaters have often big nicknamed "passion pits." Steve, I have to ask you. Have you ever tapped on a young couple's window to wake them after the second feature on a hot August night and then realized they were definitely not sleeping in the backseat of their car?

"Oh, yeah."

Today, you have to contend with Blu-ray, Redbox, Netflix and people DVRing movies at home. But, still, there's something nostalgic and fun about going to the outdoor movies.

"You're absolutely right. That's what killed the drive-in theaters in the '80s. VCRs started getting affordable. Today, people have theaters in their houses with the 80-inch screens and sound systems. You're competing with that. But you know what? Sittin' at home is not the same as sittin' at a drive-in theater in your car or in a lawn chair with the stars over your head while watching this 90-feet by 40-feet screen.

"We have 12 acres. There's room for the kids to play tag and throw Frisbees. Our concession stand offers a tremendous variety of food including our homemade pizza. We still play the National Anthem before the first movie begins. People get out of their cars and stand."

Continue, please.

"There was a time, when there were more outdoor screens than indoor screens. At one time, there were more than 5,000 drive-in theaters in this country, now there are only 330. Today, most indoor theaters have 16 or 20 screens."

Digital versus film?

"We have a new digital projector. They're going to quit making film next year. There are a number of drive-ins still using film. A good portion of the remaining drive-in theaters are going to go out of business because they can't afford $80,000 for a new projector."

Enter singer-songwriter Jimmy Buffet.

"He's big drive-in guy and doing what he can to save them by putting on a live benefit concert in Texas at a drive-in theater on June 19. It'll be available to all drive-ins across the country via satellite. We're participating in that.

"We also will have a live band that will play from 5 p.m. to 7:30 p.m., before the Jimmy Buffet concert appears on the screen at sundown.

They're a local band called Island 49. They're big Jimmy Buffet fans and will cover a lot of his songs."

I've been told you had problems with Mother Nature a while back.

"It was in the winter about three years ago. Record winds destroyed half the screen. That spring, people started emailing us wanting to help out. They were afraid of losing their drive-in. Loyal customers wanted to start fundraisers or take up collections for us. It was really touching."

Did you take them up on their offers?

"No. We had insurance. It still cost us like $50,000 out of our pockets. But we didn't take any money from anybody. We did let people know we appreciated their offers.

* * *

They don't make 'em like the '49-er Dive-In Theatre anymore. The same could probably be said about Steve and Mike Cotton.

I hope there's a mile-long line of headlights like in "Field of Dreams" come June 19 in Valparaiso, Ind. U.S.A.

Parrot Heads and outdoor movie fans unite.

Nick Petrov *(Nov. 2006)*

"Opportunity is missed by most people because it is dressed in overalls and looks like work."
-Thomas Alva Edison

I met Nick Petrov at Hanover High School. He is not a schoolteacher but he spends a lot of time there. He is the head coach of the Wildcats esteemed wrestling team. It is only September. Official practice has not yet begun but there is always open gym. Nick and wife Bessie have been married for 19 years. They live in Cedar Lake. Petrov is both energetic and charismatic.

* * *

Coach, has anyone ever told you that you talk and look a lot like

"Joe Pesci? Never."

You and Bessie have three sons who attend Hanover Schools.

"Yes. George, John, and Paul."

Wow! Too bad you don't a fourth son. You could have –

"We have a dog named Ringo. I always liked The Beatles."

What high school did you attend?

"(Thornton Fractional) South, class of '79."

Wife from Lansing, Ill., too?

"No, Bessie is from Sioux City, Iowa. She was quite an athlete herself. Bessie was an all-state second baseman and she played on a state champion volleyball team."

Petrov. What ancestry? Russian?

"My father is Bulgarian. My mother is Greek. My father escaped from Bulgaria when he was 18. It was under a communist regime at the time. My family was in the restaurant business."

Tell me about it.

"After high school, I attended Valparaiso University for two-and-a-half years. I decided I needed to do something. My dad needed help at his place in Homewood, (Ill.), Cal's Roast Beef. An opportunity came up in 1982. I opened up a little restaurant in Cedar Lake, Chicken City USA – where El Amigo is now. I continued to take some college classes, but once you start working full time... After two years, I moved my business to a different location in town. It became a bigger operation. Four or five years later, I opened up Cal's Chicken City in Crete. It's still open. I sold that business, too. I had two places for a long time. I was in the restaurant business for 18 years. It's hard work. People used to call me Chicken Nick. Some still do."

Tell me about your career as a wrestler.

"In high school, I wrestled three years at 98 (lbs). My senior year, 105 lbs. I was smaller than what I think my boys are going to be. For (Valparaiso University), I started at 118 all three seasons I wrestled for them. We were Division I. We weren't really big enough to be Division I. We should have probably been D-III. We wrestled smaller schools, but we also had Notre Dame and Purdue on our schedules. Wrestling got dropped with Title 9."

This will be your third year as head coach.

"Yes. I ran the youth program for 11 years. Scott Campbell became the head coach here four years ago. He needed an assistant coach. He figured what better coach than the guy who had been working with the kids since they were old enough to walk. I was assistant varsity coach for one year. Scott got married and moved to Indianapolis. The head coach spot opened up and I took over."

After two full seasons what is Hanover's record in dual meets?

"37 wins, 5 losses."

That's amazing. How many kids go to Hanover Central?

"A little over 500."

I love the David and Goliath aspect of high school wrestling in Indiana. But, if there was a class system like in football or basketball, you guys would be state champs or close to it every year. Were there any schools with comparable enrollments that finished as high as the Wildcats last year?

"Mater Dei. But they get kids from all over."

You once mentioned the fact that Hanover not having a football team actually hurts you as far as the bigger weight classes. I'd never looked at it that way before. You explained that if a kid wants to play football, mom and dad will send him to neighboring Crown Point even if they live in Cedar Lake.

"Fortunately, right now, we have four freshmen who are either 189, 215, or heavyweight. They probably won't start this year, but in two or three years those guys are going to have some experience under their belts. An advantage of not having a football team is our kids can be wrestling now. You look at some of the other teams – Lowell for example -- they played football all the way to the state championship. Some of those kids didn't get to start wrestling until late. I think it probably hurt them – forfeits, if nothing else. I think Lowell will have a very successful season this year, by the way. A lot of Crown Point's best wrestlers are Cedar Lake kids. But that's just how the townships are drawn up. That's how it goes. Most of those kids went through the Crown Point feeder system anyway. Scott Vlink does a great job over at Crown Point."

You've got a very dedicated staff working with you today. Two of those guys are brothers, right?

"Yes. John and Doug Willems. John is a paid assistant. Doug is a volunteer coach. Todd Staples is a volunteer coach. All three of them wrestled for Hanover. They are all giving back. That's something we preach. Giving back to the sport. We also get some help from another Hanover grad, Greg Larsen. Greg is a former State Champ (1995, runner-up '94). My coaching staff is one of the reasons we're successful."

The kids?

"I talk about my fine assistants, because they are an integral part of it. But the basis of our success, of why we are where we are today, is the work ethic of the kids. They work so hard not only during the season, but in the off season as well. This isn't a sport where you can wrestle for three months and take nine months off. Things have changed. To beat the best, you have to wrestle almost year around. Don't get me wrong, a kid needs to take a month, or month-and-a-half off to get his mind and body recouped. These kids have learned how to work hard. And it's contagious."

I've noticed what a close-knit group you are.

"Our parental group is fantastic. They are committed to the idea of their children being successful."

The battles you guys have waged against much larger schools like

Portage and Crown Point..

"That dual last year against Portage. That was the most fun I ever had losing."

Coach, I gotta hand it to you. You do your homework.

"In a dual meet you have to get the right match-ups. We pride ourselves on being prepared, knowing who the other team has, what they can do to counteract us. It's fun. Normally, what we want is to have our best wrestlers wrestle their best wrestlers. If there's a kid who was 2nd or 3rd in the state and he's a weight class above, say, Andrew Howe, we want Andrew to wrestle him. We want our guys to wrestle the best people they can go up against. We're trying to get our guys ready for the state tournament is what it comes down to."

Bigger fish to fry.

"Exactly. Even if we lose that match, that okay, we're preparing for the tournament."

Coach, you're a passionate guy, it exudes from you, and the kids pick up on it. I get the biggest kick out of watching your team. They have a job to do, and they do it. They're not a bit cocky. They're well-coached, and they're good.

"They're blue-collar kids. They're hard workin'. My boys aren't afraid to do the dirty work. That could change."

I don't see that happening. Any former Wildcat grapplers taking it to the next level?

"We've got three kids wrestling for Purdue. Eric Howe is a red-shirt freshman. There's a good possibility he could be a starter this year. Mike Sands and Roger Vukobratovich are also freshmen for the Boilermakers. Will they break the line-up this year? Probably not. But they'll be in a lot of open tournaments and those guys will get their matches."

* * *

Today, Coach Petrov is in the electrical business. He had an opportunity to learn the trade. He took the test. He got his license. He's not one to shy away from hard work. Neither are the young men who have wrestled for him. A blue-collar bunch bearing names like Previs, Sobkowicz, Vukobratovich...

Nick Petrov and his Wildcats.

Pound for pound. The best around.

David Wilson *(March 2014)*

"creepy-crawly (kree-pee kraw-lee) 1. noun: a creepy or crawling animal, especially an insect."
– Dictionary.com Unabridged

Along with his sister, Kelly, David Wilson owns and operates Monroe Pest Control, Inc. in Hobart.

Wilson, 50, lives in Hobart and graduated from Hobart High School. He earned a bachelor's degree in business management at Indiana University in Bloomington.

* * *

Did you play football for Hobart High School?

"Yes, I played for Coach Howell," he said. "We went downstate my junior and senior years and lost both years to Columbus East and then Carmel. My dad played for Hobart, too."

Indiana University?

"The Hoosiers won the national championship the year before I went to IU in 1981 and they won it the year after I left in 1987. Coming from Hobart, I didn't realize that Indiana was a basketball state. It wasn't until I lived in Bloomington that I realized I was wrong. They converted me into a basketball fanatic."

The family business?

"My grandfather bought the business off of Monroe in 1928. He kept the brand name because there was a certain client base. It was actually Monroe Chemical Distributors out of Chicago, but they had a pest control branch in Gary. My grandfather worked there. That's where he met my grandmother who was the secretary. After they were married, they bought that branch of the business.

Grandpa's name?

"Dewey Wilson."

Where was the original location?

"They started out at 7th and Washington. After my dad, Red Wilson, graduated from IU, they relocated to 8th and Adams. That would have been in the early '60s. In the mid-'70s, they outgrew that and found this place."

How does Monroe Pest Control differ from the large pest control chains?

"The large corporations like to sign up clients to yearly contracts. A lot of people don't like that. We give people what we think they need: 'You want us to take care of your wasps? We'll take care of your wasps. If you have any more trouble, here's our card.'"

Speaking of wasps, I'd bet you've been stung a few times.

"By yellow jackets and hornets? Oh, my. More than a few times. We wear protective gear."

Which species is the most aggressive?

"Yellow jackets. They have the ability to continue to sting. With that said, the sting of, say, a bald-faced hornet, is something you won't forget."

Do you remember your first job in the field?

"Yes, I went with my father on a roach job at Slick's Laundry on 5th Avenue and Broadway in Gary. It was one of our commercial accounts. The conditions of a Laundromat are good for roaches with all that heat and steam."

What did your dad use to eradicate those critters?

"Back then, we used diazinon. Before that, DDT was used. In the '50s, chlordane was used for bed bugs and termites. Chlordane was taken off the market in the mid-'80s."

I can only imagine some of the poisons your grandfather used in the 1920s and '30s.

"They used some harsh materials. I know they mixed their own roach powder from the '20s all the way to the '70s. It was sold over the counter to folks in this area."

Your busiest time of year?

"April through October. Commercial business we do 12 months out of the year – restaurants, hospitals, taverns, nursing homes, grocery stores... ."

Common culprits you deal with?

"Termites, roaches, carpenter ants, wasps, mice, rats, bats, spiders in the fall... . Bed bugs are huge right now."

Really?

"In the '50s and '60s, bed bugs were basically eliminated in the United States because chemicals like chlordane were used. Within the last 10 years – due to international travel – bed bugs are back with a vengeance. Bed bugs are hitchhikers. They get in people's luggage and clothes. It has become an epidemic in the United States. When I was a boy, there were no bed bugs. I never did a bed bug job until the last seven or eight years. Now, we're getting calls every single day."

The bed bug is actually a louse, correct?

"Yes. They're a parasite that feeds on the blood of humans. They live in mattresses, but come out in the evenings to feed on their hosts. You can pick them up in movie theaters. It's disturbing is what it is. It's difficult to eradicate bed bugs. There's a lot of preparation work that goes into having the place ready to be treated."

Termites have been known to wreak havoc.

"Where did you say you live?"

On Ramsey Road along the Kankakee River.

"I have eight or nine clients on Ramsey Road – termites."

Tell me more about the dreaded termite.

"Annually, termites do more damage to homes nationwide than tornadoes and fires. We use a product called Termidor. It's a liquid material we put in the soil. We don't have use a lot of it, so it's easy on the environment. The beauty of Termidor is the termites don't know it's there. We call it a non-repellant product. As the insects forage about, they pick up the material on their bodies and then they transport it around; it kills off the entire colony. Termites are subterranean.

"People put a lot into their houses. Termites eat the wood as a source of food. Since they live underground, they destroy the structural timbers at the lowest level. God help you if you have hardwood floors, they'll eat them up as well."

Fleas?

"People are controlling their own flea problems because they get products for their pets from veterinarians. The flea portion of our business is all but dead."

Bats?

"I've seen 140 bats come out of a single attic. Bats are protected. We don't do anything to kill them. We can only work with bats during the late summer because they have their little ones in the spring or early summer. From August through September, we exclude them from the structure. We set up ways for them to get out, but they can't get back in."

Rats?

"Mark and I went to a cattle farm that was infested with rats. The farmer was supplementing the cattle feed with a high-protein mix. The bags were stored in a shed. There was spillage. Well, the rats were feeding on that high-protein mix, too. It turned them into 'super rats.' They were the biggest rats we'd ever seen and the largest number of rats, too. You could see the feed bags moving. We walked in, and ran out."

That had to be a sight.

"It was like movie 'Ghostbusters.' Remember the scene where they walked into the library and said: 'We'll get back to you.' We regrouped, got our courage up, and went back in there. We eventually eliminated them. Then, of course, we had to collect the corpses. They were the size of ground hogs."

One of your odder requests?

"A lady called us because she said her house was infested with crickets. We went out there to do an inspection. No matter how hard we tried, we couldn't find any crickets."

What was it the lady was hearing?

"The battery was low on her fire alarm. It was doing the chirping thing."

* * *

Monroe Pest Control, Inc. is a responsible and reputable family business. All employees must continue their educations by attending Purdue University for re-certification seminars.

Sharon Speichert *(Feb. 2006)*

*"...I'm right up the road
I'll share your load..."
- Bill Withers, "Lean On Me"*

I first met Sharon Speichert at Uncle John's Flea Market where I sold home-grown organic vegetables, everlasting flowers, honey, and herbs (legal herbs). I also sold items such as hornet's nests, cattails, moss, mushrooms, acorns, pods, weeds, rocks, clam shells, and driftwood. I was laid off from the steel mill. My twins daughters needed new shoes. Sharon Speichert was my best customer.

She was born Sharon Cox and raised on Nichols Street in Lowell. Today, she is the owner-operator of Old Town Appraisers.

* * *

"Jeff, I don't know why you want to interview me; I'm boring," Speichert began.

Heard that one before; everyone has a story to tell.

"Well, I was one of 10 children. We grew up in a 900-square-foot house. My father was a steel worker at Youngstown in East Chicago. He ran an overhead crane."

I used to work on overhead cranes in the mill. It gets mighty warm in the summer time up above those fiery orange slabs of steel.

"Dad died six months before he could have retired with 30 years."

Your maternal grandmother was a Worley?

"Yes, her cousin was the father of actress Joanne Worley. There were a lot of Worleys in Lowell. You had to watch out who you married – might be your cousin.

"While still in school, my sisters and I worked for Matt and Ruby at Matt's Restaurant; which is now Neat Repeats. I'd go in early in the morning to wash the pots and pans. I was so little, Matt had to build a box for me so I could reach the sink. I also worked at the Sweet Shop and Fry's Department Store when it was down on the corner."

What about your brothers?

"They were all great guys. Two of them were lifers in the Marine Corps. A third brother flew a helicopter during the Vietnam War; he got out after four years. I had two other brothers who died in automobile accidents. My older brother, Buck, was killed when he was 28 years old. My youngest brother, Tommy, was killed while he was still in high school; he was 17. My brother-in-law also was killed in the same wreck. My hip, pelvis and lower back were broken.

"My dad was a stern man, but never got over Buck's death. He died before Tommy was killed. All my brothers and sisters are very hard workers. Our parents taught us that. I was divorced for 18 years with three babies. I always worked two or three jobs. Even now, with things being easier, I have a hard time slowing down."

What year did you graduate from Lowell High?

"Class of '62. I worked as a bookkeeper until '91 for Mason Metals. It was a family-owned business in Schererville. Great company; great people.

"But I wanted to become an appraiser. I went to school for it in 1989. It was pretty much the old boys club back then. They didn't want to let any women in. It was Art Handley, out of Crown Point, who finally took me on. I kept hounding him.

"I also kept his books for free until I could get going on my own, which took me from '89 to '94. In 1994, I opened my doors as Old Town Appraisers. I bought the building across the street with the bonus money I received from Mason Metals.

"It was Guy Carlson in '94 – I have to hand it to him – who let me work by myself without a male appraiser working over me. He gave me my chance. DeMotte State Bank has been one of my clients ever since. I will never forget what Guy Carlson did for me."

Retail is tough right now.

"When I see a place of business shut its doors in Lowell, it just knocks the wind out of my sails. Lowell is a great town. I try to help anybody I can."

Any thoughts on the town's downtown business district?

"I hope the stores get filled with businesses again. I think the new people who are moving in appreciate our town. The newcomers like the hometown atmosphere, but they want some of the urban amenities, too. They prefer to shop here rather than going to the mall. I know with growth comes everything else, but we need growth. With good people comes good ideas. I hope it goes back to retail, myself."

You were the head of the Main Street Association.

"I'm strictly a Chamber member now. There used to be three entities; the Lowell Downtown Merchants Association, the Chamber of Commerce, and the Main Street Association. The LDMA is still active. They are a great group. They are an independent group.

"I'd join them in a minute if they were a part of the Chamber of Commerce. I believe that all businesses should support the Chamber of Commerce. If the LDMA would come in as a merchant group it would make our Chamber strong – they are very hard workers. But they don't want to be part of the Chamber. I don't know why. It's been baffling me for years."

How many members of the Chamber of Commerce are there now?

"Probably close to 100, but the Chamber is really only made up of the people who work in the Chamber. Entrepreneurs need to come in as volunteers and make changes. We were trying to unify, so there wouldn't be so many groups.

"We shut down the Main Street Association as a nonprofit organization and moved – as a committee – into the Chamber when I was the president. It ended up that I was the only member on the committee. So, I couldn't get anything accomplished, but before we disbanded we ensured that the downtown area would become a historical district officially. They can never tear it down like they did in Dyer."

Do you think Lowell should become a city?

"I'm all for it. Cedar Lake has a group that's buying up everything. You won't recognize Cedar Lake in a couple years. Those people are making positive changes. They're going to run us over.

"Our past town councils should have annexed all the way to I-65. Look what's happening out there. There are thousands of acres that have been sold that are now county. They'll be developed and that tax base won't come to Lowell. Why didn't they think of that? It's not the present town council's fault. Look at Crown Point; they work well with a mayor."

* * *

There are people in Lowell who Sharon Speichert, anonymously, has helped out. She wants it that way. There have been upstart business owners who do know who Sharon Speichert is. They will fondly attest as to the many "little things" she hàs done to try to help them stay afloat.

Sharon Speichert; right up the road on Commercial Avenue.

Tom Hargrove *(Dec. 2011)*

"...If I was a coal miner, I'd want a union representing me to make sure I was safe and you did not have some of the tragedies that we've been seeing in the coal industry.

"If I was a teacher, I'd want a union to make sure that the teachers' perspective was represented as we think about shaping an education system for our future."
– President Barack Obama

About 70 years ago, President Franklin D. Roosevelt told workers the first thing he'd do if he was a worker in a factory would be to join a union.

Tom Hargrove is the president of United Steelworker Local 1010 in East Chicago. Hargrove, 67, has been married to Veronica since 1967. They've raised two sons. He has lived in Hammond all his life and is a Hammond Tech High School graduate.

* * *

Growing up in Hammond?

"We didn't get a TV until about '56," he said. "Most of our childhood was spent playing outside, which is a little different than what goes on today."

Hammond Tech?

"I think the technical-vocational high school is something we need to bring back. Right now, we're in a crisis; we need qualified electricians and mechanics.

"We really need to revive the apprenticeships and transfer the knowledge of the senior folks who are about to retire from the mills. If we lose the knowledge, it's gone forever. Apprenticeships gave us the opportunity to transfer the knowledge."

Tom, I had Pete Gyerko and Rich Ortiz for welding instructors when I was an apprentice. Those guys were old school and had burned a lot of rods. They were both bargaining unit employees.

"Jeff, like you, I come from blue-collar stock; my dad was a cement finisher. I remember my Uncle Joe living with us in the early '50s. He was working for a small company in Hammond; they ground up cornmeal."

American Maize?

"No, it was some off-the-wall company. He was cleaning a machine and, evidently, someone started the machine; he was killed.

"I remember my father going to the door; there were a couple of policemen standing there. They had to tell my dad his brother was dead. That has quite an effect. Uncle Joe had two young daughters who never got to know him."

Your uncle's entire family lived with your family in Hammond?

"No, my uncle, like my father, came up here from the South to find work. His wife and daughters were to remain down south until he got established up here."

I know you started out a welder in the mill. How long have you been president of Local 1010?

"Since '98. Prior to that, I was vice-president, treasurer, griever"

Safety-wise, has the mill changed much since the 60's?

"We're much better today. Prior to '89, when we put in the (Inland Employee Safety Program), there were only two years when we didn't have a fatality. Most years, we had multiple fatalities. Since that time, we've had 12 years without a fatality. The only thing acceptable is zero fatalities."

ArcelorMittal has employees all over the world. Global safety?

"Leo Gerard and the (International Metal Federation) and the (European Metal Federation) put together a group of union people among their company counterparts and we signed an agreement in June of '08, setting minimum standards of for safety around the world. We visit the sites... We have meetings with the unions; we listen to their concerns..."

These are all ArcelorMittal plants?

"Yes, Mittal has facilities in 60 countries. I've been to the Ukraine, Romania, Brazil, South Africa..."

How are some of those mills regarding safety?

"Brazil was the cleanest and most safety-minded facility I've been to. The worst one was in Romania; the factories there were full of dogs. Before the old dictator and his wife were killed, they made all the people release their dogs from public housing. So, there are literally thousands of dogs occupying the plant. I've never seen anything like it.

"The mill with the most pollution was Poland. It looked like East

Chicago back in the '60s. The iron oxide and pollution just hung around the city; it was so thick you could taste, see and smell it."

Right-to-work legislation?

"Right-to-work is a misnomer; it brings you no rights or work. It's a plot to disband unions. It's the top priority in the state of Indiana. It's wrong. ...

"Jeff, before you leave, I want to give you copies of the Indiana Chamber of Commerce Foundation Right-to-Work report that came out in January, and also the Higgins Labor Studies Program report from the University of Notre Dame that counters it, which came out in March."

Thanks, I'll read them. I can't imagine Northwest Indiana being part of a right-to-work state.

"In 1957, Indiana voted in Right-to-Work. We had it until 1965."

Really?

"In '65, the Democrats got hold of the Statehouse and voted it out. Once again, the Republicans are in charge, and instead of focusing on jobs, they want to focus on eliminating unions.

"Working at nursing homes, making beds, that's the kind of jobs they have in mind. The good jobs are not the ones they're talking about."

Could right-to-work lead to the demise of the middle class?

"Jeff, we want young people to stay in Indiana. The more workers are attacked, well, it gets to a point where you have to ask, 'Why would someone want to live in this state?'

"Look at Florida – seven or eight bucks an hour? These jobs in the mill or building trades are good-paying jobs where you can raise a family and send your kids to college."

Let's switch gears a little bit; solidarity among the rank-and-file?

"Sticking together works; we have to focus on supporting our retirees and up-and-coming workers. We finally have some young people in the mill, and we're trying our best to get them involved in the union."

Tom, I've always loved that painting in your office; the one with the ladle, tundish, and molten metal.

"Frank Myslivie created that painting with his left hand in the 1940s. He was born right-handed, but lost it in the mill."

* * *

Hargrove told me he's hopeful 11 fair-minded Republicans will join the state's Democrats in opposing right-to-work.

Melting Pot

Dr. Biljana Uzelac *(Jan. 2015)*

"Homeopathy cures a larger percentage of cases than any other form of treatment and is beyond doubt safer and more economical."
– Mahatma Gandhi

Dr. Biljana Uzelac is a Serbian-born, board-certified pediatrician and a clinical homeopathy and integrative medicine specialist who practices at the Franciscan Medical Specialists office in Schererville.

Uzelac, 41, lives in St. John with her husband Nenad and their eight-year-old son.

* * *

"Would you like a glass of water or tea," Uzelac began.

No thanks, I just guzzled a Diet Coke for breakfast on the way here. What is your maiden name?

"Stankovski. I was born and raised in Belgrade."

When you were a little girl was that area still known as Yugoslavia?

"Yes, then it became part of Serbia in the early '90s. My country was being bombarded about the time I was graduating from the medical school. That's why I left and came here.

"(Slobodan) Milosevic was the leader when the war was going on. Before that, up until 1980, it was (Josip Broz) Tito."

A lot of people tried to assassinate Tito, but failed.

"Correct. He died from the age. I had a really nice childhood when Tito ruled the country.

"I have a lot of friends who are Croatian and Slovenian. I am currently working on a cookbook with a Slovenian nutritionist."

When did you decide to become a doctor?

"When I was in elementary school I wanted to be movie director. But in high school, I witnessed a really bad car crash. People were badly injured. I had such an urge to help, but I had no idea how. From then on, I decided that I wanted to help people. That's when I entered medical school. In high school, I made straight A's so I received the full scholarship.

"My dad was into marketing and finance. He told me that being a doctor wasn't a good profession for a female, that it was hard work and long hours. But he saw that I was determined and didn't try to stop me which was very nice."

Your mother?

"She was a hairdresser, but since I was a small kid, if anyone in neighborhood was sick she would help take care of them and cook for them. Her father was a farmer, but he would go around and deliver babies."

Coming to America?

"I came to United States after bombing with one suitcase, a few books and a few hundred bucks. You cannot come to United States and say, 'I want to be a doctor.' So, I had to take my schooling all over."

Being a mom?

"I tell my kid that experience is much more important than 'stuff.' We haven't given anything for Christmas since he was a baby. We'd rather take him traveling – the experience. That's much better than material things."

Are you and Nenad Serbian Orthodox?

"Now we are. Christmas is celebrated January 7. When I was growing up it was communist. We weren't supposed to even talk about that kind of stuff. At Easter, if you wanted to color the eggs, you had to do it hush-hush. If you mentioned at school or wherever that you colored eggs somebody could tip off the authorities and parents could lose job."

Scary. Let's switch to medicine. I've been told you incorporate a lot of homeopathic and holistic methods as a pediatrician.

"Homeopathy is basically using the dilutions of the herbs, minerals and even animals. It's very safe and allows the body to self-heal. I practice integrative medicine. There is Chinese medicine, homeopathy, acupuncture, Western medicine... The more you know the better because you integrate that into one holistic approach. It's really beautiful.

You have two business cards. One is your Franciscan Medical Specialists card, but the other reads "Green Pediatrics."

"I'm working on a new website that is not active yet. It will have a lot of recipes for cooking well. I tell moms to make their own baby food and formulas, not to buy it. You can even make your own insect repellent and sun block.

"I grow everything from my garden and make everything from scratch. For my bread, I buy the grains, then I make the flour from the grains, then I make the bread from that flour."

Wow. Full time job, mom, chef and gardener.

"You have to organize well, but it's doable."

Anything else you'd like to tell me?

"I'm getting more and more autistic kids. It is becoming an epidemic. One in 68 kids is autistic in America. One in 42 is boys. Boys are really hit hard and nobody knows why."

Do you have a theory on that subject?

"Yes. It is multi factorial. I think it has to do with the pollutants in the air, food and our medicine. The other thing is radiation. When we were young there weren't that many laptop computers, cell phones and Ipods."

I interviewed a doctor several years ago who believes soy is killing us.

"I don't use soy at all. I don't even recommend the formula with the soy milk because it is genetically modified."

I've always loathed milk.

"I don't promote milk either. Not really that important because you get more calcium from the green vegetables and leafy stuff."

Do you ever get the urge for classic American cuisine such as a Whopper, Slider or Big Mac?

"I've never been to McDonald's since I came to this country."

Doc, it's been a slice.

* * *

A remarkable person is Biljana Uzelac, MD. She told me that she has been to 47 countries since the age of 26, and usually visits five or six a year. The woman with the delightful accent not only speaks Serbian and English, but Russian, Macedonian, Spanish, Latin and some French as well.

Before making my exit, I checked out the good doctor's food pantry. It was filled with bottles of spices, herbs, mushrooms, bee pollen and berries, most of which she'd grown, dried and labeled herself. She told me one acerola berry has as much vitamin C as 50 oranges. When I asked her if the bottle labeled "hemp" was medicinal marijuana, she said, "Ha, ha, it's not that kind of hemp, Jeff!"

Rasi Sanuchit-Smart *(Oct. 2014)*

"Fresh rice and tasty fish" (a newly married couple)
– Thai saying

I turned west off of U.S. 41 and crossed the historic Upside Down Bridge, which spans Beaver Ditch in Newton County. More than a century ago, said ditch drained what was the largest natural lake in Indiana into the Kankakee River.

A quarter-mile from the bridge is the only house remaining in the ghost town of Conrad. It is the home of newlyweds Rod Smart and Rasi Sanuchit-Smart. The old farmhouse sits approximately 200 meters from where the town's founder, Jennie Conrad, once lived. Jennie died in 1939. Most of her town was located on the east side of U.S. 41. Being harvest season, Rod was busy picking soybeans in a field that was once the bed of Beaver Lake. The progress of man.

Sanuchit-Smart speaks a whole lot more English than I do Thai. Rod's adult son Tyler helped bridge the gap for us. Tyler was sporting a heavily bandaged finger. He'd been bitten by a brown recluse spider. Not good. Because of the wound, he'd been going to the hospital for infusions every day for a week.

Sanuchit-Smart, 48, looks like she's 28. She is very intelligent and talented. For her wedding, she created scores of elegant white flowers made from crepe and construction paper that served as table settings. She made the bridal bouquets as well.

Sanuchit-Smart goes by the nickname Nok. It is pronounced the same as the word "nook."

* * *

"I was raised in southern portion of Thailand near Malaysia," Sanuchit-Smart began. "I move to Bangkok to go to university and to work at same time. Bangkok big city. Live in Bangkok about 20 year. I bought house there."

Did you earn a degree?

"Missed by one subject. My father pass away. No money. Have to take care of my mother. There are seven children. I had two sisters move in with me in Bangkok. I take care of them. I open up laundry shop and also work at import-export company."

Sounds like you're a hard worker who is very family-oriented.

"I eventually move back to gulf of Thailand where I make old culture Thai clothing and sell them at night market. After a while, my sisters and I open clothing shop and send clothing to Bangkok."

How long of a drive was it from your village to Bangkok?

"Two hour, 30 minute."

Tyler, how did your dad and Nok meet?

Tyler: "Dad had always wanted to visit Thailand. Through the Internet he started talking to a bunch of people back in 2009. Nok was one of those people."

Nok: "Rodney, he talked to me about Thai culture. I tell him everything because we friends."

Do you miss Thailand?

"No, no because I talk to my family every day on my Skype."

What kind of government does Thailand have?

"Same as here, but we have king."

Back when Thailand was known as Siam, the king was Yul Brynner, right?

"I don't understand."

Etcetera, etcetera, etcetera!

"Yeah, yeah! Ha!"

Is Rod attempting to learn your native language?

"Yeah, he is learning a lot."

What do you think of this country?

"Before I think nothing like this. Nice peoples here. American families are warm like Thai families."

Which do you prefer, rural or urban living?

"Countryside. Don't want to stay in big city."

Well, Nok, Conrad should suit you just fine.

"After my father pass away it was very hard. My mother no job. Everybody had to stop studies, go to work."

Did your father have a heart attack?

"He kill himself because he sick a long time. Two year, three year. He cannot walk or move arm."

He must have been partially paralyzed from a stroke. That had to be rough on everyone.

"Yeah."

Favorite Thai dish?

"Ka-nom-chine. It is noodle with curry fish and coconut milk. It very spicy. We eat the rice every day. I no eat beef. Eat chicken. I eat vegetarian food two days per week. I was born on a Saturday. My father pass away on a Saturday. I eat vegetarian on Saturday. Don't want anything to be killed no more on Saturday. Every week we also have Buddha Day, full moon – no meat."

Saturday's child works hard for a living...

"Excuse me?"

It's from an old American nursery rhyme.

"I would like to know why you interview me? Because I'm foreign people, right? Thank you so much for interest in small foreign people like me. Sorry, I know my English not good. I will go to study English soon."

Nok, we improved as a nation the day you set foot on this soil.

* * *

A week or so before my interview with Nok, I talked to Rod over the phone. He told me a story about how he tried to mess with Nok by telling her about an American custom or tradition known as "Heart Healing Days." He explained that two days after a man gets married it's his duty to seek out all his former girlfriends and break the news to them. With his chest flared up like a king cobra, Rod assured his wife there would be dozens of broken hearts out there that would need healed.

Stoically, Nok mused, then burst her hubby's bubble: "That good. Want to go with. I like to see happy women smile."

I really believe Rod Smart and Nok Sanuchit-Smart were meant for each other. The English translation for the Thai word sanuchit? Smart or smart mind.

Fresh rice and tasty fish.

Eamonn Frampton *(March 2008)*

"I couldn't stand it longer, so a-hold of him I took,
And I gave him such a welting as he'd get at Donnybrook.
He hollered 'Milia Murther,' and to get away did try
And swore he'd never write again 'No Irish Need Apply.'"
– Anonymous 19th Century

Eamonn Frampton, 64, spent more than a quarter-century in salt water. But for the last 18 years, he's been a "sweet water sailor" in the Great Lakes. He's a merchant marine for ArcelorMittal.

The beginning of Eamonn's first name is pronounced the way the first letter of our alphabet is pronounced. He lives in a green-colored house in Munster with his wife, Eileen Pender; they have raised one child.

Being as Eileen speaks both American and Irish, she served as interpreter for the guy who was born on the bayous of the Kankakee River and the fella who grew up in Waterford, Ireland.

* * *

What did your father do for a living on the Emerald Isle?
"He made kookers," he said.
Come again?
"He made kookers."
Eileen?
"Eamonn's father worked in a factory where they made stoves," Eileen said.
Eamonn, are you a member of Local 1010?
"No, we're AMO – American Maritime Officers. Our local office is in Toledo, Ohio."
I realize Lake Michigan is off limits this time of year, when will

you be back at sea?

"Soon. Probably around St. Patrick's Day. Basically, we do 60 days on and 30 days off. But some guys do 90 or 100 days aboard ship."

Are you on one boat all the time?

"Last year I was on two; mostly the Wilfred Sykes – a steamer. The ship was built in 1949. I also work on the Joseph L. Block; I left her in December. The ships are laid up in Wisconsin right now near Green Bay – Sturgeon Bay."

What's your actual job title?

"I'm a 3rd Mate – a watch keeper. There's three watches on a ship: from midnight to 4, from 4 to 8 and from 8 to 12. You do two watches a day. You do eight hours, basically. The third man does the 8 to 12. That's from 8 in the morning until midday and from 8 at night to midnight. I put down our position on the chart to make sure we are where we're supposed to be – navigation."

What materials do you ship?

"We carry a lot of limestone or slag on the Wilfred Sykes from either Burns Harbor or Indiana Harbor over to Grand Haven and Muskegon, (Mich.). The Block is loaded with iron ore pellets."

Rough seas?

"If we have bad weather, we'll hug the shoreline if we can. If we're in a real bad spot, we'll anchor someplace. It depends on which way the wind and the sea is comin' from. Normally, if it's out of the north we go up along the shore and inside 'Illie' (Isle) Royale up into the Canadian waters by Thunder Bay. Then we'll sneak around that way back to the Sault (Ste. Marie)."

How big are the ships you work on?

"The Sykes is 670 feet long; the Block is 730."

Did you have a similar job when you lived in Ireland?

"I was an AB."

AB?

"An able bodied seaman – a deck hand. We would be gone nine, 10 months at a time. We sailed around the world. We'd come into Navy Pier when it was a working dock. I became an AB abowt farty-five years ago."

Eileen?

"About 45 years ago," she said.

Eamonn, when did you become an American citizen?

"In 1994."

Do you like baseball?

"Not really. I have a hurley and a sliotar downstairs."

Eileen?

"I have a stick and a ball downstairs," Eileen said. "Eamonn enjoys the sport of hurling; it is similar to lacrosse."

Education?

"I graduated high school in Ireland. The closest I got to a college was a school trip to Trinity College in Dublin."

Tell me about Waterford.

"It's on the south coast. Where I come from it's called the Sunny Southeast because it doesn't get quite as much rain as the rest of the country. That's not sayin' much. The population was about 28,000 when I was in school. Waterford is world renown for making lead crystal, but that industry has downsized as well."

Is St. Patrick's Day a big deal in Ireland?

"Oh, yeah. We have parades. But it's more of a holy day in Ireland than it is here. Everything is closed on St. Patrick's Day."

Do the Irish peoples eat corned beef and cabbage on St. Patrick's Day?

"Bacon and cabbage."

The economy in Ireland today?

"Bad. I got half me family livin' in England. I have three uncles buried in London. Some relatives went to Australia. There's no work in Ireland. A lot of Irish people are emigrating to Canada. I read Irish newspapers and listen to Irish radio on the internet."

Siblings?

"Two living and two who died at the ages of three months and six months."

That was probably a fairly small family in Ireland.

"One of me pals, Paddy Coady, was one of 22 children."

Can you speak Gaelic?

"Not much now. I can say my prayers in Gaelic; the Christian Brothers beat that into you."

During the mid-1800s, Irish immigrants who came to this country were sometimes discriminated against – No Irish Need Apply.

"Yeah, they used to post those signs around Boston and New York. It didn't mean much because most of the Irishmen couldn't read it any way – they spoke Gaelic. African, Irish, Italian, Polish, Greek,

German, Russian, Hispanic, Asian.... Nobody came into this country on the top. Everybody came in on the bottom."

* * *

Every two or three years, Eamonn Frampton returns to the "auld sod" to visit his family and friends.

May all your St. Patrick's Days be green.

Yolanta Flowers *(Aug. 2005)*

"I write to find out what I know."
-Flannery O'Connor

She was born Jolanta Szychniewicz. Friends and neighbors know her as Yolanta Flowers. Yolanta lives in Lowell with her 7-year-old daughter Monica. She moved to the United States from Poland 12 years ago. Yolanta has a delightful accent and an extraordinary English vocabulary. She loves to laugh and enjoys stand-up comedy. She is honest and open when discussing more serious subjects.

* * *

So, Yo, did you learn any other foreign languages besides English while growing up in Europe?

"No. I was forced to take eight years of Russian. I made sure I didn't learn it."

You must still remember some Russian?

"No. Absolutely nothing. When you have a mental block, you have a mental block. I got my grade. I passed. Because Poland was still communist at the time, we had to take Russian. It was mandatory until 1989."

When the Wall fell, it kind of went down with a whimper.

"Technology and spread of information. You can not prevent democracy when you have spread of information to the people – like Internet. That is why we have such huge changes in political systems. It is hard to maintain a totalitarian country when you have educated people. We would listen to Free Europe out of Washington, which is different than what they tried to make us listen to. We had one station in Poland. They would tell us their version of what they wanted us to believe – or tell us nothing at all. Polish people are extremely defiant. In other communist countries they would try to control church. In Poland, communist government could not control church. We had Pope, eventually. They could not suppress our religious beliefs."

Help me Yolanta, it sounds like the majority of the hard working, church going, defiant Poles probably didn't want to be under communist rule, but...

"Our leaders were generals. We had very strong police force. Strong Red Party. They had the guns. Also, Jeff, you must realize, after World War II we were so poor, a lot of people believed communism was the way to go. Poland was economically, physically, emotionally, devastated. You must remember that communism lets workers believe in equality. We are equal to aristocracy – it all belongs to us. Poles remember before World War II, when they had to work for somebody under horrible conditions, many hours, with one person making a lot of money, and yet they didn't have anything to eat."

Communism offered them a better life than they had.

"When you read Marxism, it's not that bad – the core of it. But because of ideology and greed, it got twisted."

In this country, during the Great Depression, there was a fella, a Hoosier, actually, by the name of Eugene V. Debs. He was a labor leader – like Lech Walesa. Debs ran for president of the United States as a Communist while locked up in a prison cell. He received more than a million votes. What do you think of Walesa?

"He isn't president anymore, just the leader of a small party. When he became president, he couldn't keep up. He was good for what he was intended to do – to lift workers to fight against communism, but as a politician, he was not good."

He was a warrior. A revolutionary.

"Yes."

What did your father do for a living?

"He worked in another communist country – Hungary. He was seldom home. It was better money in Budapest. On black market, he would buy American dollars because whatever zloty was worth today is was worth nothing the following day. Very bad inflation. He would bring the dollars home and sell them in Poland. He would hide them in the house. If we needed a TV, he would take a 100 dollar bill and sell it. It was like taking your own currency, changing it into dollars, and keep it. He would smuggle goods, too. Many things he would give away to friends and family because they were all struggling."

He was smart and also kind.

"He was smart, and a lot of other people did the same thing."

You taught English in Poland.

"Yes, I taught for one year then came to America. I was 24 with 500 bucks in my pocket and a backpack."

Where did you go to school in Poland?

"I went to finish up masters degree at Institute for American Studies in Warsaw. I was 19 when Wall fell and graduated high school at age 20."

All those consonant blends in the Polish language baffle me.

"Did you know that English language is the only language that pronounce their W's with a woo sound? Most other countries pronounce W's like Americans pronounce V's.

I "vhant" to be alone... Have you ever worked any jobs other than teacher since coming to the states?

"My favorite job was as a cashier for Menards in Hammond. I love interacting with people. Then I began studying accounting at Purdue. When we moved to Lowell in 2000, I continued my studies at Davenport. I got my CPA in 2003. I will go for my doctorate in October at Argosy University in Chicago. I want to continue teaching. I love teaching."

You're such a brain!

"Oh staaahp it. You know vhat they alvays say, 'One percent is talent and the rest is perspiration.' I study like crasy. I have this strong belief in human mind. You can accomplish so much if you stay focused."

Hobbies?

"I like manual work."

Yikes. You know, what amazes me about you, Yolanta, is how you're so good with numbers, but you were originally an English teacher. Look at all these books you have... Fitzgerald, Roth, Ginsberg, Bellow, Nabokov, Mailer, Updike, Eco, Sartre, Proulx, Poe, and you have Proust in Polish!

"My original dream was to become either an author or an actress. I love English language. It's so different than Polish. English language is extremely descriptive. I noticed that I could better explain myself in English more than in Polish, not that it's more dynamic than Polish. English grammar is simple. I can explain English grammar in two weeks. I cannot do that with Polish language. The simplicity of an English sentence, yet such an exuberant wealth of meaning – each word. When you read Hemingway, simple childish sentences, and you think, 'Oh my gosh.' It's wonderful."

Ever notice how many of those writers were drunks? It's uncanny.

"It comes from the pain. There is so much going on in their heads. How does one relieve it? For me, the reason I write, it is the only way I can obtain some type of perspective. I've got so much in me, I get very emotional and need some way to process it. The way I can process the world around me is through writing. Because then I see it in black-and-white, and then I don't have such a heavy burden anymore. I love to write."

What happened, Yolanta? I mean, that would have been so cool if you would have chosen the path of a writer!

"That doesn't mean I won't be. When I came to America, I wanted to study American Literature. That is my dream and it will always be my dream. To study philosophy and American Literature. Being from a foreign country, I cannot support myself living on English writing. I had to think of something in the meantime."

Money and Art – far apart.

"I happen to be good with numbers. I actually like logical thinking. In future, once I become established in my career as an accounting instructor at the university level, then I will take classes, explore my writing abilities. I write very well, about an hour every day in my journal."

It's been said that one of the great common denominators of many of the world-renown authors is that they traveled. Hemingway and Joyce had to leave their native soils before they could really write about their respective homelands. You write every day and you've spent time in various parts of the world. Yolanta, I realize I'm changing the topic of conversation, but what do you miss most about Poland?

"I miss my friends. I miss having a history. All my friends here in U.S.– who I love – we don't have the past. I miss when we would just go from one house to another and simply have a cup of coffee. Polish people work hard, but we also like to just sit and talk at coffee table, like this. We constantly socialized. You go for groceries and you would stand for two hours, yakking about what's going on. Here, it's different. I love individualism, but it's not always good. Individualism can be lonely. It's like, 'I need my personal space. Stay three feet away from me.' You see, when I'm with people, I hug. I will kiss them on the cheek. And I notice, that sometimes that makes people very uncomfortable. I constantly have to remember that American people don't always like being that close."

Yolanta, I think this country, a generation or two ago, was probably more like the Poland you grew up in. Families sticking it out – two or three generations living together in the same house. Neighbors, that might as well been family. The American front porch has become nothing but a dew-claw on a Dalmatian, a rudimentary appendage serving no useful purpose.

"Exactly. And entertainment! Americans have to *do* something for entertainment. Where is the interaction? We didn't have to go snowmobiling, go to big league ball games, boating. Here, it's like you have to *do* something. Maybe, I'm just..."

* * *

Maybe she's one of the most beautiful, honest, human beings I've ever met. I hope she continues to write. I'm sure it would be fascinating stuff, reading what she puts down on paper.

Reading what Yolanta Flowers knows.

Gloria Tuohy *(April 2014)*

"England and America are two countries divided by a common language."
– George Bernard Shaw

I met with ballet instructor Gloria Tuohy at photographer Edda Taylor's studio within the Old Courthouse in Crown Point. Gloria was raised in London, Edda was raised in Paris, and I'm from Sumava Resorts. A linguistics expert would've had a field day eavesdropping on our conversation.

Tuohy, 66, is founder and artistic director of Indiana Ballet Theatre NW Inc. She lives in Crown Point with husband Mike Tuohy; they have raised two children who are now adults.

In a valiant effort, Gloria also is in the process of renovating the historic old Nurses Home near the government complex in Crown Point into a Classical Arts Centre.

She could use your help.

* * *

Memories of England?

"I go there often," she said. "I'm still very much English. My father was one of the Grenadier Guards at Buckingham Palace."

Very interesting. You were born just after the bombings during World War II.

"Yes, but there was still the aftermath. Food continued to be rationed. "

When did you immigrate to the United States?

"I was 25 and went to work for the British Consulate in Chicago for two or three years."

Differences between England and America?

"People cook at home much more than they do here. Families are closer in England; they do more together. You call it the 'trunk' of a car, we call it the 'boot' of a car."

You use the "loo" and I go to the "john."

"The cockneys in the middle of London have their own language. They have nicknames for things."

Examples, please.

"Instead of saying 'up the stairs' they say 'up the apples and pears.' Your sister is your 'skin and blister.' The cockneys are the real Londoners. They are the ones who have the markets."

They're not royals.

"Absolutely not. It's the same as in France. The people who don't have money are almost romantic. It's not a shameful thing to be poor, it's just a different thing to be."

At what age did you become a ballerina?

"I started lessons when I was 5. I did it for health reasons, actually. I had asthma. The doctors suggested that I take ballet to help with the breathing. I've been doing it ever since. I now have 10 teachers and over 200 students."

Tell me about Indiana Ballet Theatre?

"I founded it 34 years ago and have created nine different classical ballets. We perform at the Star Plaza Theater twice yearly now."

You operate two schools.

"Yes, one in Merrillville and one in DeMotte. We do jazz, tap and the whole bit. More than 8,000 students have been trained. More than 300,000 individuals have been reached through 40 productions of classical ballet and contemporary and modern dance presentations in Lake, Porter, Jasper, Newton and LaPorte counties in Indiana and in Lake County, Ill."

That's fantastic.

"But we have outgrown our current conditions. Our studios have no soundproofing and poor lighting. Storage space for scenery, props, and costumes is non-existent. Simply put, we're bursting at the seams."

Enter center stage: The old Nurses Home.

"Yes."

The history of this Gregorian Revival "Grande Old Dame"?

"Beginning in 1930 the Lake County Nurses Home housed caregivers for patients at the former James O. Parramore Hospital here in Crown Point. It was a tuberculosis sanatorium. The preservation of the 20,000-square-foot Sanatorium Nurses Home will not only preserve our history, but create it."

Is the building in bad shape?

"It had been abandoned for more than a quarter-century. All the windows had been knocked out and there was a big hole in the roof. So far, I've raised about $340,000. We have a new roof, the windows are done, and the asbestos is removed. It's the last remaining nurse's home in the United States that hasn't been fully renovated. There weren't that many of them to begin with.

Is the Lake County Sanatorium Nurses Home going to be for ballet only?

"Oh, no. Dancers, musicians, writers, children, teenagers, parents, grandparents and statesmen will relish the Classical Arts Centre. It will be a place like so many other countries have to enjoy – right here in Northwest Indiana."

Continue, please.

"The Classical Arts Centre is a three-story building with a basement sitting on three acres. The top floor will be the ballet company, the middle floor will be the other arts, and the ground floor will have a black-box theater. On the other end we'll have a carvery."

Carvery?

"They are very popular in England and Europe. It's where you have a small space, but can still have a full meal. It would go out onto the balcony. We'll have a tea room. There will be gardens and a very unusual sculpture out front."

Can a guy get a shot and a beer?

"The sculpture will be of an upside-down woman doing a backbend."

Now, you're talkin'.

"She'll be 12 feet tall, white, and have waters going over the top. People need a destination. People need cultural activities. There will be a children's natural playground as well.

"And there will be no class distinction in this building. Everybody can come to this building and enjoy a day out.

"The grand opening is scheduled in 2016."

Gloria, have you ever dined at Marti's Place on the Kankakee River in Jasper County?

"Oh, yes. I love it there! Now that, reminds me of England."

* * *

A sanatorium is defined as an establishment that provides therapy combined with a regimen of diet and exercise for treatment or rehabilitation.

I'd like to see the building at 2323 North Main St. receive some much-needed architectural therapy. A Classical Arts Centre would do wonders for the good the people of Northwest Indiana, too.

May Gloria Tuohy's dream come true.

Father Joseph Ivans *(June 2013)*

"Let us touch the dying, the poor, the lonely and the unwanted according to the graces we have received and let us not be ashamed or slow to do the humble work."
– Mother Teresa

Father Joseph Ivans lives at the Albertine Retirement Home near Bishop Noll Institute in Hammond. The place is run by the Albertine Sisters, a group of Polish-born nuns.

Ivans, 89, stands in at 5 feet, 2 inches tall and weighs 115 pounds soaking wet. He arises at 5:15 every morning and says his prayers for about 90 minutes. Then, he attends Mass. And then he has breakfast. Some days he goes to the Carmelite Monastery in Munster to hear confessions. He still makes visitations at local hospitals.

* * *

In what part of India were you born?

"In the State of Kerala," he said. "It means 'land of the coconut palms.' Kerala is located in the southwest corner of India. I was born as an Eastern rite Catholic. I belong to the community known as St. Thomas Christians."

Being Catholic you had to have been in the minority.

"Yes, 80 percent of India is Hindu; 10 percent Muslim. About three percent are Christian."

You're old enough to remember India's caste system.

"The caste system was very strong in India. There were four major castes. The educated people were known as Brahmins. St. Thomas, the apostle, preached only to the Brahmins. Brahmin means 'God's people.'"

What about the bottom rung of the social ladder, the

Untouchables?

"You have heard of Mahatma Gandhi?"

Yes.

"Gandhi said the Untouchables were God's people. By law, the caste system was officially banned. With that said, some of the upper classes still take advantage of the ignorant to this day.

"I remember when Gandhi came to Kerala. He was a well-educated man who lived a very simple life. Although a Hindu, he was a believer in the teachings of Jesus Christ."

Father, I consider Cesar Chavez and Mahatma Gandhi two of the greatest men who ever lived.

"Gandhi was spat upon by a British man."

And?

"He gently took his handkerchief and smilingly wiped the saliva from his face. He then reminded the man that Jesus taught that you should not return evil acts with vengeance. You must forgive them."

When were you ordained?

"In 1952. I attended Madras Christian College. It was the most prestigious college in all of India. As a student, I was involved in protests. We would march and shout out slogans. Gandhi told us to push out the British gently, but not to harm them."

Mother Teresa?

"She used to visit Kerala often. Mother Teresa was so popular in those days. She was always invited to big Catholic gatherings that would last a week. People thought so highly of her because of the wonderful things she was doing."

Let's switch gears. Sports in India?

"Soccer was very popular. Cricket was for the upper classes."

Your thoughts on author Rudyard Kipling?

"'Oh, East is East, West is West, and never the twain shall meet.' He was a typical British imperialist."

Your father?

"My father was a very prominent businessman – a merchant. We were upper middle class. My father would always give the beggars alms. When the ordinary people had complaints, they would come to him and he would return the petitions to the government. My mother was a very devout Catholic. She would pray and pray all the time."

What year did you come to the United States?

"In 1976. I was invited by our previous bishop of the dioceses of Gary, Bishop Grupka. That was a time of turmoil in the entire Catholic Church. There was a shortage of priests throughout the Western world."

Favorite traditional Indian meal?

"Rice and curry. Rice was a standard meal at home. In our language – not as here – curry is the food that is mixed with the rice, such as fish or vegetables."

First assignments in America?

"St. James in Highland for three years. I also taught theology at Bishop Noll High School and was at Sacred Heart in Gary."

* * *

I'm not a Catholic, but whether interviewing Sister Peg Spindler, a Catholic nun; Rabbi Michael N. Stevens, a Jew; Moanes Khawalid, a Muslim; Mineko Hirata, a Buddhist; Rev. Charles Edward Adams II, a Baptist; Patricia Riley-Churilla, a Pagan; Rev. Roger Brewin, a Unitarian; or several atheists, I have learned something from each and every one of them.

And when I interviewed this humble man who was born Varakukala Dominic Joseph, a man who knew Mahatma Gandhi, I was touched by his compassion as he told me the story of how an Archbishop told St. Teresa of Calcutta, a native of Albania, that he was not worthy of kissing her feet.

Father Ivans wept.

History Books

Edith Sautter *(March 2010)*

"The right of citizens of the United States to vote shall not be denied or abridged by the United States or by any state on account of sex."

– 19th Amendment of to the U.S. Constitution

On March 4, 1909, Theodore Roosevelt's term as the 26th president of the United States ended.

Meanwhile, little Edith Meyers was celebrating her second birthday.

Another decade passed before women were allowed to vote, after the 19th Amendment was passed by Congress on June 4, 1919, and ratified Aug. 18, 1920.

Edith Meyers Sautter,103, was married to Emery Sautter for more than 76 years before his passing. They raised two sons, Robert and Jim. She lives in Lowell, but is currently staying at Saint Anthony Home in Crown Point, where she is recovering from a broken hip.

* * *

"I was born in Creston," Sautter began. "My father, Eddie Meyers, was a farmer."

Please, Edith, finish your lasagna before it gets cold. Then, we'll begin.

"Food means nothing to me. My mother's maiden name was Barber, but that's the American way; in France, it was Barbier. My grandfather was from Alsace-Lorraine. I don't think I'll make a good story."

Knock it off.

"My paternal grandfather was born in Germany, but he died young; I never knew him."

What about your dad?
"He's buried in Plum Grove, across from the State Police station on (Indiana) 2."
Tell me more about Creston; my buddy, Ken Travis, grew up there. He said it was a sad day when the post office closed and Creston became part of Lowell. Did you know the Travis family?
"Oh, sure; we lived on the west side of town. Floyd Vinnedge ran the post office."
How do you spell the last name?
"V-i-n-n-e-d-g-e. My teeth don't fit right."
Edith, you're doing just fine; your memory is incredible.
"We made our own butter. On horseback, I'd take the butter and our hen's eggs, from Creston to Lowell and trade them with the grocer for items like sugar.
"When I was in sixth grade, we moved to the east side of the Lake Dale area. There was no lake back then; it was a saw mill.
"Then, after a few years, we moved to Crown Point. I graduated from Crown Point High School, Class of '24. There were 38 of us; I'm the last one left. My best friend from Creston, Ardetta Burnham, just passed away. I was born in '07."
First car?
"It was a Ford, the one that came out before the Model T. I drove until about a year ago."
Did you remain loyal to Henry Ford?
"No; I have a (Chevrolet) Malibu."
When you were in your early teens, women weren't allowed to vote.
"Correct; that wasn't until about 1920. I've always voted."
Do you lean a certain way?
"I'm a Republican."
Have you ever voted for a Democratic presidential candidate?
"No."
Not even Harry S. Truman?
"Nope, and I didn't vote for this one, either."
Who is the first president you can remember?
"Roosevelt, maybe."
Franklin Delano?
"Teddy."

When you were a young girl, did you think a man one day would land on the moon?

"Heavens, no. Didn't even consider it. We didn't have electric lights or indoor plumbing."

Do you remember Charles Lindbergh's historic trans-Atlantic flight in 1927?

"Oh, yes. I remember all that. That was terrible when their baby was kidnaped."

The Great Depression.

"I was married then; my husband was out of work. We managed. Emery started out laying tile and carpet. Later, we had a furniture store in Lowell where the Midtown Hardware store is today. We moved to Lowell in '56. I attend Lowell Church of Christ; they've been so good to me."

To what do you attribute your longevity?

"We lived the simple life. I loved to keep my house clean; I worked hard at that all my life. I still scrub my floors on my hands and knees. I also worked at the National Tea Co. in Crown Point."

World War II?

"I don't remember much about that period of time; but I remember World War I like it was yesterday."

Were you a pretty good cook in your day?

"I thought I was, not anymore."

What was one of your specialties?

"Chicken and homemade noodles. I baked a lot of pies."

Personal favorite?

"Probably lemon."

Mine, too. Are you a reader?

"I used to read a couple of books a week from the library, but my eyes aren't what they used to be. I liked biographies and the classics, romantic things mostly, like 'Wuthering Heights.'

"I have subscribed to the Post-Tribune for 50 years or more. I take the Lowell Tribune, too. My son brings my newspapers to me everyday. By the way, you look different in person."

I get that sometimes. Edith, you took a nasty fall.

"Yes, I slipped in my breezeway. I crawled to the outside door and hammered on it, but nobody heard me. It was 10 o'clock at night.

"I knew I couldn't stay there because it was cold. So, I crawled about 20 feet to the kitchen. The telephone is on the desk. There was a little bitty edge sticking out; I was able to pull the telephone down toward me and call 9-1-1. I did more damage to my hip by crawling on it."

You probably would have froze to death if you had stayed in the breezeway. You did what you had to do.

"Yes, I had to. Did I mention that I've belonged to the Daughters of the American Revolution for 54 years? Jeff, I'm grateful I've been able to keep my mind in my old age."

* * *

I, too, am grateful – that I was able to sit and listen to Edith's good story.

Barney Wornhoff *(Sept. 2012)*

"This (stock market) crash is not going to have much effect on business."
– Arthur Reynolds, chairman of Continental Illinois Bank of Chicago, Oct. 24, 1929

Bernard Wornhoff was born in 1918; on Nov.11 of that year, World War I ended.

The next fall, the Chicago White Sox threw the World Series to the Cincinnati Reds in the infamous "Black Sox Scandal."

In 1919, Dad could buy a new Studebaker for $675, and Mom could pick up a chuck roast for less than 30 cents per pound, a quart of milk for 15 cents and a pound of sugar for a dime.

When I interviewed Wornhoff, he was in the process of moving in with his son, Greg, who lives in the old Cook neighborhood which is now part of Cedar Lake.

Wornhoff was married to Junella for 66 years; they raised four children.

At 94, the old-timer is a as sharp as the proverbial tack.

* * *

Barney, tell me about the town of Leroy during the Roaring Twenties.

"Actually, we lived in a rural area called Southeast Grove before the family moved to Leroy," he said.

Southeast Grove?

"It's in Eagle Creek Township, east of Lowell. I went to three grades of school in Southeast Grove. There were only four or five kids in a class.

"Across the road was a cemetery; all the old-timers were buried there. The cemetery is there yet, but the school is gone."

What was the name of the school?

"Center School on Range Line Road. Horses pulled our bus, which was a converted wagon. I went to Hebron High School for two years. At age 16, you could do anything a man could do; you went to work."

Was your father a farmer?

"Yeah; I was one of six kids. I stayed home with Dad and Mom working on the farm until I was about 24. It was hard work back in those days; everything was done manual. We bought our first tractor back in the late '40s."

What make?

"Allis-Chalmers."

Life after farming?

"I bought a gas station in Leroy back in the early '50s. A few years later, I opened up my garage-repair shop in Cook. It was a block building with a barrel roof on the southeast corner of U.S. 41 and 133rd Avenue.

"My house sits right there. They tore it down to build a CVS (pharmacy). My father-in-law, Adam Schafer, had that house built in 1913."

How long did you operate the garage?

"Oh, 40-some years. I retired in the 1990s. I also drove a school bus for 32 years until about 1991."

Have you seen a few changes to the Cook-Cedar Lake area since the 1940s and '50s?

"Oh, yeah. I used to go dancin' at the old Midway Ballroom. Ron Coby used to direct the square dancing out at Midway. That was out on the water and a lot of people were kinda leery because that floor would waver back and forth, but it never caved in.

"Roller skating was a big deal around here back then. I never was much of a roller skater, but my wife and her lady friends would frequent the rink often."

This neighborhood where we're sitting is really nice.

"The main section of this house and the main section of the house across the street were once owned by the railroad. Across the street, was the conductor-station master's house and this was the section crew house when they had steam engines. They were moved here in the 1940s."

Interesting; what about harvesting ice out of Cedar Lake?

"As a kid, I worked that job. They had a big saw that was pulled with horses. They would cut the ice into large chunks. Then they would pull them through a channel and into the ice house with a conveyor.

"The ice was packed with sawdust. It would keep all the way into summer."

Amazing. I bet that was exhaustive work.

"Oh, it was hard work. Those old bosses we had, they didn't take pity on nobody. Herman Jebens was one of them; he was an old German and an iceman here. He was the one who sold the ice in the summertime."

Barney, my memories don't go back as far as yours, of course, but I recall a beer-and-wine joint back in the late '70s; it was located on U.S. 41 in Cook. It was called Saco's.

"Oh, gee, that was like a wild west saloon."

Yeah, through the grapevine, I've heard that my grandfather used to shoot craps in there when a fella named Harry Bixman ran the place during the 1940s.

Today, that establishment is known as Carlo's Restaurant, Pizzeria & Sports Bar.

* * *

While sitting on the front porch with Barney and his son, Greg, Barney turned around in his lawn chair, pointed, and informed me that the front door of his son's place was recently salvaged from his house at the southeast corner of US 41 and 133rd.

At almost a century old, the handsomely crafted door, made in 1913, is quite a piece of work.

So is Barney Wornhoff.

Cullen Ben-Daniel *(July 2013)*

"Where after all do universal human rights begin? In small places, closest to home – so close and so small that they cannot be seen on any map of the world. Yet they are the world of the individual person: The neighborhood he lives in; the school or college he attends; the factory, farm or office where he works. Such are the places where every man, woman and child seeks equal justice, equal opportunity, equal dignity without discrimination."
– *Eleanor Roosevelt*

Cullen Ben-Daniel wore a yarmulke while I interviewed him, he's the son of an interracial couple, and he's married to a man named David.

OK, we got that out of the way.

Ben-Daniel, 36, also is a historian by trade, an artist, and one of the most interesting human beings I've ever met. And he lives in a gorgeous, solid brick, three-bedroom, two-bath, Tudor Revival home with hardwood floors on Lake Street in the Miller neighborhood of Gary on Lake Street near the Big Lake.

* * *

Nice digs.

"An old Norwegian family named the Balogs lived here before me," he said. "Betty Balog was an English teacher at Wirt High School. I walked past this house all the time on the way to Lake Street Beach as a kid. I'd see Betty in the yard gardening and I'd wave to her.

"I found an old coffee mug in a cabinet when I moved here. It said, 'You can always tell a Norwegian, you just can't tell them much.'"

That's funny. If you don't mind me asking, how much did you pay for this gem?

"I paid $21,000 almost two years ago. It was built in 1937."

Your husband?

"David works in Cook County. He's a cartographer – a map maker."

I know what it means.

"We got married two year ago in New York City. It was the same summer that New York passed marriage equality. We'd already been living together for a couple years.

"What makes it difficult is he and I don't have any marriage protection in Indiana. If I got in an accident and had to go to the hospital, he couldn't make any medical decisions for me. As far as the state of Indiana is concerned, we're strangers."

I believe that will change soon.

"We're only a few years away. The Supreme Court will force it. My parents were an interracial couple back in the early '70s. They moved here because Miller was a tolerant and liberal place to live."

Historic William A. Wirt Senior High School?

"There were really great teachers at Wirt. Teachers like Kittie Bjorklund-Cozza who had an amazing impact on my life. She taught English and directed plays. As a historian, I write a lot. Many of my writing skills come from having her as a teacher."

College?

"I have a bachelor's degree in history and a master's degree in world history. I work for Roosevelt University in Chicago in its Center for New Deals Studies. It's a division of the history department that is dedicated to preserving the legacy of Franklin and Eleanor Roosevelt."

Early Miller?

"Miller is more than a half-century older than Gary. I believe Gary annexed it in 1919. Most of Miller belonged to the Potawatomi tribe by law. There was a particular Potawatomi individual and his wife who owned what became downtown Miller. They sold if off to a person named Ewing. It was called Ewing Subdivision.

"Miller was settled around 1850 as a railroad town. It was called Miller Station and Miller's Junction. At first, there were just squatters – people who hunted and fished in the dunes. The French fur traders were the first Europeans to settle around here."

Very interesting.

"Then, after the Great Chicago Fire, there were a large number of

Swedes who settled here. The Swedes opened up the Lutheran Church which is on Lake Street. It's actually the oldest church within the boundaries of Gary. Miller was a small, sleepy town."

I love the history.

"The area nestled between the lagoon, Miller Woods and Lake Street Beach contains the oldest beach homes and dune cottages ever built in Miller. It has recently been dubbed Cottage Row.

"During the early 20th Century, most of the land around Lake Street Beach was owned by Robert and Drusilla Carr. They built Carr's Beach, a lakefront recreation Mecca which included a dance hall, several night clubs, a miniature railroad, a shooting gallery, a roller rink, a boardwalk, and a pleasure boat. By 1917, the Carrs had built more than 100 cottages on their property which they rented out for $100 a year. By the Roaring Twenties, Carr's Beach was the most popular vacation destination in all of Lake County."

Tell me more.

"When I moved back to Miller, I wanted to do something to help preserve, protect and promote the history of this area. People who have lived here all their lives don't know that Miller was once a Swedish community or that in the 1950s, a large population of Jews lived in Miller."

I know several who still do.

"Yeah, we lay low. In 2010, I got together with some local citizens; we started a historical society in Miller. We still have our town hall which is on the National Register of Historic Places. It has been vacant for 20 years and the city has done nothing to keep it up. It's a beautiful building that sits on the corner of Grand Boulevard and Miller Avenue.

"One of the goals of the historical society is to do a full historic preservation and restoration of that building and turn it into a welcome center with a small museum in it."

How often does the Miller Beach Historical Society meet?

"The last Saturday of every month at the Paul H. Douglass Center here on Lake Street. We usually have lectures and programs on various aspects of history, not just Miller history. We're history buffs who sometimes get together and watch documentaries."

Miller today?

"I've lived in several places, but none of them felt like home. Miller is home. Miller is a place where you know your neighbors, and you like them."

Final thoughts?

"Miller is a diamond in the rough. It's racially and socioeconomically diverse. There is so much potential in this community. It's an area that is surrounded by a national park right on Lake Michigan. And my commute to Chicago is a snap with the South Shore within walking distance.

"The area between Grand Boulevard and Lake Street is the historic core of Miller Beach. It contains some of the oldest structures in the entire city. Our historical society has designated this area the Grandlake Historic District. The houses are an eclectic mix of early 20th Century architectural styles including Tudor Revival, Spanish Colonial, Craftsman-Style Bungalows and even Sears Catalog Homes."

The future?

"Within five or 10 years, I see downtown Miller and the residential neighborhoods around it, being one of the most artsy and hippest places to live in the entire region. Our best days are ahead of us."

* * *

Ben-Daniel also gave me the dime tour of his backyard where he raises a wonderful urban vegetable garden and maintains a pond that was built along with the house in '37. When I ribbed him about the pair of plastic pink flamingoes near the pond he told me they were there before he was and they deserve to stay. I like the way he thinks.

And it is nice to know Cullen Ben-Daniel has come back home.

Jim Kersting *(Aug. 2014)*

"If you build it, they will come."
– from the film "Field of Dreams"

Kersting's Cycle Center & Museum is located out in the middle of a 40-acre cow pasture just off Hwy. 39 about four miles south of North Judson in Pulaski County. But folks from all over the world have signed Jim Kersting's guest book. The museum is really something to see. A nominal donation of $5 per person is appreciated.

Kersting, 78, lives in North Judson with Bobbe, his wife of five years. He and his first wife, Nella, raised three children before her untimely demise.

* * *

Lived in this area all your life?

"Yes, I graduated from North Judson High School," he said.

I read on your website that as a boy, you took the motor out of your mother's washing machine and attached it to a motorcycle frame.

"Sure did. I still have it. My mother wasn't too pleased because she was still using that Maytag. Her maiden name was Bau, but that was shortened from Bautista. I'm half Italian."

Did you ever race motorcycles?

"Racing is what got me so hooked into motorcycles. I qualified third-fastest at Daytona in 1969."

How did you get started in this business?

"I started out here as a tractor repairman and had a filling station. We were right here by all the fields. The farmers wouldn't have to go into town. But I had read an ad in Popular Mechanics magazine about becoming a Harley-Davidson dealer around 1960. I filled out the ad and sent it in."

And?

"A couple of years went by. I forgot I even sent it in. I was working on the transmission of a tractor in my shop and had grease up to my elbows when one of the district managers from Harley-Davidson Motor Company approached me and said: 'Jim, we've heard you'd like to become a Harley-Davidson dealer.'"

What did you say to that?

"I said: 'Naw, I think I'm gonna just stick with rebuilding these old tractors.' Well, after some coaxing, the D.M. talked me into it. That was 1962.

"In '68, Kawasaki came along. I figured we needed a smaller bike in our area. Not everybody wanted a Harley. By the mid-'70s, Kawasaki was our main bread and butter."

How were Harley sales going in the '70s?

"In the '70s, Harley-Davidson kind of took a thug mentality. The Harley-Davidson world was a pretty rough world in the '70s. A lot of people didn't want to be associated with Harley-Davidson. During those years it was a good thing we had Kawasaki. In 1980, we purchased the Yamaha dealership.

"Things got really tight here at the dealership in the early '80s. That's the way the museum got started. In order to get stuff sold, I'd have to take anything in trade because nobody had a lot of money in the early '80s. You couldn't afford to finance money at 20 percent interest. People would bring in junk that had been sitting around in their garages or barns. I'd take it in trade just to get a new bike sold and stay in business."

Interesting. Harley-Davidson's comeback?

"Some of the key people in the company bought Harley-Davidson back from AMF in '82. By '84, they had a well-designed motorcycle that would hold up. Harley-Davidson started cleaning up its image.

"It was in the early '90s when I started cleaning up the old stuff I had amassed so I could show it off. As the economy got better, some of my collection became valuable. People wanted to buy the old bikes, but I said no. In fact, I added to it. I started going to auctions."

Not counting the new motorcycles for sale in the showrooms, what would you estimate your collection in the museum is worth? Monetarily speaking.

"Well, I have it insured for about a million-and-a-half."

What makes do you sell new?

"Harleys and Yamahas. We used to sell Kawasakis."

That tongue-in-cheek replica of Harley-Davidson you have displayed out front must be close to 20 feet tall.

"I built that myself."

How about the dime tour?

Those leather jackets with Moonlight Rangers across the backs?

"They were a motorcycle club out of Kankakee, Illinois."

Do you have any dirt bikes in your collection?

"Not too many. Here's a nice 1970 Husqvarna on display."

Some of these American-made Indians are beautiful machines.

"Yes, they are, with that big skirted front fender. This one is a 1927. Indians were made in Springfield, Mass. The company went bankrupt in 1953.

"I also have motorcycles from at least 10 different countries in here. I've ridden them all at one time or another."

One of your favorite motorcycles in the museum?

"This 1910 Harley. It's pretty much all original. I ride it occasionally."

Was 1910 the first year Harley-Davidson produced motorcycles?

"No, that would be 1903."

Jim, I read the memorial plaque set in the brick outside the building.

"I get emotional when I talk about Nella. It happened just down the road a little ways. She was sittin' behind me on the motorcycle. A three-quarter ton pickup truck drove right out in front of us. He had a stop sign. We had a through road.

"I had just read an article where the writer said you should go faster through an intersection. That way you won't be in there so long. Well, I had just turned up the throttle... Boom!"

I'm so sorry. Were you hurt bad?

"Yeah."

Broken bones?

"Lots of 'em."

Final thoughts?

"I've traveled the world because of motorcycles. I'm an absolute true motorcycle enthusiast, not loyal to just one brand. Anything on two wheels."

* * *

My interview with Kersting was cut short because he had forgotten he needed to attend a funeral. But before I left Kersting's Cycle Center & Museum, I had a nice chat with Jim's youngest son Jason in the backroom of the Harley showroom.

Jason said: "During the '80s, when things were pretty tight, Dad was off on other ventures trying to make more money, trying to keep the place alive. My Mom was here running the store. If it had not been for Nella Kersting, the store wouldn't be here today. Dad was always the front man, the P.R. guy. Mom was behind the scenes keeping things together."

Dolly Millender *(July 2014)*

"...And I said good-bye to the Mayor of Gary and I went out from the city hall and turned into Broadway. And I saw workmen wearing leather shoes scruffed with fire and cinders, and pitted with little holes from running, molten steel, and some of them had bunches of specialized muscles around their shoulder blades hard as pig iron, muscles of their forearms were sheet steel, and they looked like men who been somewhere."
– Carl Sandburg (1915)

Dharathula H. "Dolly" Millender is founder and CEO of the Gary Historical & Cultural Society, Inc. At 94, Millender is a walking, talking history book. She's a retired librarian originally from Terre Haute, but has lived in Gary since 1960.

Our interview took place in her office at the Genesis Center on 5th & Broadway in downtown Gary. Her daughter Naomi was in attendance.

* * *

When did the GHCS come to fruition?

"In 1976," she said. "They were giving out grants all across the United States for people to put together programs that had to do with the bicentennial of the country. I thought to myself, 'Well, maybe I can write about Gary and the 47 different ethnic groups who peopled this area.' I had never written a grant before.

You had to get approval from your city council and a community committee had to back you up to get the grant."

How did that go?

"When I did my presentation, the place was packed. To back up a little bit, I had to talk to the councilman of the 6th District first. He told me,

'I don't think you're gonna get anything out of this, but you can try.'"

And?

"We took Fred Chary who was getting his PhD in different ethnic groups and a professor named Nicholas Kannelous who played the guitar. He was Mexican, I believe."

Greek, probably.

"I wrote a song called 'Gary Was Made For You & Me.' Eugene Kirkland – who was a powerhouse in the city council – told me, 'It's your turn to try to convince these people to accept your idea.' He told me, 'Good luck' – halfheartedly. Eugene lived in the Morning Side district of Glen Park where the rich white folks stayed.

"I told the audience how we were trying to pay tribute to the different ethnic groups who were living in Gary. We wanted to make sure they all got recognition and how this grant would bring all the people together. I started singing my song."

And?

"I can't sing."

What are the odds? You and I are probably the only African-American and Italian-American on the planet who can't carry a tune.

"Fred's little boys were beating away on sticks and Nick was playin' the guitar. He could really play."

Belt it out for me, Mahalia!

"It's been years. Here goes... 'I saw before me, an opportunity, Gary was made for you and me. So, now we're all here, from many cultures, don't let those outside, divide us inside, we chose to stay here, and build our city, Gary was built for you and me... '"

Dolly, Woody Guthrie would be in tears.

"They were all looking at me in shock. I guess they were thinking, 'What's with this crazy old lady?' I shouted out for them to join in with me."

Yeah?

"They joined in and we got the grant."

Great story. Where did the GHCS meet in the early days?

"My good friend unionist Larry Regan's mother had a restaurant right across from (Indiana University Northwest) called Jenny's Cafe. Larry is one of our board members. We'd go to Jenny's on Sunday afternoons. If the Lithuanians were gonna tell about their culture, Jenny would cook Lithuanian food. All the different cultures would come and discuss their backgrounds on Sundays. They were still all here then."

Dolly, I've always been both fascinated and appalled by stories about "The Patch."

"When U.S. Steel decided to build this mill here there was no city. There was an Aetna, Glen Park, Miller, Tolleston and a Clark that surrounded the area. In the middle was to be Gary. The area was just a bunch of weeds and sand. Judge Gary came in and said: 'We need a building so we can start to plan things."

The Gary Land Company building.

"Correct. It's still standing and is Gary's oldest building. It also has been reopened as a museum and visitor's center."

Reopened?

"Yes, the Gary Land Company building was a museum before we got it. There was a historical society before us as well. It was called the Gary Historical Society. Everything was going fine, but when Richard Hatcher won that second term on his own, the people who had the museum took everything out of there.

"Jeff, some people think that all white people hate black people. Not true. There were whites who had stuff in that museum they wanted others to see. They were very upset when that group took everything away."

Back to the fledgling days of the Steel City and the notorious Patch.

"U.S. Steel recruited in Europe because over there they had ironworkers and all those sturdy men."

Kind of like today, where agribusiness hires sturdy men, women and children from south of the border to do the dirty work for less pay that Americans refuse to do. I digress. The Patch.

"Like I said, they recruited all these different ethnic groups to come over here and build the city. They'd introduce the immigrants to those from their cultures who were already here. They'd tell these tradesmen: 'This man also is Croatian and he has a grocery store. This man speaks German like you and he has a bakery.'"

And this man is Italian and he make-a-the-shoe.

"They decided that 5th & Broadway would be the main drag. They also decided it was going to be fancy, so they had a lot of theaters. By 1927, they had the Gary Hotel which cost several million dollars to build. Yeah, they really thought they were going to have themselves a snazzy town."

Even the best laid plans… .

"They forgot the hoi polloi consisted of the lowly foreigner and blacks from the Deep South. Upper management thought when the workers finished building the city they'd leave. Where were they gonna go?"

The Patch, perhaps?

"The Patch was an area near downtown."

I knew I'd get it out of you.

"It started at about 10th Avenue and went to about 13th Avenue just past where the railroad goes over Broadway."

That would've been the extreme southern end of Gary back in the day.

"Yes. There were no restrictions in The Patch. They could have a million bars and grills down there. There was all kinds of funny looking housing down there. It was a terrible area – squalor and disease. Everything went on in The Patch. They had one saloon for every 10 people."

Dolly, the GHCS is not your average historical society.

"Our mission is to enrich the lives of Gary's citizens of all ages through programs that preserve and promote local history and culture, improve access to educational opportunities, teach respect for ethnic diversity, develop positive citizens, and promote Gary pride."

* * *

I but scratched the surface regarding the incredible, selfless, nonagenarian Dolly Millender.

A person can learn a lot when he or she sits down and really listens to someone else's point of view.

Fuzz Campbell *(Aug. 2013)*

"Spittin', whittlin', tellin' lies
Sittin' on the ol' dead pecker bench
Drinkin' an R.C. and eatin' Moon Pies
Singin' Mabel on the Hill"
– Author unknown

Fuzz Campbell, 77, lives a couple miles west of Gifford which is about 10 miles north of Rensselaer. He is a retired autoworker and a widower. He and Linda raised three children.

I first met Campbell about a month ago at the Rensselaer Public Library where I was doing a presentation of the documentary film "Everglades of the North: The Story of the Grand Kankakee Marsh." He approached me afterward, telling me that he had worked with my Uncle Joe at Ford for many years.

Being a dipper of snuff, Campbell kept his spit cup nearby while we conversed.

* * *

I'm going out on a limb here and assume mother Campbell didn't name you Fuzz.

"My real name is Forrest with two 'r's," he said. "My last day on the job at Ford, a guy I worked with more than 30 years asked me, 'Fuzz, what the hell is your real first name?'"

Were you born in Gifford?

"Yep. Take Gifford Road two miles due east. I went to grade school in the nearby town of Newland."

What was the population of Gifford when you lived near town as a boy?

"About 50."

Today?

"About the same. Back in those days, believe it or not, the town of Gifford had two stores. My dad owned one of those general stores. Everything is big box stores these days. You can't compete. Can you believe as big as Medaryville and San Pierre is they don't have a grocery store?"

Tell me more about your childhood in Gifford.

"There was a lot of people coming from the South and they all had seven, eight, nine kids. We all went to school and played together. But in the evenings, when things got kinda slow, the old farmers, trappers and hunters would sit on my dad's store porch and tell their lies.

"I'd say 75 percent of the time, I was sittin' right there with them while the rest of the kids were playin'. I liked listening to their history."

How old were you?

"Probably about 7 or 8."

One of the more memorable characters who would frequent the store's porch?

"Dicey Zook."

How do you spell that?

"Well, I don't know. Dicey probably was his nickname. I never did know his real name. But then again, those old-timers had some funny names, so maybe Dicey was his real name."

What about the spelling of Zook?

"Just Zook."

Z-O-O-K?

"Yeah. How else would you spell it?"

How old was Zook when he'd tell his tales to you?

"Well into his eighties."

What did Dicey do for a living?

"He was a professional hunter."

I love this kind of stuff.

"I remember me and Dicey was sittin' on the old Gifford Ditch before they cleaned it out and ruined the fishin'. We'd fish together for hours at a time.

"Dicey was born during the Civil War. As a child, Dicey played with the Potawatomi boys whose families remained after removal. Those Indian kids play like any other kids."

I'd imagine so.

"In the spring of the year, as soon as the ice was off, my dad and Dicey would take rakes and an old boat and collect frog legs. Dad paid for his first car from money he got shipping those frog hams to Chicago."

Can you imagine the wild game in this area back in the day?

"Some of those Chicago restaurant owners would come down here wanting to know who was the best shot on the marsh."

Why?

"That was who they'd hire to shoot the game for them. The restaurant people would furnish the ammunition. Dicey told me they gave him a few cents for a rabbit, a few more cents for a pheasant or a duck. A goose paid more than a duck.

"You shot year around in those days. There wasn't any laws. They'd pack waterfowl into wooden barrels and put ice on it."

The Grand Kankakee Marsh – "Chicago's food pantry."

"The men responsible for draining the marsh should have been prosecuted." *Men like Benjamin Gifford?*

"BJ Gifford named Gifford after himself, obviously. He also built the town of Kersey. He had his own railroad and had 35,000 acres of marshland. He drained the marsh with a floating steam dredge. He run it 24-7 until he cut all these ditches, then he leased the ground into individual parcels and encouraged his tenants to grow onions. That's where his railroad got the name the 'Onion Line.'"

Tell me one more of those "Dicey" stories.

"Dicey used to hang around old man Granger's boys. The Grangers were a rough bunch who lived on the river. Dicey told me about a time when he was hunting with one of those Grangers in a canoe; there were game wardens by then. Anyway, they was shootin' ducks out of season when they heard a strange noise coming from somewhere else in the swamp. Granger says, 'Dice, I'm gonna let you out on this island. I'll be back.'"

That's kind of odd.

"Dicey thought so, too. After about 10 minutes, Dicey hears the report of a shotgun. Soon after, Granger returned just like he said he would. Dicey asked him, 'What did you shoot?' Granger replied: 'Oh, never mind. Everything's alright. We won't be bothered no more.'"

He shot a game warden?

"You didn't cross the Grangers."

Let's switch gears. Did you attend Rensselaer High School?

"No, I went to Wheatfield High School. DeMotte, Fair Oaks, Tefft, Mt. Ayr, Kentland and Morocco all were in our conference. It would always come down to the nitty gritty between us and the Morocco Beavers."

Of which sport are you referring?

"Football. I was starting quarterback all four years. We played six-man football. Can you imagine that? Back in those days the quarterback didn't throw that much because it was a running game. In four years, I don't believe I threw the ball a dozen times. You had to gain 15 yards to get a first down."

Fuzz, it has been a slice.

"When you see your Uncle Joe, tell him he better not mess with me. I've been drinking this special muscle milk."

Will do.

"And, Jeff, tell him to stop on by next time he's near Gifford. I miss that ornery cuss."

* * *

After our interview, I checked out the hamlet of Gifford. There were a couple dozen modest houses and not a soul in sight. I made a u-turn near the Gifford Church of God and started back home.

Like Lot's wife, I couldn't resist the urge to look back. In my rearview mirror, I yearned to catch a glimpse of a weatherbeaten market hunter telling tales on the front porch of Campbell's General Store.

Didn't happen.

But just as sure as the Onion Line once chugged through a vanishing swamp, a lad named Forrest did see such things 70 years ago.

And I'm grateful a retired autoworker called Fuzz told me all about it.

Floyd Johnson *(Jan. 2013)*

"And David put his hand in the bag and took out a stone and slung it. And it struck the Philistine in the head and he fell to the ground. Amen."
– From the movie "Hoosiers"

Floyd Johnson, 90, lives in Kouts. He was married to Velda two weeks shy of 65 years before her passing. He is a World War II veteran, a retired school teacher and was quite an athlete in his day.

* * *

"I grew up in Hebron," Johnson began. "I graduated from Hebron High School in 1940."

You're tall man for your generation, did you play basketball for the Hawks?

"Yes, but we didn't have very good gymnasiums in those days. Kouts didn't even have a gymnasium. But in 1938, they finished a nice new school here in Kouts.

"The principals at Kouts, Boone Grove, Morgan Township and Hebron decided to have a holiday tournament on Jan. 1. It was a blind-draw tournament. There were two games in the afternoon and two in the evening; there was a consolation game."

Who won?

"Hebron won the first South County Tournament; we beat Morgan Township in the championship game. Morgan had a bunch of big, strong farm boys. Our victory was somewhat of an upset."

Did you play center?

"Yes, I was a sophomore."

World War II?

"I joined the service when I was 20, and did a little more than three years – South Pacific naval duty. I was involved in all the major invasions on an amphibious transport. We landed Marines on islands."

Like an LST?

"No, the USS Sheridan was a bigger ship than that. We had about 500 crew members and could carry about 1,000 troops."

Name a few of the invasions with which you were involved.

"One of the first we made was in the Gilbert Islands, then the Marshall Islands. We made landings in Sai Pan, Guam, Okinawa, three in the Philippines... ."

Did your ship get torpedoed?

"No, I never received a scratch; we were well-protected. But we were under attack many times. We had destroyers, cruisers and aircraft carriers around us all the time. In the Philippines, we did get involved with some kamikaze planes which hit our convoy, but we escaped. The ship next to us got hit."

Any other World War II memories?

"We would unload our battle troops, then serve as a hospital ship. We'd take the wounded back to places like Pearl Harbor. One of the things that I remember that still bothers me about the war is burying guys at sea. We didn't have the refrigeration back then."

Were you married to Velda while you served?

"No, but we did get engaged while I was on leave in '45. We got married in '46; I was working at U.S. Steel. I decided that was not the life for me. I always liked school and decided I wanted to be a teacher."

At what college did you attend?

"I started at Valparaiso University, but decided that was a little too close to home. After a year, I transferred to Ball State University. It's a very good teachers' college. While at Valpo, I played varsity baseball."

Let me guess, first base?

"That's right. When I was growing up, softball was a big thing. Every little town had a lighted softball field. There wasn't any television back then. Evening softball games were a big deal. I missed a lot of that while in the service and was all gung ho to catch up on all that.

"It didn't take me long to figure out that I was married and had better settle down and get to work."

Where was your first teaching job?

"In southern Indiana, a town by the name of Williams near Bedford; I stayed there two years. Then I went from Williams to a town named Cayuga. Then I had a chance to come to Kouts High School. I taught at

Kouts for nine years, and finished my career at Portage High School."

What years were you at Portage?

"From '64 to '82."

Did you know a football coach by the name of Les Klein?

"Sure, I know Les Klein well."

Les grew up with my parents; like you, he was quite an athlete in his day.
What subjects did you teach?

"Business and Physical Education. I finished as an assistant principal at Portage."

Did you ever coach sports?

"In my early years, I coached basketball, six-man football and track."

What year did you retire?

"In 1982. I taught for 33 years and have been retired for 30."

Did you and Velda travel in retirement?

"Oh, yeah. We spent some winters in Arizona. I got to go back to Hawaii and see some of the sights I'd seen when I was in the service."

Floyd, its been great talking to you. Is there anything I didn't ask you or something you'd like in your story?

"Well, I tried out with the Brooklyn Dodgers in 1941. They sent me home, saying, 'We're not going to keep you this year, but come back next year.' But the war was going on by then and I joined the Navy."

* * *

I received an e-mail from a lady I don't know regarding interviewing Floyd Johnson. She told me everyone in Kouts thinks the world of him and felt the same about his beloved wife, Velda.

During the middle of our interview there was a knock at Floyd's door. With the aid of a walker, the old-timer made his way back to the kitchen with a plate of goodies. I asked him, "Meals on Wheels?"

Floyd replied with a smile, "No, just a friendly neighbor."

You've lived a good life, Mr. Johnson.

Lydia Grady *(Nov. 2010)*

"I do not hesitate one second to state clearly and unmistakably: I belong to the American resistance movement which fights against American imperialism just as the resistance movement fought against (Adolf) Hitler."
– Paul Robeson

Lydia Grady has lived in Gary since 1945, the last 40 years in the Miller neighborhood. She was born in Detroit and twice has been widowed.

Grady, 94, has raised a son and daughter both graduates of Horace Mann High School.

Grady watches one program on televison per day, the news, and reads three newspapers: the Chicago Tribune, the New York Times and the Post-Tribune. She enjoys folk music.

Our mutual friend, Robin Rich, helped set up the interview. Rich, a union organizer, sat in on our conversation. Also on hand was retired Indiana University Northwest professor Ruth Needleman who is interested in oral histories. Needleman didn't remain retired long; she recently has started a program at Calumet College of St. Joseph called leadership and social justice.

Uncharacteristically, I might have been the most conservative person in the room.

* * *

"My parents were born in Poland," Grady began.
What year did they arrive in the United States?
"About 1915."
Tell me about Detroit?
"The Purple Gang was active not far from where I lived."

I've read about the Purple Gang, a murderous mob of bootleggers in the Roaring Twenties.

"Yes, a Jewish version of La Cosa Nostra. I grew up in an atheist household and attended a socialist Jewish school in Detroit from the ages of 10 to 14."

That's fascinating.

"I have to tell you something about my mother."

Please do.

"She called all clergy parasites. When my father did attend temple, she'd drive him there and wait in the car."

When did your family move from Detroit?

"About the time I started high school; we moved to Butler, Pa., about 35 miles north of Pittsburgh. It was a blue-collar town.

"My dad was a tool-and-dye designer. He took a job in Butler at the Austen automobile factory. The Austen was a British car that got a lot of miles per gallon, but it never took off in this country. After the first year, my father had to work for half wages. By the third year, they told him he could keep on working, but they weren't sure if they could pay him."

The Great Depression was taking its toll.

"My parents moved back to Detroit."

Did you go with them?

"No, I attended nursing school in Chicago at Michael Reese (Hospital). Then I lived in New York City for a while."

Tell me about the "Big Apple" during the Great Depression.

"For a nickel, you could get into the theater. I attended Columbia Teacher's College in New York for a year. I ended up getting my degree at Indiana University Northwest – $7 a credit hour."

World War II?

"I was a nurse in the Army and spent a year in England. I had a wonderful time. I went to Scotland and heard Myra Hess play the piano. I went to London to get rye bread."

Lydia, there was a war going on, it couldn't have been all Myra Hess and rye bread. Air raids in England?

"Oh, yes. I had to jump in a ditch a couple of times. We had German prisoners; they had a hard time understanding my particular brand of German."

Why's that?

"I spoke to them in Yiddish."

What did your first husband do for a living?
"He was a doctor."
Tell me about the Jewish community in Gary during the 1940s and '50s.
"We had two temples and one of them had a rabbi, Gary August, whose sermons were so good that people who weren't members would listen to them."
Maybe even a few atheists?
"Maybe. Rabbi August was very socially conscious. He got in trouble."
Because he was extremely liberal?
"Yes, he had to tone it down some."
McCarthyism?
"My first husband was very outspoken. There was a period of at least six months where he had no patients except for a couple of die-hards."
Julius and Ethel Rosenberg?
"I was at the Crown Theater watching a film about them and two young people were sitting in front of me. At the very end of the film, one said to the other, 'I think they (the Rosenbergs) might have been real people.' Can you believe it?

"During the 1950s, I was involved in the breakdown of segregation at the Methodist Hospital in Gary. Being head of the department, I hired the first black nurse.

"If a black person was critically injured in the steel mill, Mercy (Hospital) would allow them on the first floor only. If a family doctor from the black neighborhood admitted his patient to the hospital, a white doctor had to admit the patient as well. Again, first floor only. I also helped desegregate Marquette Park Beach."

Lydia, in Mark Spencer's play "Steel Waters," which told the story of Gary's first 100 years, there was a scene that depicted the protest that went on regarding that very topic.
"I attended that play at West Side High School; my niece was in it."
So was I.
"Who were you?"
A Polish immigrant named Joe Wolek; your niece portrayed Joe's granddaughter.
"Well, about seven of us brought a young black man to the beach.

He ran toward Lake Michigan and jumped into the water."

And?

"The cops came and said the beach was closed."

The Froebel High School strike by white students in '45?

"I got thrown in jail over that one; I'd been in Gary like one day. I had just gotten out of the service. I told the kids who were striking, 'This is not why we had a war.'"

Did you ever attend a performance by the Weavers?

"No, but I saw Pete Seeger live."

Name two people from the past who you've really admired.

"Paul Robeson and Franklin Delano Roosevelt. Paul Robeson came to my house in 1948; he sang 'My Curly Headed Baby' to my daughter when she was 2." *Lydia, that's incredible. Let's fast forward two decades. Do you remember the campaign to get Richard Hatcher elected as Gary mayor?*

"Sure, I was part of it."

Did Miller residents support Hatcher?

"The Jews from Miller did. I think Hatcher's daughter is a little premature (about her mayoral campaign)."

That's what some folks said about a young senator from Illinois named Barack Obama. Speaking of whom, what do you think of the president's performance so far?

"Some people expect miracles. I housed workers during the Obama campaign; they slept here and ate here."

The present generation of young progressives?

"Today's 20-year-olds need to stop listening to and playing with all these electronic things. Are these children involved in any social issues? Where's their passion?"

* * *

Politically speaking, Lydia Grady is one of those folks you're either for or against. Nobody can say she hasn't been socially involved and passionate in her beliefs all these years.

Like Jim Hightower once said, "The only thing in the middle of the road is a yellow streak and dead armadillos."

Terry Stoner *(Dec. 2009)*

"We can do it."
-Rosie the Riveter

A 55-foot-tall pine tree stands in Terry Stoner's front yard in Lake Dalecarlia. For years, until about three Decembers ago, Stoner would wrap a 100-foot extension cord around one shoulder, shimmy to the top of said conifer, and then attach a star to it.

But relatives decided that Great-grandma Terry shouldn't do that any more. After all, she's 86.

While on a 300-mile bike ride in Ohio at age 79, she took a spill and broke her collar bone and three ribs. She still enjoys cross country skiing.

Our interview took place on Pearl Harbor Day.

* * *

"Jeff, yesterday I told my daughter I wanted to call this interview off," Stoner began. "Don't you feel this is presumptuous of me?"

Terry, this is no time to be humble.

"I was born Teresa Michiels on Chicago's northwest side. All four of my grandparents were born in Belgium. My husband and I moved to Lake Dale in 1950; we raised four children here. I've been a widow for more than 15 years."

Your early days in Chicago?

"I was raised Catholic, but graduated from a public school. I have five brothers; I don't think my parents knew whether to raise me as a boy or girl. I probably shouldn't say that.

"My father was in the Naval Reserves; he was conscripted into the service – that's different from being drafted. He was assigned to the USS Sacramento and was its second-highest ranking officer."

What time frame?

"The ship was assigned to duty in August of 1941. They went through Intercoastal Waterway to the Atlantic Ocean and then south to and through the Panama Canal to the Pacific Ocean. He had been ordered to Pearl Harbor, Hawaii."

What about you?

"He made arrangements for all of us to move to the Kaimuki District of Honolulu, about seven miles from Pearl Harbor. We arrived in October of '41; I was 18 years old."

Dec. 7?

"I was writing a letter to my friends back in Chicago. My mother and the two younger boys were at church. My brother, Bernard, and I ran outside just in time to see the second wave of Japanese planes going by; they were so low you could see the Rising Sun painted on them.

"Mom was told to get back home; we were under Martial Law – don't get caught in the streets if you were told not to."

Your father?

"A gunnery officer had gone ashore with the keys to the ammunition storage. My father had to smash it open with his fist. He used a machine gun to shoot at the Japanese planes as they dove toward our battleships – the Sacramento was a gunboat.

"We didn't hear from him for two weeks. But mother stayed positive; she kept saying, 'Bad news travels fast.'"

How long did you live in Hawaii after the attack?

"Three more months."

Animosity between Japanese and Americans living on those islands?

"Bernard was 17 and itching to join the service like his older brother. Our ice man was Japanese. He made a delivery soon after the attack."

Yeah?

"Bernard came from the kitchen with a knife in his hand, glaring at him. My mother was embarrassed."

Al Stoner?

"We got married in Dallas, Texas, in February of '43. Two months later, Al was assigned to Bremerton Naval Yard near Seattle. He also was assigned to the USS Liscome Bay, which was being converted to a escort aircraft carrier."

The home front?

"After a week of training, I started out as a bucker within the nacelle of a B-17. The riveter was on the outside."

Bucker?

"The bucker held a metal bar against the perforated aluminum sheeting so a rivet could be flattened. I earned 86 cents per hour."

Rationing?

"There were gas ration books and food ration books. We collected everything from scrap metal to cans of lard.

"I remember blue stars in residential windows – gold ones, too. We scoured the newspapers to see if we could learn about our loved ones. That's how I found out the 'Lizzy' was torpedoed on Thanksgiving of '43. I was pregnant."

The Liscome Bay?

"Yes; there were more than 700 men aboard – 200 survived. Al gave his life jacket to a man who was badly burned. Then, he swam for two hours before being rescued by a U.S. destroyer.

"After a 30-day leave, he was assigned to a troop carrier that was struck by a kamikaze attack while he was aboard. Many of our men were killed on that ship also.

"Al was given another 30-day leave and finally got to see Al Jr., who was a year old by then.

"Like my father, Al received the purple heart. He took a jagged scar across his forehead and a bum knee to his grave."

* * *

Terry Stoner is a Democratic precinct committeewoman who has voted for U.S. presidents such as Franklin D. Roosevelt, John F. Kennedy and Barack Obama.

And as an octogenarian, she is part of what Tom Brokaw deemed "the greatest generation."

Should old acquaintance be forgot, and never brought to mind?

Judy Kanne *(March 2014)*

"Yeoman (yo-man) n. 1. An independent farmer, esp. a member of a former class of small freeholding farmers in England. 3. An attendant, servant, or lesser official in a royal or noble household. 6. A diligent, dependable worker."
– Noah Webster

My interview with Judy Kanne took place at the Jasper County Historical Society Museum in Rensselaer. She is curator there. County genealogist Sue Caldwell and intern Ben Kessler – a senior at St. Joseph's College – were on hand.

Kanne also is county historian appointed by the Indiana Historical Society and is involved with the Prairie Arts Council which has a gallery in Rensselaer's Carnegie Center.

Kanne, 72, is a graduate of Indiana University Bloomington who taught at St. Joseph's College as a visiting professor where she was in charge of student teachers. She lives in Rensselaer with her husband Michael; they have raised 2 adult daughters.

Kanne is a German name that rhymes with the word "rainy."

* * *

You're not a native of Rensselaer.

'"No, I was born in Greencastle. My dad had a drugstore there. When I was 7, we moved to the east side of Indianapolis where I attended Howe High School."

Any memories of Greencastle?

"I really do. It's sad, a few years ago I went down there to visit my folks' grave. Our house was torn down. I was a little girl who lived in an old house. Luckily, we live in an old house here in Rensselaer. You kinda get hooked on those. In Indianapolis, we lived in one of those wonderful little bungalows."

As a youngster, did you live near DePauw University?

"Yes, I remember trekking through the campus on my way to get ice cream at the drugstore."

Your husband is a judge.

"Yes, he was a local state court judge here for 10 years. For five years, he was a district judge in Hammond appointed by Ronald Reagan. Now, he's on the 7th circuit court of appeals in Chicago."

The honorable Judge Kanne is a lifetime Rensselaerian.

"Yes, that's why we live here. His father owned Kanne's Restaurant on the square."

You were a schoolteacher.

"When Mike was in law school, I taught at a two-room schoolhouse with outhouses. We have an old schoolhouse at our fairgrounds that is under the auspices of the JCHS. So, I kind of get back in the groove of being an old schoolmarm."

Judy, let's delve into some Rensselaer history. There's a statue of a man in town. Who is he?

"Brigadier-General Robert H. Milroy, a veteran of the Civil War. We have President Lincoln's signature here. Lincoln signed documents approving some of Milroy's promotions. We figure the signature is worth about $8,000.

"After the war, Gen. Milroy ended up Superintendent of Indian Affairs in Olympia, Wash. During the Civil War, he fought in several major battles in West Virginia and Virginia. Gen. Milroy wasn't exactly well-liked in that part of the country."

Why not?

"Because he treated the blacks better than the whites of that area. In fact, he brought an African-American couple home to Rensselaer so they could be educated. Here's a photo of them."

Let me read that cutline: "Benjamin Summit was a freedom-seeking slave sent to Rensselaer, Ind in 1861. Summit was taught to read and write by the general's wife, Mary Milroy."

"The Confederate Congress offered a $100,000 dead-or-alive bounty on Milroy at that time."

Tell me about this building.

"It was built by the Free Will Baptists and originally stood on the northeast corner of Susan and Van Rensselaer Streets.

"In 1902, the building was purchased by the Methodist Protestants and moved to this site. In 1916, it was sold to a David Yeoman. That was the only year taxes were paid on the building. The structure eventually was sold to the Christian Science Society in 1918. The Christian Science Society's congregation dwindled and the few remaining members donated the building to the historical society in 1982."

Quite a history.

"The original Jasper County Historical Society goes back to the 1930s, but we do not know where those records are. We have not heard who was in charge. You'd think we'd come across that, but haven't."

When was this Jasper County Historical Society formed?

"In 1966, about the time a log cabin was discovered inside a barn in Barkley Township and taken to the fairgrounds. Now, there's also the old schoolhouse, post office and a blacksmith shop."

Very good.

"I'm also a member of the Newton County Historical Society, White County Historical Society, DeMotte Historical Society and Kankakee Valley Historical Society. I guess I'm snoopy."

You folks sure have a fascinating collection of antiques, heirlooms and relics displayed here.

"Sue and Ben are working on a very special collection of cards that nobody knows about. In 1918, there was a survey of women taken by the Women's Committee Council of National Defense. The information on these cards is unbelievably detailed. We have 3,212 of them."

Great find. When I interviewed Jessica Nunemaker (little Indiana), she told me the woeful tale of pioneer Joseph Yeoman.

"It is by the (Iroquois) river bridge and the Tastee Freez where Joseph Yeoman and his family built a cabin in the fall of 1836. They started farming. That first winter, I don't think they had four walls.

"James Van Rensselaer wasn't a very successful businessman back East. So, he came to Indiana to find his fortune. Van Rensselaer made it to Lafayette, but it was his son who came up here. He was taken by the beauty of that spot on the river and anxiously brought his dad here from Lafayette to see it."

Yeoman was a squatter.

"More or less. The Van Rensselaers purchased the land properly and the Yeomans were booted off their farmland."

Nunemaker told me that Yeoman actually took Van Rensselaer in for the remainder of a harsh winter so he wouldn't freeze to death.

"I hadn't heard that part of the story. It's quite possible. James did stay here. He's actually buried at our Presbyterian Church. After the patriarch died, the rest of the Van Rensselaers left the area for good. But we have hundreds of Yeomans in Jasper County; they've been here forever. I've always felt that Rensselaer should be named Yeoman."

* * *

Jasper County pioneers Joseph and Sarah Yeoman had a son born Sept. 26, 1841 on the old Yeoman homestead. At the beginning of the Civil War, young David Yeoman, son of Joseph and Sarah, enlisted with the 48th Indiana Regiment and fought valiantly at the battles of Shiloh and Iuka. Toward the end of the war, Capt. Yeoman was part of the Atlanta Campaign, the 100 days fighting, and from Atlanta, followed Sherman to the sea.

It was that same war hero, at the age of 75, who purchased what it now the Jasper County Historical Museum. For more than a half-century after the war David Yeoman was a successful farmer and a well-respected citizen in Jasper County.

He was a diligent, dependable worker.

Yet, you'll search in vain for a Yeoman Street in Rensselaer.

Ed Camblin *(Aug. 2014)*

"I may not be as strong as I think, but I have many tricks and I have resolution."
– Ernest Hemingway, from "The Old Man and the Sea"

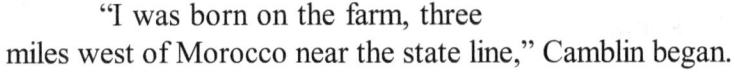

If Ed Camblin isn't the greatest J.C. Murphey Lake bass fisherman who ever lived, he's certainly the most venerable. The lake is part of Willow Slough Fish & Wildlife Area.

Born Aug. 17, 1920, James Edward Camblin has fished "the Slough" since its creation in the 1940s, and still fishes it every day possible.

Camblin is a retired mailman who lives in Morocco with Marcheta, his wife of 71 years.

* * *

"I was born on the farm, three miles west of Morocco near the state line," Camblin began.

The area you describe in Beaver Township is very near where Potawatomi chiefs Turkey Foot and Bull killed each other in a fight. They were "buried" sitting up against two trees facing each other.

"As a boy, I had a bushel basket of arrowheads. But there was a man named Ed Hamilton who was paying a penny apiece for them. This was back in the Great Depression. A penny was a lot of money. ..."

Were you in the service?

"Yes, I was in the Navy and the amphibious force. We were the ones who put 'em on the beach. I was on a landing craft tank.

"I got married when I was on leave in '43. I came back home in '45. My wife has always maintained that was the best two years of our marriage."

Do you care to talk more about the war?

"I was in the European Theater, but started in Africa. This headband was what (German Gen. Erwin) Rommel's men wore around their hats."

"AfrikaKorps." Where did you get that?

"Off a prisoner. Our first invasion was into Sicily. We were also in major battles at Salerno, Anzio and Southern France. Plus, minor battle at the island of Elba."

I can only imagine what was going through your mind during those major battles.

"I've seen a lot of Fourth of July celebrations, but unless you've sat ready to storm the beach, ready for your orders to go. ... You look up and see all those tracers, well, they look like flocks of ducks with lights on them. You can't explain it. You have to be there. It's something that stays with you the rest of your life. I got hit in Salerno."

Did you go back to farming once the war was over?

"Yes, the first year that I farmed, I used an old F-20 (tractor) and four head of horses. I planted all my corn with the horses."

When did you become a mailman?

"I started turning mail in 1950. I was still farming. In '52, the doctor told me: 'If you want to live to be 40, you're going to have to quit one or the other.' I was farming 435 acres back then."

The early days of Willow Slough?

"Bill Madden was the first manager of the Slough. He was my best friend. In '89, the year after he died, the boathouse at Willow Slough was dedicated in Bill's honor."

Tell me more.

"We used to pole our boats around the lake because when they built the Slough, they never cut any of the trees. You couldn't row your boat with a set of oars. There just wasn't a whole lot of open water when they first flooded it."

Bass fishing?

"Once the bass bug bites you, there's no cure for it. Whenever someone asks me how I learned to be a fairly good bass fisherman I tell them, I learned from the best – the violators. You see, during the Depression, the people who were catching and selling fish were breaking the law.

"For four years, my dad was a game warden. He caught a lot of flak because he didn't arrest some of those folks. A couple of those poachers, whose names I won't mention, had five kids apiece. Dad figured if he put those guys in jail, the county was going to have feed them."

I'm sure you remember Dutch Swartz who ran the bait shop on State Line Road.

"Dutch turned out to be a decent fisherman, but he had emphysema real bad. He was constantly coughing and couldn't conceal his honey holes. If the wind was right, you could be a half-mile from him and know he was catching bass back in the cattails.

"There were two women who loved to bluegill fish at the slough. One was Mrs. Bryant who ran the A&P and the other was Doc Purkey's wife. Whenever I'd spot the gills on the beds, I'd let them know where."

A couple of your favorite lures?

"The bait I caught the most bass on at Willow Slough was a black Johnson Spoon with a green and white skirt. Me and Madden would buy them off Dutch by the dozen."

Your biggest bass out of the Slough?

"It was 7 pounds 1 ounce. Caught him on a purple worm."

Favorite top-water bait?

"Ever heard of a man named Leo Packner out of Momence, Ill.?"

Yeah, the guy who made homemade lures. His daughter married professional bass fisherman Roland Martin.

"Well, Leo invented the Walkie Talkie. It's a little plunker. If you reel it straight it has action like a Jitterbug."

You and the Slough today?

"About two or three years ago, my wife and daughter made me quit taking my canoe out to the Slough. You see, I tipped the canoe a time or two. Plus, I've had complications with my bad leg and hip."

Mementos of Salerno?

"Yeah. I fish out of a jon boat these days. Still take my push pole, though. The last time I went in the drink at Willow Slough was in October, took me over an hour to get to Mormon Hill. The canoe filled with water. And that water was cold. I started doing jumping jacks trying to get warm. I looked up to the sky, and what do you think I said?"

Please dear Lord don't let me get hypothermia. At age 90, I promise to never take my canoe to the Slough again?

"No, I said: "Madden, you son of a bitch, I know you're up there laughing at me, but I sure could use a stiff drink right now!"

* * *

In 1962, Outdoor Life did a big write-up on bass fishing at Willow Slough. The two anglers featured?

Bill Madden and Ed Camblin.

Merritt Coffin *(May 2014)*

"Those were the days, my friend
We thought they'd never end
We'd sing and dance forever and a day..."
– Lyrics by K. Podrevsky, performed by Mary Hopkin

Merritt Coffin has been on this planet as many years as there are keys on a piano – 88. A widower, he lives in Cedar Lake with Pam and Chuck Kouder, his daughter and son-in-law. Although "Arthur" (arthritis) has crippled up Coffin quite a bit, the aged entrepreneur is as sharp as the proverbial tack.

Like his father before him and his son after him, Coffin was the owner-operator of the former Coffin's Shady Beach Resort on Cedar Lake.

* * *

"I met Betty at the old Lowell High School," Coffin began. "We ran off and got married. I was 17 and she was 15."

Early memories of Cedar Lake?

"I was born in what was an old chicken coop here on the lake. Dad built some living quarters above it."

When did your father create Coffin's Shady Beach Resort?

"Just before he went to fight in World War I. He deeded it over to his mother before for he went to war."

Your first job?

"Cuttin' ice."

You refer to harvesting ice from the lake before refrigeration.

"Yes. They had me workin' out in the field, that was cold out there. I talked them into loading the (Monon Railroad) cars. The Monon Depot is gone now; they put the condos up."

Merritt, in the early '80s, I remember when Coleman's Corner was still standing. That establishment looked like something out of the Wild West.

"They had good chicken dinners there. Yeah, it saddens me when they tear down those old buildings. We had some corkers around here. At one time, there were 21 taverns around the lake.

"I told Betty that was the worst thing I ever done, selling that resort. But these guys come along with their big fat pockets and bought the whole shootin' match."

Tell me about those early days of Shady Beach Resort, when your father, Cordie Coffin, started the business.

"It was basically just tents. Then Dad built a few decks, you know. People could pitch their tents on the decks – easy living. Then he built one-room cabins for the people to rent for one or two weeks. We had 500 feet of lakefront."

Were most of the resort customers Chicagoans?

"I would say so. Dad charged 50 cents to park for the day. We had two piers and a boat launch, a sandy beach, picnic tables, campfires, diving boards, swings and teeter-totters. When I owned the place, we designed a toboggan slide. It was for summer and for winter. We charged 75 cents for toboggan rides.

"Later on, after we built the pavilion we had a juke box, pool table and pinball machines. I started C.L. Vending.

"I used to pay the local kids who did odd jobs for me with marked quarters. I'd paint them with red shoe polish. I'd tell them they could use the quarters to play pool or the pinball machines, but they couldn't buy any pop or candy with the red quarters."

Why not?

"Because I made 100 percent profit on pool and pinball machine money, I didn't make that much money off the pop and candy."

You thrifty rascal, you. Tell me more about the pavilion.

"In the early '60s, Coffin's Shady Beach Resort was the place to go for dances. I built a concrete block building into the side of the hill with a Flexicore roof on the top of it. A lot of the local kids would show up and have a good time."

So, your place and Midway Ballroom were competitors.

"I catered to the kids and Jim Kubal catered to the adults."

Did you and Betty cut the rug a few time at Midway Ballroom?

"Oh, yeah. We had many a good times there. Jim and I were responsible for the first fireworks on the lake. We shot them off from a boat. I remember going to a couple of tavern owners conventions with

Jimmy; those were some pretty wild affairs."

Will Cedar Lake ever return to its heyday as a resort community?
"I don't think so. Resorts are a thing of the past."

* * *

The Lake of the Red Cedars Museum sits along the shore of Cedar Lake. It was built by the Armour Bros. in 1895 and includes 11 special exhibits highlighting the resort area's past. One exhibit showcases photographs of the men who harvested ice from the lake. The actual tools used to harvest the large blocks of ice are displayed as well.

It somewhat saddens me that Merritt Coffin has never been to the museum to see all that. But then again, the Coffin family of Cedar Lake lived it.

Those were the days.

Dante D'Apice *(June 2013)*

"I took a walk along the historic coast of Normandy in the country of France. It was a lovely day for strolling along the seashore. Men were sleeping in the sand, some of them were sleeping forever. Men were floating in the water, but they didn't know they were in the water, for they were dead."
– Ernie Pyle

The above quote is from a column written by Ernie Pyle of Dana describing Omaha Beach on June 8 or 9, 1944.

Dante D'Apice of Dyer landed at Omaha for the first time at about 6:30 a.m. on June 6 – D-Day.

D'Apice, 88, and his wife Vera have raised three daughters. He was born and raised in Chicago Heights, Ill, and attended Bloom Township High School. His sister, Nadia D'Apice, has been my father's significant other for more than 30 years.

* * *

"When we were kids, we were on welfare," D'Apice began. "There were 11 of us. Two died when they were 1 and 2 years old. They had what they called a Spanish disease."

Influenza?

"Yeah, that's it. I didn't graduate from high school; I went to work. Vera graduated."

When there was work for your father, what did he do for a living?

"He was a painter. When I got back from the war, he taught me the trade. I did it for 50 years."

June 6, 1944?

"I was 19 when we went to Normandy. We were assigned to the (Landing Ship, Tank) 286. It was 325 feet long. We ate breakfast at around 4 a.m. about 2 miles off Omaha Beach. By 6:30 a.m, I was operating one of our six (Landing Craft, Vehicle, Personnel). LCVPs were made of plywood and could hold 30 men.

"During the battle, we continued to bring in The Big Red One (1st Infantry Division), the 29th Division, the 45th Division and the 101st Airborne Division."

Dante, I can only imagine what must have been going through your mind and all the rest of the men's minds aboard that LCVP.

"A lot of guys got sick on the boat. I did, too. It was rough water. The invasion was planned for June 4, but the weather was so bad, they had to postpone it.

"I had one guy who wouldn't get off the boat. Being the coxswain in charge of the crew, I decided rather than arguing with him while under heavy fire, to take him back so I could pick up 30 more soldiers for the next wave. They probably court-martialed him."

Then what?

"The second wave took heavier fire than the first wave. Machine gun bullets whizzed by everywhere; bombs exploded all around us.

"Returning for the third wave, we took the wounded back with us to the LST. Now, the deck of my LCVP was not only covered with puke, but blood as well. As coxswains we tried not to hit the dead floating in the water. But there was so many of them... . I could hear a thumping noise when I hit one of them."

Horrific.

"After the third wave, the trucks and tanks were coming in and they didn't want to run over our dead. The beach still wasn't secure, but we were ordered to land and stack bodies. We'd pick them up like sacks of potatoes and throw them against the wall. I think 4,000 of us died the first day."

How long did you serve?

"I was in for 33 months. We were a hospital ship toward the end in Europe. We took a lot of guys in; they would operate on them on the kitchen tables.

"Vera's twin brother, Guido, was a paratrooper with the 101st Airborne. In January of '45, the Western Union man came to the door. Like mine, Vera's parents were Italian immigrants. Her father accepted the telegram, but couldn't read English. He took the message to the corner grocery store where a woman had to tell him his son was killed in action at Bastogne, (Belgium). Guido's body was returned to America after the war. He's buried in Steger, Ill.

"My brother Bill was three years older than me. He was a an infantryman with the 4th Marine Division. Bill was at Iwo Jima and Saipan. There were 20,000 GIs killed at Iwo and 23,000 Japs. The war pretty much ruined him psychologically. Years later, he sorta snapped out of it."

What about you, after Omaha Beach?

"I was shipped to Okinawa; where we were preparing to invade Japan. Good thing they dropped that bomb. There would have been a lot more dead people. And nowadays? Everybody buys Toyotas and Volkswagens."

Have you ever seen the film, "Saving Private Ryan"?

"Oh, yeah. They overdone it a little bit, but it's pretty realistic. Do you ever watch that (former Arkansas Governor Mike) Huckabee on TV? He was a senator. Him and his wife went to Normandy. When he was telling the story on TV, he was crying. He said they saw dried blood in the sand. I believe it."

Any final thoughts?

"I felt sorry for the guys who didn't make it. We had one guy who was wounded three different times. And they still had him stay there to get killed. Three Purple Hearts... . It's been almost 70 years, some things I forget. And some things, I'll never forget."

* * *

Dante D'Apice was awarded two Bronze Stars while serving his country. The former coxswain carries his liberty pass in his billfold to this day.

Nick Thiery *(Oct. 2011)*

"We will not have any more crashes in our time."
– John Maynard Keynes

No, John Keynes wasn't an early Indy 500 driver when he made the above prediction in 1927; he was a British economist.

Nick Thiery, 98, was a tremendous artist until his eyes went bad a few years ago, and he was a great athlete when he wore a younger man's cleats. Thiery also was named Best Volunteer Fire Chief in Indiana in 1953.

He lives in St. John, is a widower who has raised four children, and is a longtime member of the Dyer Historical Society.

Thiery stays busy doing yard work around his house and is still as sharp as a tack.

* * *

"I was born in Chicago," Thiery began. "We lived on Roby Street; it's now called Damen Avenue. We moved to Dyer in 1920."

What year were you born?

"In 1914; I remember the (World War I) armistice in 1918. I was scared; Dad took me to the Loop -- I always say the Loop, but I'm not sure there even was a Loop back then. Anyway, there were a lot of people who were all going crazy because the war had ended."

Ancestry?

"French and German. Some of my family came from the Alsace-Lorraine area. Part of my ancestors were coal miners and some were furniture designers.

When did you move to St. John?

"In 1935. I wanted this high ground, but the owner, John Behrens, wouldn't sell me these two acres until he sold me the two low-lying acres next to it. So, I bought the low ground first. I didn't have any more money. Behrens said if I paid 50 cents per week on the high ground until I got up to $200, it could be my down payment."

One of your first jobs?

"I was a filling-station attendant in Dyer at the age of 12; gas was 11 (cents per gallon).

High School?

"Dyer; I was class president in '32. As you can see, I don't throw anything away. Anybody who went through the Great Depression is a saver. There was no money back then; it was the barter system."

Nick, my dad is 80, he's been known to rib one of his brothers on occasion: "Joe, you came into this world for a cord of wood." That's how my grandfather paid the doctor.

"Everyone wonders why their taxes are so high; one reason is everybody wants something, but they want it for nothing. You don't get anything for nothing in this world – somebody has to pay for it.

"I might not see it, but I have a feeling something is about to happen in this country that but a dwindling few of us have lived through."

Where did you find employment after high school?

"The Shell refinery in East Chicago on the south side of Chicago Avenue.

You were quite an athlete at Dyer High.

"In track, I was in all the dashes and a jumper, too. They used to call me 'Speed' Thiery. I had infantile paralysis when I was a kid; I wasn't ever supposed to walk. They called it polio for a while. But I was stubborn and determined to do what the other kids were doing."

Good for you, "Speed."

"I was elected to the Lake Central High School Athletic Hall of Fame."

What about baseball?

"I played shortstop."

Do you root for one major league team?

"My dad was a White Sox fan and I was a Cub fan. I knew all the Cub players in the late '20s: Charlie Grimm, Rogers Hornsby, Gabby Hartnett, Hack Wilson, Kiki Cuyler... .

"I had an aunt that I'd stay with in Chicago; she knew I knew my way around and let me do as I pleased. I'd go to the Art Institute in the morning and get all the free lessons I could, then I'd take in a Cub game in the afternoon. My cousin Violet loved to dance; she'd take me to the Aragon Ballroom."

Did you play any ball after high school?

"That's the only reason Shell hired me; they wanted me to play on their industrial league team. They told me I was a hillbilly because I was from south of Route 6. My job was to do landscape work across the street from the refinery where the staff houses were located."

Staff houses?

"That's where the bosses lived."

Did you ever get a "real" job inside the refinery?

"Yes, but the refinery shut down in '39. I hired in at City Service and then it shut down in '73."

How old were you when City Service closed its doors?

"Almost 58; I couldn't sit still. I had nothing to do."

What did you do?

"I went to the superintendent of the high school and ended up getting a job as a janitor at Kahler Middle School (in Dyer). I worked there for about 17 years."

Wow, you were still working at age 75. How long did you serve on the St. John Volunteer Fire Department?

"It's right here on this certificate of appreciation – 69 years."

Nick, do you remember when Teibel's Restaurant was established?

"Sure do --1929."

First U.S. president for whom you voted?

"Franklin Delano Roosevelt, 1932."

Another fellow who didn't let polio stop him.

"No, he did not."

Who's the lady in that photograph?

"That's my mother; she was born the year of the World's Fair in Chicago – 1893."

Also the year that began the worst depression this country had known; it lasted about five years. Only the stock-market crash of 1929 was worse.

* * *

Nick Thiery told me he used to like talking to his neighbor, a pilot in World War I. The guy told Nick when he and his colleagues ran out of ammunition, they'd throw bricks and milk bottles at the enemy from their planes.

As a boy, Thiery would sit on the curb in Dyer and talk to members of the Grand Army of the Republic.

There's something to be said for talking and listening to old folks.

Characters

Chuck Hegan *(Sept. 2014)*

Al Czervik: (tees off) *"Fore!"*
(His ball hits Judge Smails in the crotch)
Al Czervik: *"I should have yelled, 'Two!'"*
– from the 1980 film "Caddyshack"

Chuck Hegan is 88 years young. He owns Summertree and Pheasant Valley golf courses, leases Oak Knoll golf course, and recently sold his equity in Indian Ridge Country Club to his son Paul.

Our interview took place at the Pheasant Valley pro shop in Crown Point.

* * *

Married?

"Three times," he said. "They're all deceased. I live with a woman who also has been married three times. All her husbands are deceased."

What are the odds of that?

"My grandmother, a little Scottish gal, was about 40 when a doctor told her he'd have to amputate her foot because of diabetes. She told that sawbones: 'I came into this world with that foot, I'll go out with it.' She outlived three of her doctors. The diabetes finally killed her at 105."

Lived in Crown Point all your life?

"Just about. I was born in Chicago, but went to high school at Crown Point."

College?

"Indiana University. I majored in accounting. I was a distance runner for Crown Point and IU. When I was in my 50's, I'd jump off my tractor at Oak Knoll and take on the Crown Point cross country runners and kick their butts. The coach would say: 'Are you guys gonna let that bearded old man beat you?' I've always been real active. That's probably why I'm still going."

They say that running slows the aging process.

"Years ago they said the opposite. When I was about 26, I had to take a physical for a CPA firm I was going to work for. The family doctor told me I had an enlarged heart from running and that I was going to die young."

In high school, what your best time in the mile?

"About 4:20."

Chuck, bear with me, I'm a bass fisherman, links lingo is a foreign language. Are or were you a decent golfer?

"I was an avid golfer back in the '60s. A lot of gambling went on. I did pretty well. I'd admit to maybe $50,000 on my tax returns."

Your best score?

"I shot a 69 at the Youngstown Tournament."

Did golfers use carts in the early '60s?

"No, we used chariots."

Come on, you're not that old.

"We walked."

Name one of the best local golfers you've known.

"Bob McCall. He and (Arnold) Palmer were roommates in college. Palmer wanted McCall to go on the circuit with him, but Bob figured the steel industry was more stable. McCall was probably just as good as Palmer."

Odd or humorous occurrences on the fairways?

"A lot of oddities. One time I was driving toward my golf course and I look across the road and see these two golf carts on the green. I get in my golf cart and head toward them. Here are these two guys and two girls having a great time."

And?

"The girls were wearing high heels. It was their first time golfing. I told them they had to take off the heels and golf barefooted. They were making holes in the greens."

Tell me another one.

"I had a 20-feet-wide bridge going over a culvert and these two guys – drunk as heck – missed the bridge and ended up in the peat bog on the back nine. I go out there and here they are up to their waists in muck trying to pick the cart up out of what was practically quick sand."

No way.

"I asked them, '*What the heck are you doing in there?*' The one guy took his muddy arm and wiped his eyeglasses with it which completely blackened the lenses. They decided to go on strike and just sit there refusing to leave the premises. I had to call the sheriff."

What was the first golf course you purchased or leased?

"Oak Knoll in 1961. The clubhouse was a Quonset hut."

When was Oak Knoll created?

"In 1926. I started working there in 1938 as a parking boy, then I caddied for a while."

Indian Ridge?

"I leased it from '65 to '78, then somebody else bought it and took it over. In '74, I started building Summertree. About five years ago, I bought this place at a sheriff's sale for $975,000 and put another $1.3 million into it. I got back at Indian Ridge in '93."

The most challenging of your courses?

"Right here. Pheasant Valley is the most aesthetically beautiful as well. Summertree has better greens and undulation, but this is a better course."

Celebrities who've golfed at any of your courses?

"Ron Kittle, Ernie Banks, Willie Nelson... There was a singer that had real pretty blue eyes... Seems like he had a French name..."

Robert Goulet?

"That's it. His wife had just divorced him. He was out there in 40-degree weather wearing just a T-shirt. I asked him if he needed to borrow a sweater. He told me no thanks and also stated that he was very depressed."

Have you ever attended the Master's Tournament?

"Several times. Television doesn't do it justice. The course down in Augusta (Georgia) is breathtaking."

One last golf-related story.

"I was golfing at course called Lost Tree in Florida. Jack Nicklaus and his son just happened to be right behind me. I was playing from the regular tees and Nicklaus was playing from the back tees. I hit my next shot and pretty soon Nicklaus' ball is rolling up behind me. In other words, he was outhitting me about 80 yards off the tee.

"Jack is real polite. That night, I was having dinner and he came to my table, sat down, and chatted with me. That made me a happy man. He gave me his autograph. I had always considered Jack Nicklaus the greatest golfer who ever lived. Still do."

* * *

    The octogenarian Scotsman is quite the raconteur. Being a storyteller myself, I left Hagen with a story of my own. Can't remember where I read it, but there was this rich dame driving her convertible down Rodeo Drive in Beverly Hills when she sees this Hispanic guy pruning shrubs and pulling weeds in front of a mansion. The woman pulls up to the curb and asks the landscaper what his hourly rate is. He smiles and tells her: "Lady, I live here."

    The happy gardener was Lee Trevino.

Roby Joe *(Feb. 2014)*

"Well I was born in a small town
And I live in a small town
Prob'ly die in a small town
Oh, those small – communities"
– John Mellencamp

When I worked at Inland Steel Co., there was a chap of Eastern European descent who was referred to as "Alphabet" because none of us could pronounce his 13-letter last name. Well, with a surname like Boguszewicz, it didn't take long for guys at American Maize to nickname my interviewee Roby Joe.

Today, Roby Joe lives in what is known as the Water Gardens which is in the Robertsdale neighborhood of Hammond, but he was raised in what was once known as – you guessed it – Roby.

Roby Joe, 77, is a widower who works out at the YMCA three days a week. His regimen is one hour on the tread mill, lifting assorted weights, and throwing 50 punches. He also does 75 sit-ups before leaving his house.

Roby Joe has served as a deacon at New Life Christian Church in Whiting for the past nine years.

* * *

"When my dad started at Standard Oil, the foreman asked him his name," Roby Joe began. "Dad replied: 'Boguszewicz.' The boss said: 'What? Where do you live?' Dad told him: 'In Roby.' The boss said: 'O.K., you're Roby Joe.'

"Then, I worked at American Maize for 44 years and also was known as Roby Joe. I'd say 75 percent of the people I worked with didn't know my real name."

Roby Joe, of what ethnicity is your real name?

"Lithuanian. My dad was born in Chicago, but his dad took him to Lithuania when he was real young and he stayed there until he was 18. Then Dad came back to the United States. He was an American citizen because he was born here. My dad could speak nine languages.

"Jeff, I never did finish high school. I went on the road with the rodeo. It was a rodeo and wild west show from Farmer's City, Ill. I hooked up with a guy by the name of Bob McKinley. My dad had to sign the papers because I was only 15. I rode bucking horses and bulls. Plus, I'd help set up the show. We moved from Illinois to Indiana, Missouri, Michigan, Ohio, Wisconsin.... It was interesting."

I've been told Roby was a wild and wooly place in the early days.

"They tell me that after my grandfather had a couple of hookers, he'd go down 5th Avenue – that's our main drag – and shoot his gun into the air. My dad was rough and tough, too."

A couple of hookers?

"Drinks."

Oh.

"My grandfather used to drive alcohol for Al Capone. There was illegal gambling on 5th Avenue. It was like a syndicate. Old man Utich got shot behind the gambling joint. They killed him. It was one of them kind of deals."

Tell me more about this fascinating enclave known as Roby.

"Before my time, there was a race track in Roby – midget cars. I remember when we had our own grocery store in Roby. There were some good restaurants like Peter Levent's. I used to park cars there. Roby had the smallest post office in the world. It's in the Guinness Book of World Records, you can look it up."

Continue, please.

"Well, I was born at 1128, 5th Avenue in Roby. My dad built a boathouse that was our home; it was called Roby Joe's Boats and Bait. Right next to us was a fireworks place."

Why not? You only lived in one of the most potentially explosive areas on the planet.

"We had outside toilets. Ma and Pa was painted on the roof. We also had a hand pump in the house – no running water. We did have electricity, my dad had to put all the posts in and run the wire himself. During bad weather, we'd wait inside the Roby Tavern for the school bus.

Did you fish Wolf Lake?

"A lot. I fished for bluegills, northerns and big buffalo carp. I used to love to catch bass with the fly rod. It was exciting with surface baits. We used to do a lot of duck and goose hunting on the lake, too. Everything we killed, we ate. My dad used to trap muskrats along the lake. My sister and I could skin them. We ate muskrats, too."

I've eaten muskrat. They're a clean animal – vegetarian.

"Trapping was a good sideline for my dad. He made pretty good money at it." *How many people lived in Roby when you were a kid?*

"About 60."

Let's switch gears. American Maize?

"It's called Cargill today, but when I started there at 18, we had our own horses. After the Roby Riding Stable closed up my dad and I built a big barn for people to board their horses. I'd ride my horse to the plant gate which is about a mile from where I grew up. The horse would meander back home along the railroad track and go back into the barn. It was a barn-soured horse."

A barn-soured horse?

"A horse that doesn't want to leave the barn."

What was your job at American Maize?

"I started out at the bottom, but I worked in the welding shop for 10 years. We were Local 7210 CIO. That's the Oil, Chemical and Atomic Workers. I ended up teaching welding. There were a few fires while I was there. A couple of people got killed. One kid got burned real bad, but survived. All it takes is a spark."

Final thoughts?

"Jeff, I made a print while they were building the Walmart several years ago and pinpointed where the house I was born in sat. It would've been where the chicken and fish department is today."

* * *

The world's smallest post office, race track, riding stable and Roby Joe's Boats and Bait are no more. But I can picture them.

Thanks to the man born Joseph Boguszewicz.

John Schutz *(May 2011)*

*"If a guy is over 25 percent jerk, he's in trouble. And Henry (Ford II) was
95 percent."*
— Lee Iaccoca

In 1925, Calvin Coolidge was president of the United States, a young science teacher by the name of John J. Scopes was being tried for teaching the theory of evolution to his students, the Thompson submachine gun was selling for $175 in the Sears, Roebuck and Company mail-order catalog and the Chrysler Corp. was founded by a chap named Chrysler.

And, on May 25, 1925 in the Cook neighborhood of Cedar Lake, John A. Schutz struck a deal with blacksmith Mike Schillo. Schutz purchased the village smithy's shop and Center Garage was born.

I interviewed John G. Schutz, the grandson of John A. Schutz. John G., 58, has been married to Terry for 37 years; they have raised two sons and are the owners of Center Garage just east of U.S. 41 and 133rd Avenue in Cedar Lake. They also are members of Holy Name Catholic Church, across the street from their dealership.

* * *

Has Center Garage always sold Chrysler and Dodge products?
"No, my grandfather started out selling Fords and Willys Knights. Today, we also sell Jeeps."

You're the third generation of Schutzes to run the business. What about your sons?
"They weren't interested; both of them live out of state. One is a

glorified ski bum, but he don't ask for no money and he's living his life. He says, 'Dad, I don't have much, but I don't need much.' He skis all winter and drives a shuttle van. In the summer, he's a white-water raft guide in the upper Colorado River."

What's his name?

"John P. Schutz; we call him Jay. His brother, Sean, works for Allied Bank in Texas."

Lived in Cedar Lake all your life?

"I grew up in this neighborhood behind the dealership and I've never left. We like Cook; it's close to church and it's close to work. I have no reason to leave. Cedar Lake is my town."

College?

"'The School of Hard Knocks.' My first job here was hauling out 30-gallon lube containers that we used as garbage cans. I'd put them on an old baby-buggy frame and wheel them out back. That's when you still had metal in the oil cans.

"I'd separate the metal from the garbage and the trash. I also filled the pop machine for a whopping 25 cents per hour and a free bottle of Kayo chocolate drink. It was good."

How long have you been at the helm?

"I've been running the business since 1986 – through attrition. My uncle, Eugene Busick, passed away in '85; he ran the body shop. My dad, John N., died in '86."

Care to talk about the fire?

"We burned to the ground in '89. The only thing left in the showroom was Mike Schillo's anvil and the stump it sat on. The front wall fell on three or four cars; we lost a couple dozen cars altogether because of smoke damage or whatever. We also lost a lot of mementos – neat old advertizing stuff."

Tell me more about Cook.

"At one time there was Cook Lumber, Cook Building & Salvage, Cook Lounge.... Grandpa Schutz was a board member of the Cook Civic Club."

John, I've interviewed some interesting folks from this area.

"A lot of people call Cedar Lake, Cedartucky. I take offense to that. I was at a meeting one time and there was a guy from Munster who said something derogatory about Cedar Lake. And after that meeting, I gave him what for. Then, I took him to lunch at Tobes and for a boat ride on the lake. I stand up for myself and my town.

"Jeff, all-American (University of Illinois) high jumper Greg Shroka came out of little old Hanover Central High School. Andrew Howe is an all-American wrestler for the University of Wisconsin right out of little old Cedar Lake, Indiana."

I know those guys. Greg is amazing; there aren't many people on the planet under six feet tall who can high jump seven feet. Andrew is a machine. John, you took a hiatus from work a while back.

"With the boys not being in the business, I got tired of working 60, 70, 80 hours a week. We put a deal together in '07, but in December of 2010, I had to take the dealership back."

You've had some health issues.

"In January of 2010, I had quadruple bypass surgery. It was a piece of cake. But in December of 2010, I had a stroke. That about did me in. I'm back to driving a car now and I'm here at the dealership six days a week."

Center Garage sells new and used cars, and does mechanical repairs. Anything else?

"We sell a tremendous amount of tires."

When were some of your best business years?

"The '90s were good. I ran a sale one year between Christmas and New Year's; we just happened to get hit with a big snowstorm at the time of sale. We sold every Jeep and four-wheel drive vehicle on the lot.

"I had a friend in Michigan City who was running a dealership there; I bought five more Jeep Cherokees from him. We were smokin' busy that year. I've made a good living through the years selling 30 or 40 vehicles a month."

The secret to your success?

"I surround myself with good people. I know people who have been in the business years. If I'm having some type of problem, I can call them and ask for advice. It's good to rub elbows.

"In the old meetings at the trade association, the people you wanted to sit by were my grandfather, Paul Heuring from Hobart and Milford Christenson. Them boys could tell some stories. Milford is my friend to this day; he's a great guy."

You enjoy what you do for a living.

"Jeff, I love people and I love the car business. I think it has helped me to use my brain again since having the stroke. I wouldn't change a thing, other than having my loved ones back. My uncle, my father, and even Grandpa – some of our arguments were doozies."

I'm sure you've dealt with a wide variety of customers.

"Yeah, I've had old farmers come in and pull out a musty-smelling wad of cash wrapped in baling twine. I remember Adolph Niemeyer coming in with a shoe box full of money.

"I had a retired banker from Crown Point, John Hershman, who would buy a car from me every year. People would fight over Hershman's trades because they had hardly any miles on them. I also had a local woman who I sold a new Concord."

Yeah?

"She came in just bitching away at me, 'This car is falling apart!' I got behind the wheel, looked the car's door panel over and then shut the door. I thought I heard a little something.

"She said, 'No, you have to slam it like I do.' So, I slammed the door and noticed a plastic map pocket with a plastic ice scrapper in it. I grabbed the scrapper, got out the Concord, and said, 'You crazy, old woman; this is your rattle!' But I've known Edith all my life and I can talk to her like that."

John, when it comes to purchasing a vehicle, my dad is probably the greatest haggler who ever lived. He learned from one of the best – my Grandpa Vito. I'd love to videotape you and my old man while wheeling and dealing.

"You know what I'd tell your dad?"

What's that?

"Sticker's quicker."

* * *

Like a phoenix, Center Garage arose from the ashes and is back in the hands of a Schutz.

And, maybe, somewhere at that dealership up in the sky, Grandpa Schutz and old Mike Schillo finally have come to terms on a shiny, new Willys Knight.

Kayo for everyone!

Tom Johnson *(June, 2014)*

NUTHATCHES: (Family Sittidae): Small stout tree-climbers with strong woodpecker-like bills, strong feet. Nuthatches climb down trees headfirst. The white-breasted nuthatch is known by its black cap and beady black eye on a white face. The undertail coverts are chestnut. Food: Bark, insects, seeds, nuts; attracted by suet, sunflower seeds. Range: Canada to Mexico. Habitat: Forests, river woods, shade trees; visits feeders.
– Roger Tory Peterson (from his field guide, "Eastern Birds")

Along with his buddy Andy Cullimore, Tom Johnson is trying to get Indiana's state bird changed from the cardinal to the white-breasted nuthatch. Johnson, 32, is single, unemployed and rents part of an old house in Valparaiso. Cullimore had to work the day of the interview.

* * *

Did you grow up in Valpo?

"Yes, but I attended Chesterton High School," he said. "We lived just north of the district line. It was Jackson Township. Care for a soda?"

No thanks. Were either of your parents raised in the South?

"No."

I thought I caught a trace of a southern accent in your voice. Plus, you use the word soda rather than pop.

"I get that a lot. Most people say I sound and look like Matthew McConaughey. They say I have that persona."

Hobbies?

"Biking. Originally, I bought a mountain bike because I wanted to do a lot of trails. Now, I mostly pedal around town. The longest distance I go is about 30 miles. I also like to play volley ball and throw the Frisbee, but Frisbee golf annoys me."

College?

"I went to Ivy Tech for a semester and didn't like it. After a couple of years, I moved to Los Angeles. I attended the L.A. Recording School. It was a pretty intense 10-month training course. I had everything from live sound to talent management to equipment maintenance to recording mastering – every aspect of the recording-music industry. I ended up with a certificate."

How long did you live in California?

"Almost three years. It was a crazy transition from here to there. I can think of few not so polite ways to describe California. People out there are different. They're the polar opposite of people on the East Coast. Whenever I've been to the East Coast it seems people are uptight for some reason. I like living here near Lake Michigan. Like they say, we're the 'Third Coast.'"

Have you picked up any recording jobs?

"When I moved back from L.A., I spent four or five months trying to get a job in audio, mostly in Chicago. In that business it's kinda who you know more than what you know. I took my resume to all these studios and the most I was offered was an unpaid internship. I don't have the money to drive back and forth from Valpo to Chicago just to come home empty-handed. You know?

"I've done some live shows for local bands like Chester Brown. And I've done some board work."

Board work?

"Soundboard. The sound guy is the extra musician. It's the band's job to play their songs to the best of their ability. It's the sound guy's job – the audio engineer – to make it sound as good as it can in the space it's being played.

"I did floor coverings for about six years. Andy is a laborer with Local 81. I'm trying to get in there right now."

Tell me a little bit more about Andy.

"He's about the most generous person I've ever met. He wanted to go on this long road and knew I was unemployed and asked me to tag along with him. I told him I couldn't afford it. He told me not to worry about it. Andy said, 'If you can cover most of your meals, we're good.' We drove out to the Hualapai Mountains in Arizona. They're always green."

What's with this nuthatch pipedream?

"On facebook we're calling it White-breasted Nuthatch for Indiana State Bird. I don't know if it's worthy, but it has kinda picked up and we like where it's going."

How did this idea originate?

"Andy's quite a birder. One day he and I were sittin' around drinkin' a couple bottles of wine and he started talking about what an interesting bird the white-breasted nuthatch is."

En vino, veritas.

"Come again?"

In wine, there's truth.

"We usually drink beer. Anyway, we set up the facebook page and formed this group. People have shared the link. We've got almost 800 likes so far."

Have you contacted any state representatives?

"They all have facebook pages now. We've pretty much canvassed them. We've shared our link on their pages, but so far we haven't had any response or got any politicians to sign on. Some of them make you wait to be approved because they don't want people posting nonsense on their sites."

There are some real nuthatches, I mean nut cases, out there.

"A couple of people have been real close-minded about it which is kind of surprising to me."

Example of an anti, please.

"One lady said, 'That's Indiana's history, you can't mess with that.'"

A traditionalist to be sure. Maybe you should have mentioned to her that Indiana's state flower was the zinnia from 1931 to 1957 before it was changed to the peony.

"Indiana didn't even have a state bird until the late 1930s. That's when we adopted the cardinal."

Let me play devil's advocate. Why the nuthatch as the new state bird and not the American goldfinch, wild turkey or the habitat-threatened bobolink? What's wrong with the cardinal?

"There are seven states that have the cardinal for their state bird. The white-breasted nuthatch is more unique. Indiana is a unique place to live, especially Northwest Indiana. Like the sign says: We're the crossroads of America.

"A lot of people converge here and a lot of people go different ways from here. You know, the nuthatch has kinda done that, too. You'll find nuthatches spread out all over this country."

Continue, please.

"The white-breasted nuthatch is here year around and it's real adaptive. It can set up a nest just about anywhere and be happy with it. Nuthatches are tough little birds that don't bail out in the winter. In the summer, they eat a wide variety of food and are good for people who have gardens because they pick the bugs out without harming the plants."

* * *

I figured this one for a tongue-in-cheek interview before setting foot in Tom Johnson's modest home. But the more I listened to him, the more I got to liking this young man. I hope he gets a job with the union laborers where he can earn a decent living right here in Northwest Indiana, a place where unique folks are real adaptive.

Tough little birds.

Aubrey Fullerton *(Dec. 2015)*

"There are two reasons why I'm in show business, and I'm standing on both of them."
– Betty Grable

After interviewing Aubrey Fullerton I was a bit red-faced. In her 28 years on this Earth, I believe she has seen and done more things than I have in 58.

Fullerton is a single mom who is a professional photographer, make-up artist and the owner of Tokyo Rose Pinups.

Her Hobart home with its green exterior and pink flamingos in the front yard is quite quaint, but it's the interior with its fabulous '50s decor that is really something to see. Her house is her studio and her studio is her house.

* * *

You are my first Aubrey.

"It's a boy's name in Scotland," she said. "It means 'keeper of the elves.'"

Tell me about your childhood.

"I grew up along the Kankakee River on Ramsey Road in Jasper County and graduated from Kankakee Valley High School. My sister and I were raised rough around the edges, but also were taught to be polite and to give respect to everybody. Let's just say we were taught to handle our own."

Taught to handle our own?

"If we were left out in the wilderness somewhere, we were taught to start our own fire. We can throw tomahawks, hunt and do whatever we need to do to survive. Even here in Hobart, I chop my own wood and grow my own vegetables.

"Mom's maiden name is Radaszewski. She was the eighth of nine kids. None of them had any money. My busha (Polish grandmother) never worked outside the home. My grandfather eked out a living. They made duck blood soup and raised their own animals for consumption near the Kankakee River in extreme southern Lake County."

Aubrey, I grew up near your parents. Your father's family lived on a large sand hill in northern Newton County. At one time, that property was known as Bogus Island which was located in the middle of the largest natural lake in Indiana – Beaver Lake. The foundation of the house your father grew up in is still there. The Nature Conservancy owns the land today.

"My dad's long hair and bushy beard are grey now, but there was a day when it was black as coal. Dad was a chiseled-out stud who worked on Triumph motorcycles for a living. Today, he's a maintenance man at St. Catherine's Hospital in East Chicago."

What does mom and dad think of your tattoos?

"When I came home after I had my arms done, my mom cried. I told her, 'I'm still me. It's just art on my skin.' Now, I think both my mom and dad want tattoos."

Life after high school?

"I moved to Florida about a year after I graduated high school. I went to school down there for special effects and makeup."

How long did you live in Florida?

"About nine years. I lived in a warehouse for a while in St. Petersburg with my miniature pig and a Chihuahua. I started out doing makeup for commercials and television shows, but I hated the industry and got out of it. After that, I worked for myself doing freelance makeup.

"I also worked on a golf course, in bars, and in a surf shop. I did woodwork, metalwork and construction, too. And, I worked for Xerox as an account manager."

That's a diverse list of occupations.

"Plus, we had a store where I sold vintage clothes and new clothes. The store also had a soda shop. When I got pregnant we closed the store down and moved back to Northwest Indiana. That was about three years ago."

Tell me about your business.

"I do pinup photography, vintage-style shoots and avant garde. But I do family stuff like weddings and senior pictures, too.

"Every month I build a different set. I have clients who come in every month to shoot on each set. We do wardrobe and pinup parties. Anywhere for five to 12 girls come at once. We do their hair and makeup and then dress them up vintage-style. You know, like the '20s, '30s, '40s and '50s. I do Great Gatsby shoots. I just did a Roaring '20s family Christmas shoot."

Continue, please.

"I pretty much use my entire house to shoot. Everything is kind of retro '50s. My stove, fridge, TV and the rest of the furniture is from that era and still functioning. This is my son Simon's tricycle; it's from the '40s.

"People come in here and I'll have cookies on the stove. They'll ask me: 'Are those real?' I'll say, 'Yeah, they're real. Don't you bake?'"

Explain pin-up art?

"Traditional pin-up art was posters of women like Marilyn Mornroe, Betty Grable or Bettie Page. During World War II, they would send those kind of posters to our soldiers overseas."

I'm not familiar with Bettie Page.

"She did more risque type of stuff. Bettie broke the mold for a lot of stuff. She did bondage kind of stuff."

Tell me more.

"To me, pin-up has a whole new meaning today. A lot people are drawn toward the nostalgic. I live like this, but a lot of people who live normal lives in the modern world say they've always wanted to dress up like a '50s girl. So, I make it happen."

What do we have here?

"This is my steampunk set."

Steampunk?

"Steampunk is pretty much a mixture of old and futuristic. A lot of it has to do with either Western- or Victorian-style clothing, but a lot of clocks, gears, futuristic types of guns and different stuff are incorporated. Have you ever seen the movie 'The Wild Wild West' with Will Smith?"

No, but I remember the TV show. It was billed as a mix between westerns and science fiction. Back in the '60s, I dug it. Robert Conrad was a cool cat.

"'The Wild Wild West' was very steampunk."

Describe one of your custom-designed jobs.

"I had a lady contact me saying her son was turning 11 and that he was really into plants and science. The mother wanted me to do a mad scientist shoot. No problem. We had a fog machine, plants, science books and different colored bottles with liquid in them. The kids wore lab coats."

Very cool. How much did it cost to make this steampunk set?

"About $5. The antique telephone was donated by a client. The stuffed pheasant came out of my parents' garage. That old portrait of that couple came out of the attic of this house. I collect lots of stuff. I'm really good at working with what I got. That's the way my parents raised me."

How much do you charge?

"My standard shoots are $150. That includes makeup and hair."

What's this?

"It's a hobo dobro. I'm learning to build my own banjo from a 1968 hubcap." *Kid, you're something. Anything else?*

"I specialize in zombie pin-up shoots. Oh, I also sponsor 30 roller derby girls."

* * *

Two words come to mind when I think of the life Aubrey Voyles Fullerton...

Good stuff.

Ralph Knapp *(May 2013)*

"A flying saucer results when a nudist spills his coffee."
– author unknown

Ralph Knapp couldn't come to the phone when I made the initial call to set up an interview with him. He was hand-milking Harriet who had just given birth. Harriet is a shorthorn-black Angus cross. At the ripe old age of 16, her udders are too saggy to do  the job properly. And, according to Ralph, a baby calf should have mama's milk the first week of its life.

Knapp, 72, is a truck farmer who lives in Thayer with wife, Joanne. They have raised three adult children.

Knapp also is a former justice of the peace, has served on the Newton County Police Merit Board for the past 26 years, is the only remaining active charter member of the Lincoln Township Volunteer Fire Department and is the nephew of Alois Knapp, an Austrian immigrant who founded a nudist colony in Roselawn he named Zoro Nature Park in 1932.

* * *

Ralph, what's one of your main crops?

"Asparagus," he said.

This sand country is ideal for acid-loving crops like blueberries. Asparagus likes an alkaline soil.

"We have to add limestone every few years."

Other crops?

"Tomatoes, sweet corn, green beans, peppers, pickles and cucumbers, pumpkins, gourds, strawberries... . The strawberries come in about the time the asparagus goes out."

Last fall, you were given an honorary gold card and axe for 50 years of service as a volunteer fireman.

"Yeah, after 50 years, they gave me the axe."

It doesn't take a mathematical wizard to figure out that you were with the LTFD on Halloween of '94.

"I heard what I thought was thunder. Soon thereafter, Joanne received a phone call that a plane had gone down by the Prohosky farm. I met the boys at the station, we hopped in the fire truck and drove to the site. At first, all we saw was part of a tail section of a plane in that soybean field. It was complete destruction."

American Eagle Flight 4184.

"We didn't realize until about an hour later that it was a commercial airplane with 68 people on it. We wanted to believe it was a cargo plane that had crashed, but that wasn't the case."

You guys from Lincoln Township were the first responders.

"They wanted to set up a morgue at North Newton High School, then they thought better of it because it was going to take quite some time to take care of the situation. The Remington National Guard Armory was decided upon."

I know there were locals who helped with the identification process during the ensuing weeks.

"Yes, there were."

Horrific. Ralph, let's switch gears. Coming to America for the Knapps. "Uncle Alois came here first in 1910. He was from Austria. My father, Herman, and Uncle Peter didn't emigrate to New York City until 1924. Soon after, they started farming on property just west of Roselawn.

"My father told me when they came to the United States, they were often looked down upon as those 'damn foreigners who came to America.'"

Why was that?

"Because Germany and Austria sat side by side and things were getting kind of hairy in that part of the world. During World War II, there were certain ethnic groups in America who were suspicious of people with surnames like Schultz or Schmidt."

You mentioned your Uncle Alois. I can think of another Austrian named Alois who named one of his sons Adolf. Later, that son liked to be called "Der Fuhrer." Tell me about Alois Knapp.

"Uncle Alois was married to a woman named Lorena whose maiden name was Jensen. She liked to write poetry and things like that. I remember when she passed away in 1951. Alois went back to the Old Country and married a woman named Ursula. We really liked Ursula."

Wasn't Alois Knapp on a TV show back in the late '50s or early '60s?

"Yes, he appeared on 'What My Line?' The panel couldn't determine that he owned a nudist colony, by the way."

Did Alois do anything else for a living?

"Yes, he was an attorney. He earned a law degree at Northwestern University. He had practices in Chicago and Crete, Ill."

When your immediate family would pay a visit to Uncle Alois and Aunt Ursula would they be naked?

"Yes, Alois was proud to be out there without clothes on. I believe it was in 1967 that my uncle sold the place to the Drost family. Dick Drost was paralyzed from the waist down. The Drosts immediately changed the name from Zoro Nature Park to Zoro Nature City and then to Naked City.

Ralph, from what I've read or been told, when Alois Knapp owned the nudist colony it was a classy place. The members were sun worshipers; it was like their religion. What about when the place changed hands?

"Dick Drost started the Miss Nude America contest. I was justice of the peace here at that time. Drost asked me: 'Since you're judge around here, would you be one of the judges of our first Miss Nude America contest?'"

You turned him down, of course.

"No, I agreed to be a judge. The Chicago news stations came out here to cover it. They had to black out the nudity, obviously.

"Being so close to I-65, Drost started catering to truckers. There would be dozens of them parked out on what used to be the air strip that was on the property. There were nude waitresses. Shows were performed and one 'lucky' trucker was permitted to spray whipped cream on whatever part of the body of the nude waitress that he wanted to."

You don't say?

"And remove it however he wanted to remove it. It was a novel sort of thing. The county raided the place. Drost ended up being exiled from the State of Indiana. Today, Naked City is called Sun Aura."

What about Ponderosa Sun Club across the street?

"A man by the name of Harvey Schmidt had a falling out with Uncle Alois, so he started his own nudist camp. But in Uncle Alois' later years, when he'd return from Florida to Indiana in the summertime, he realized what Naked City had become. Uncle Alois chose to stay at Schmidt's nudist camp and they ended up becoming good friends. The true nudists followed suit and also moved to Ponderosa Sun Club."

Interesting.

"We sell produce at Ponderosa in the summertime. My good friend Cecil and I raise some of the produce together. Cecil took his wife in there one time while selling our wares. I asked him, 'Did Thelma take her clothes off while she helped you hawk the vegetables?'"

Old Cecil's reply?

"'Nope, she woulda scared off the customers.'"

Ralph, when I was in high school, there was a girl whose family lived in Naked City. The school bus would pick her up on Ind. 10. She asked me if I would be her prom date. She was really pretty and a very nice person. You're not going to believe this, but her last name was Smelly.

"I didn't know the Smellys. Did you take her to the prom?"

No, I ended up going to the big dance with what would become my first wife. I shoulda went with Penny Smelly.

* * *

There is a memorial in remembrance of the victims of American Eagle Flight 4184 at the station of Lincoln Township Volunteer Fire Department in Thayer. As the weather warms, nudists will emerge from their cabins in Roselawn. Ralph Knapp's asparagus crop will sprout from the soil. Harriet's calf is doing fine.

Life goes on.

Mike Dalkilic *(March 2014)*

"Deve bir pula, devebin pula."
(A camel for a dime, a camel for 1,000 dimes.)
– Turkish proverb.

The above proverb has been used to show the irony when a person could not afford something even when it was very cheap, but later can afford it when it's 1,000 times more expensive.

Although Miray "Mike" Dalkilic was born the son of wealthy parents in Istanbul, Turkey, he struggled mightily while first married in this country. Through hard work and being the possessor of a brilliant mind, he has gone from ditch digger to successful entrepreneur.

Dalkilic, 76, is the founder-president of Midtech Hydraulics, Inc. in Cedar Lake. He lives in Crown Point with wife Sandra who worked for the Internal Revenue Service for 37 years. Today, she runs a thriving real estate company and shares office space with her husband. The Dalkilics have raised a son and a daughter. Mehmet is a professor at Indiana University in Bloomington, and Samantha, who owns Steeple Gallery in St. John. "Sam" appeared in this column several years ago.

* * *

"I came to this country when I was 17," Dalkilic began.

Did you attend college in America?

"Yes, the University of Texas and eventually St. Edward's University, both in Austin, Texas. St. Edward's is the second oldest Catholic university in the United States."

Are you Catholic?

"No."

Are you Muslim?

"No, I'm not a religious man. At St. Edward's you had to be at least 32 years old. We were a class of 72. We had colonels who were flying B-52s; we had general managers of IBM. I graduated second in my class."

Impressive.

"I was kicked out of history class at the University of Texas."

Really?

"One of the slippers I had was broken, so I went to class barefooted. I was a pure, unadulterated Turkish hillbilly. The professor looked at me and said, 'Mr. Dala, Dalka, Dalak... .' He couldn't pronounce my name. It took my wife 20 years to pronounce my name."

Is Sandra a native Texan?

"Yes, her maiden name is Hitchcock. The professor asked why I was wasn't wearing shoes. I told him, 'Is broken.' He said, 'We will not accept that.'"

Tell me more.

"At first, I hung around with Turkish students. After a year, I started messing around with the Americans. I played piano in a bar. In 1958, a bald-headed Turk playing piano was very impressive to the ladies. It became a problem. I flunked out of school. But I had beautiful fun. Booze and women, it was wonderful.

"By luck, I met my wife. I was struggling; the immigration office was after me. I had what was called an F-Visa which was for students."

Continue, please.

"For about four months, I dug ditches for $1.25 an hour. Then, I cleaned shit for 18 months on the night shift of a mental hospital. Finally, Sandy told me that I needed to go back to school. I told her they would never accept me because I had flunked out three times.

"Sandy wrote a magnificent letter. I took the letter to the dean. After reading it, he asked me if I wrote it. I lied and told him yes. I was desperate with a wife and son. He stepped out for about 15 minutes, came back with a piece of paper and told me to read it and sign it."

What did you sign?

"If I made any grade less than a B, I would never again step into the 40 acres known as the University of Texas. Plus, I had to take a minimum of nine hours and the classes would be picked by my counselors. I got my degree in sociology. I made one B and the rest A's."

Wow.

"Plus, I was working 40 hours at the time. I did not see my wife and son five days a week. I went to classes, studied and worked 20 hours a day."

What were you doing for a living while attending the University of Texas for the fourth time?

"A menial job cleaning chips that came from lathes in a machine shop. Being a foreigner, that's the only job they would give me although I had a couple of years of college. After about six months, I overheard the supervisors fretting about the fact that the draftsman was sick and his assistant was on vacation."

And?

"I said, 'Sir, I can draw.' In college, I started out to be an architectural engineer. They told me to draw something. I did and they made me assistant draftsman. In eight years, I was their sales manager. Eventually, I was pegged to be in charge of human resources as well, but needed to get my graduate degree. That's when I decided to apply at St. Edward's University."

Tell me about your business today.

"For 32 years, I buy hydraulic components – cylinders, mostly. I sell them to the steel mills. My concentration is mostly on continuous casters. The reason I have survived is I check my principles as if I'm using the cylinders myself. My cylinders have warranties above and beyond what steel mills normally get."

Example, please.

"When a customer wants some assurance beyond the standard warranties, we provide a warranty that fits the customer's needs. In steel mills, tonnage produced is the most important component of the warranty. Our warranties are based on tonnage produced. This is a critical element in the continuous caster environment."

Very good. Mike, do you care to talk politics?

"Sandy and I were extremely liberal. We worked for (Lyndon Baines Johnson) when he was running for the presidency. We put leaflets in every door when Hubert Humphrey ran for president.

"My wife and I turned conservative when the peanut farmer said on the radio that we were the reason the country was going to hell. He said the people of the United States didn't have the capability of kicking ass."

I voted for Jimmy Carter twice and don't remember him saying that.

"Then comes the B-grade actor."

Dutch Reagan.

"And he said, 'What? We're the best!' The country believed it. I believed him. For eight years, I was thrilled with Ronald Reagan. He allowed people like me to generate wealth."

It's your interview, Miray.

"When Obama ran the first time, I did not mind that he got elected. Change, change. What change? What the hell changed?"

You're right, things are almost as bad as when the Texan was running the show. Speaking of which, how were you treated during the '50s and '60s in the Lone Star State?

"They called me a camel jockey. I told them the first time I saw a fucking camel was in the San Antonio Zoo."

* * *

I but scratched the surface with Mike Dalkilic. Years ago, he was named an honorary Texan by the Governor of Texas. More recently, in honor of his 70th birthday, Mike Dalkilic Day was officially celebrated, a proclamation signed by the Mayor of Crown Point.

Dalkilic has missed but four University of Texas home football games in 24 years albeit he's lived in Northwest Indiana since this country's bicentennial year. He detests the University of Notre Dame.

Dalkilic worships Ataturk, the first president of Turkey, and George Washington, the first president of the United States. The first Republican president, "Honest Abe" Lincoln, is his ultimate hero.

Dalkilic has enjoyed sailboats and Harley Davidsons for 40 years. He collects oil lamps from around the world, some of them date from before the birth of Jesus Christ.

Mike Dalkilic earned an Eagle Scout badge in Turkey and marched with migrant workers in Texas.

He's a Turk who wears cowboy boots.

And quite a piece of work.

Ron Kittle *(April 2013)*

"When I was a kid growin' up in Gary, I remember a few Cub fans coming home from Wrigley with a little quiche and white wine spilled on the lapel of their suit coats. Sox fans came home from Comiskey with mustard and beer stains on their blue jeans."
- Ron Kittle

Ron Kittle grew up in the Aetna neighborhood of Gary and graduated from Wirt High School, where he was a three-sport athlete.

Kittle, 55, and his five siblings are the sons and daughters of an ex-Navy man and an ironworker who migrated from West Virginia in search of work in Northwest Indiana.

In 1983, Kittle was named American League Rookie of the Year while playing for the Chicago White Sox. He also played in Major League Baseball's 50th All-Star game that year. It was held at old Comiskey Park.

For the past year, Kittle has lived in Mokena, Ill. Our interview took place at Cracker Barrel just off Kennedy Avenue and Interstate 294. Once we polished off biscuits, gravy and grits, that is.

* * *

So, Kitty, how do you like our chances of taking the American League Central?

"The White Sox have a very good chance of winning the division, if they stay healthy," he said. *Childhood memories of Gary?*

"We had good neighbors and friends on the block. And we lived across the street from Aetna Senior League Field."

You worked as an ironworker for a while.

"My graduation present was a piece of paper that said: 'You are an apprentice ironworker, you start tomorrow morning.' I went to work the next day.

"When I was out on that iron, I would never let anyone outwork me. It was pride. I saw how hard my dad worked despite being being beat up with cancer and emphysema at the time."

Professional baseball?

"I went to tryout camp while I was working and did well; the Los Angeles Dodgers organization signed me to a contract. I played my first year in Clinton, Iowa."

Cool.

"I broke my neck in my very first game."

Not cool.

"I hit a double in my first at bat; Mike Scioscia (current manager of the Los Angeles Angels of Anaheim) singled me in. A late throw came in as I was sliding across the plate. The catcher jumped for the throw and landed on me while I was getting up."

Then what?

"I had surgery. It took me a long time to realize that things happen for a reason. You have to move on."

What did you do next?

"Went back to work with the ironworkers and got as strong as I could. I used to carry a pair of 50-pound boxes of welding rods, one under each arm, and run up 30 flights of stairs at the coke plant to beat the elevator. People used to bet on me."

The Chicago White Sox?

"I tried out at old Comiskey Park and missed the first pitch completely. I took a deep breath and then proceeded to hit the next pitch way out of the ball park. People stopped what they were doing and gathered around the batting cage to watch. Bill Veeck (White Sox owner at the time) told one of the brass: 'Don't let him leave the park until he signs a contract.'"

You and your former teammate and White Sox hitting coach Greg Walker were good friends.

"Absolutely. We were roommates. Greg is probably my best friend. He probably knows me better than my brothers know me. I pretty much spent half my life with the guy."

Walker was a great natural left-handed hitter. You were a slugger. Your seven roof shots at old Comiskey Park are a major league record.

"Babe Ruth hit the first one, I hit the last. You never felt it when you hit a roof shot. It was just a pure thing. It was like it was an extension of your forearm.

"You have to hit it 500-feet plus just to get it on the roof. I hit one that went completely out of the entire stadium which is about 700 feet. I can say it on record – no one has ever hit a ball farther than I have. The only park I never hit one out of is Yellowstone."

Who gave up the 700-footer?

"Dave Rozema. It was a 3-2 curve ball."

Another one of my favorite players was the late Kevin Hickey from South Chicago. I believe he was working for Republic Steel when he tried out for the Sox.

"Kevin was a guy with mediocre talent, but he had heart the size of a blast furnace. Hickey would go out to that mound and challenge you. He had some big games for us."

Harold Baines?

"Harold was about 150 hits shy of 3,000, which is a sure trip to Cooperstown. If I could give my hits to him, I'd do it in a heartbeat. Harold Baines is that good of a guy.

Your photograph graces the cover of legendary hitting instructor Charlie Lau's book.

"I had a good swing and I did a lot of things right – except stay healthy. I have three fused vertebrae and two that are ruptured, one above the fused ones and one below them, I've had two taken out of my lower back. I also dislocated my shoulder and broke my collar bone running into the left-field wall. That bothers me to this day. But I keep going."

Something the average fan might not know about you?

"I was in Playgirl magazine. They had a bunch of ballplayers together and put our pictures in one of their spring issues. We wore shorts. They gave us $500 each. Then, they offered me something like $50,000 to pose naked for the centerfold. Ma told me not to do it. Heck, today, I'd do it for 20 bucks."

Kitty, you're killin' me. Early on, you were told by an old scout you'd never make the majors because you wore glasses.

"Yep, that made me want it just a little bit more. I don't like being told I can't do something."

You played in old Yankee Stadium.

"That was a thrill; the aura of the place."

Steroids?

"I never took any. The people who took steroids blemished the records and the game itself."

What else do you have going on since you've hung up the spikes?

"More than you have space to write about; people can go to ronkittle.com. One of my latest endeavors is making red, white and blue-colored baseball gloves. I'm a firm believer in products being made in the United States.

"I also work for the White Sox. They gave me a job title called ambassador. If Mr. Reinsdorf gave me a job picking up peanut shells, I do it to the best of my ability."

Is Reinsdorf a good boss?

"He's a good man. One of the best owners in all of sports – very caring."

Do you miss playing the game?

"I miss the camaraderie and the pressure of succeeding or failing."

Kitty, there's only one thing that kept me from playing for the Chicago White Sox.

"What's that, Kankakee Kid?"

Talent.

* * *

Who knows what kind of career numbers Kittle might have put up if had played without injury for 16 or 18 years? He actually has a home run to at bat percentage higher than Lou Gehrig's.

Kittle also told me he didn't want to go to one of his major league tryouts because it took place on a Saturday and he was scheduled to work a double-shift that paid double-time for the entire 16 hours. His father told him to go to the try out. Out of his own pocket, Mr. Kittle paid his son the money he would've made that day.

In 1989, Kittle founded Indiana Sports Charities. To date, ISC has raised more than $2 million toward cancer research and education.

And I like to imagine there's a rough-and-tumble ironworker, a former Navy man and Native West Virginian, smilin' from that I-beam in the sky.

Dr. Neal Haskell *(May 2013)*

"Agent Starling, meet Mr. Acherontia Styx, better known to his friends as the Death's-head moth.... Somebody fed him honey and nightshade, kept him warm. Somebody loved him."
– from the film "The Silence of the Lambs"

I met Neal Haskell, 66, at The Pub, an extremely popular restaurant and bar next to The Ritz movie theater in Rensselaer. While noshing on lunch and sipping iced tea, we had a delicious discussion about six-legged creatures that must have three parts to the body (head, thorax and abdomen) to qualify as insects.

You see, Dr. Neal H. Haskell, PhD., B.C.E. is a world-renown forensic entomology consultant to hundreds of law enforcement agencies across North America and Europe who also teaches about 10 classes at St. Joseph's College. And I'm a little-known high school graduate who just happens to be a former Newton County 4-H entomology grand champion.

Talking about blowflies the size of dried fruit and maggots munching on carrion doesn't bug guys like us.

* * *

Could you pass the prunes and fried rice, Doc? Thanks.
"I've lived in Rensselaer all my life," he said.
Childhood memories?
"Growing up on a farm, I was a driving a tractor by the time I was 6. By the time I was 10, I was doing the work of men. Dad grew corn and beans and raised cattle on 800 acres. My mother taught art and music in the Rensselaer school system for 37 years."
Did you become interested in insects at an early age?
"Yes, I started collecting them when I was about 10. They were

everywhere; that's what fascinated me about them. I remember the first time I encountered major maggot masses, I was about 8.

"There was this 350-pound calf that had died; it was all bloated up and encased in maggots. I was totally repulsed. Little did I know, 20 or 30 years later, these would be the guys my livelihood would depend on."

Is there a certain group of insects that really grabbed your interest early on?

"I liked the beetles. There are more than 330,000 species worldwide."

I'd use Ma's bleach as a form of euthanasia when preparing to mount by bugs.

"In my college days, we used to carry around jars of potassium cyanide. We had enough cyanide in our killing jars to kill 40,000 people. They trusted us with that. Amazing."

Tell me more about your college education.

"Over four decades at Purdue University. I got my bachelor's in the '60s, did post-graduate work in the '70s, earned my master's in the '80s, and my PhD in the '90s."

As a college freshman, did you know going in that you were going to be an entomologist?

"I started out in biology, but one of the dean's talked me into coming over to entomology."

Forensic entomology?

"For me, there wasn't really any forensic entomology. Nobody had ever studied it. I'm the first academically trained forensic entomologist in the world."

You've appeared on television.

"More than 45 television programs, not counting court TV."

Can you expound upon your particular niche a little more?

"One of the main things that we do is determine how long a person has been dead based upon the growth and development of the insects feeding on them."

You were the forensic entomologist for the prosecution in the Casey Anthony case down in Florida.

"We had the car that was found July 15. It had been abandoned and then put in an impound guard. When the grandmother picked the car up, she called the police and said: 'It smell's like there has been a dead body in here.' That's when the police became involved – no one had seen the little girl in 31 days and she wasn't reported missing."

Proceed.

"An investigation ensued. The police opened the trunk and some 'fruit flies' flew out and that was that."

Or was it?

"I finally learned of the 'fruit flies' about two months later. I said, 'Boys, those weren't fruit flies, they were coffin flies feeding on the decomposing fluids that remained in the trunk that car.' That's what gave it the smell."

And?

"I was able to prove with a reasonable degree of scientific certainty, that she had probably died the 16th of June and was in the car no longer than the 18th or 19th of June. In my estimation, she had been wrapped up in a blanket and put in the trunk of the car.

"At 130 degrees in a trunk of a car, the girl's body would begin purging fluids from the nose and mouth. Hence, the smell."

Another of your more prominent cases?

"I did the Danielle van Dam trial out in San Diego. I was testifying for the defense in that one."

Another little girl. So sad. How many times have you been under oath?

"About 125. As far as I know, that's more than anyone else in forensic entomology."

A local case?

"I was involved with the McCowan case up in Porter County. Obviously, my problem with that one was they had insect evidence and the county decided that it wasn't important. I don't know if the kid murdered the girl or not, but the insect evidence could have told the story."

One of your more bizarre cases?

"I call it the Bates Motel case which took place down in Indianapolis. This guy had been taking care of his sister and aunt. All three of them were in their eighties. The two women had fallen and broken their hips. They were bedfast.

"Well, the guy had a normal itinerary everyday and the people that he'd usually see, hadn't seen him for three or four days. So, they went to check on him."

Yeah?

"They found him dead on the living room rug. So, they checked on the women of the house."

And?

"They were really dead. These ladies had been dead at least two years. I estimated that the aunt died in late September or early October; she was pretty much consumed by blowflies – the soft tissue was cleared off. The mummifying of the sister would have been brought about by a period of time when the insects weren't flying. I figured she died in the months of December, January or February."

The brother-nephew obviously had mental issues.

"I believe he had taken care of them for so long, he couldn't bring himself to depart with them. He was buying groceries as if there were three of them living there."

Wow. Any parting thoughts?

"Maggots are our friends."

* * *

What a wonderful opportunity; a chance to earn a master's degree in forensic science at nearby St. Joseph's College in Rensselaer under the tutelage of its native son and his hand-picked, blue-ribbon panel of experts.

Dr. Neal Haskell. A man who has given hundreds of scientific lectures and seminars all over the world, yet has remained close to his roots.

Mayre Williams *(March 2009)*

"Come and read a story by a man named Jeff;
A blue-collar scribe, ain't many of 'em left
Poor river rat raised on the Kankakee;
He packed up his Ford and drove to Beverly;
Shores that is, big lake, fancy cars."
-Jeff Manes

Mayre Williams' first name is pronounced "May-ree" with equal emphasis on both syllables. She owns a purebred, snow-white bichon frise, pronounced BEE-shon Free-ZAY.

I remember playing with my white dog as a boy. Cotton was a rat terrier, mostly.

I only had done drive-bys of Beverly Shores until recently, when I turned north off of U.S. 12, toward Williams' home, nestled near Lake Michigan.

Having passed by the road sign for Sumava Resorts many times in the past, Williams confessed that she once turned east off U.S. 41, just south of the Kankakee River. Out of curiosity, mostly. She thought Sumava was kind of spooky because there was only one way in and out; she said it made her feel as though she was trespassing on private ground.

I had a similar feeling entering Beverly Shores.

* * *

"I must say, earlier today, I was not up for this," Williams began. "This interview was one of the two things I did not want to do today, the other is going to the gym."

Were you reared in this locality?

"No, I was raised in Munster and graduated from Hammond High School in 1964. I attended DePauw University in Greencastle; my junior year was spent abroad in Germany. When I was quite young, I wanted more than anything to have an international experience.

"I also did a semester of graduate school at Vanderbilt University, didn't like it all, but I met a couple of singers who were in from New York City. I decided to move to New York with them so we could form a singing group. We sang together for about two years; it wasn't successful, which was fine with me."

Then what?

"Wall Street. I went to work for an investment bank. From Wall Street, I went to Harvard business school. I also worked for CBS television network in advertising sales. Then, I went on to syndication television sales, where I sold 'Entertainment Tonight,' 'Lifestyles of the Rich and Famous,' 'Star Search'... I lived in New York for 22 years.

"In 1990, right after my father died, I was transferred to Chicago where I ran a very small sales office. I had a great gig and a great apartment in New York, but Chicago is a wonderfully liveable city. My romance with corporate America lasted from 1970 until '94."

It appears you've maintained your love of reading; this is quite a library.

"Many of those are the great books produced by Encyclopedia Britannica. My parents bought them knowing that we would be sent to college among other things."

Tell me a little about your parents.

"My father was of Welsh ancestry; he was a Methodist. He moved to this area during the late '30's from Youngstown, Ohio. He was a supervisor at Youngstown Sheet and Tube in East Chicago. My mother would always say that her husband was not a steel man; he was a gentleman. Mother was a schoolteacher."

You're an adjunct professor at Indiana University Northwest in Gary.

"Yes, I teach professional writing skills because I love the students. I teach them the etiquette and social importance of using writing to achieve their goals. When you write a complaint letter, for instance, you don't just rag at the person; it's basically a sales letter – a letter of persuasion. I teach students the formulas for writing effectively to get what they want done. I also teach sailing for a time-share company in Chicago.

When did you move to this beautiful home?

"In '99. Before that, I spent a couple years with my mother in Munster as she became increasingly frail; she died in '98. When I decided to buy, I didn't want to move to the suburbs. As a teenager, we came out here all of the time. I remember the Diana of the Dunes stories; this just seemed like a cool place to live. I've always been drawn to this area.

"Once I did move back to the Midwest, I bought a 45-foot sailboat. By spending so much time around Monroe Harbor, where I keep the boat, I discovered a new career – driving a tender boat."

Tender boat?

"A tender boat looks like a tug boat without the cabin; it's used to go back and forth between the ship and the port for supplies or people."

It must be seasonal work.

"Yes, from May 1 through Oct 31. I work five days a week. It's a demanding, physical job. The wheel and gear shifts are stiff, probably like driving a tractor. I have to check the engine and oil levels. Mind you, I'm not a mechanic, but I do have to crawl down in and make certain the bilge pumps are running OK."

How long have you been a boat captain?

"I'll be starting my 10th season. July 3 is our big day, that's when they have the fireworks display at the harbor. I've never lost a passenger into the water, but on that day, I'm basically praying that I don't."

Are some of them a bit inebriated?

"Um, yes – falling-down drunk."

Mayre, it's been a pleasure. Mine is a liberal, diverse column featuring folks from all walks of Northwest Indiana life, including conservative, white Anglo-Saxon Protestants such as yourself. You mentioned that you pray you don't lose a passenger into the water. You're a religious woman, I'm sure.

"I just saw Bill Maher's 'Religulous.' He's begging nonreligious people to make their voices heard; he also makes a few quotes about our Founding Fathers not being churchgoers."

Well, he has a right to his opinion. I've read that Maher and his antithesis, Ann Coulter, are about to meet vis-a-vis on TV.

"I completely agree with Maher."

Come again?

"He will squash that bitch. She's not smart enough to go up against Maher."

But...

"I remember vividly when 'under God' was inserted into my pledge of allegiance. My father, who voted Republican every election, thought that was wrong. My mother was scandalized.

"And, besides, it was George Bush, a Christian, who took us to the fucking war in Iraq.

"I was one of 200 people who protested in Michigan City the night we went into Iraq. Was there any press coverage of that event? No. Was there any press coverage of any events leading up to the Iraq War? No. Nothing. All we got from the 'liberal' press was: We need to go to war!"

And I had you pegged for a Rush Limbaugh right-winger.

"I'm a Lincoln Republican. Today's Republican party has no relationship to the Lincoln Republican. You can be a liberal Republican; I'm also a big believer in small business and supporting small business, but what happened during the Reagan era was not the downsizing of government, it was the outsizing of corporate America. Reagan was not a capitalist; he was a corporatist.

"This is going to be just lovely when my neighbors read this one, but what the hell, I don't know any of these people anyway. Did you know they have a bow-and-arrow cull to kill the deer here? I like the deer. And I don't like the thought of a half-culled animal jumping over my fence, going hog-wild, and kicking one of my dogs! Jeff?"

Mayre?

"Being interviewed wasn't so bad after all."

* * *

Williams owns one other bichon frise; it came from a raided puppy mill. And there's an incongruous black mongrel that was abandoned. The poor creature wandered along the beach road for weeks, she said.

Today, that lucky dog also makes its home in Beverly Shores, thanks to the kindness of a Lincoln Republican.

Brenda L. Cole *(Dec. 2011)*

"According to a recent survey, men say the first thing they notice about a woman is their eyes, and women say the first thing they notice about men is they're a bunch of liars."
– Author unknown.

I recently stopped at a liquor store in Crown Point and grabbed a couple dozen business cards. In my line of work, I do that on occasion.

There were cards pertaining to window cleaning, chimney sweeping, a gift basket specialist, "Wanted! Old Guitars" and so forth.

One of the business cards read: "Surprise Parties: Brenda L. Cole, Surprise Lady." I thought to myself, "This is something new. What a neat idea; a woman who helps folks throw surprise parties."

Cole, 43, has been married to Marc Cole for six years; they live in Crown Point. She has three sons, ages 24, 16 and 7.

Our interview took place at the VFW in Dyer where Cole volunteers her services. She also is a server at the Aspen Cafe in St. John.

* * *

"I was born on Mother's Day, 1968," Cole began. "Mom chased an ice cream truck for two blocks at a family picnic and went into labor."

Did you grow up in Crown Point?

"No, I grew up in Blue Island, Ill.; I loved Blue Island."

High school?

"Dwight D. Eisenhower."

Childhood memories?

"I remember we used to walk everywhere. Walgreens used to have a counter; Rosie worked behind the counter. Every payday Mom would take us to the restaurant in Walgreens. It was a big deal. I loved their fresh strawberry pie."

Anything else?

"I worked at Kline's Department Store and Iverson's Bakery. Iverson's is still there on Western Avenue and Blue Island."

What is your maiden name?

"Martino. When I was a kid, we lived at the Blue Island Hotel. My parents didn't have much money and it was cheap. It was just one room."

How long did your family live in the hotel?

"About a year. Only a couple of my girlfriends knew that we lived in a hotel. Kids can be cruel. My mom and dad always tried to do the best they could. One year, for Christmas, my sister and I got a gift apiece from a thrift store."

What did your dad do for a living?

"He had lots of jobs; he worked at numerous pizza places."

The VFW?

"I do taco dinners, steak dinners, pork chop dinners. I also shuffle Marines around. We got a phone call from a colonel recently from an Air Force base in Germany. One of his Marines needed a ride from Monee, Ill., to Merrillville where he was meeting another colonel who would take him home to Massachusetts. I picked him up; he was a very polite, young man by the name of Luis Costello. I was honored to help out."

How did you meet Marc?

"While bartending here at the VFW. We got married here. On our first date, we went fishing. We both love to fish. I recently caught a five-pound bass in Wisconsin.

"I'm very outdoorsy; when I was younger, we used to camp out at the Potawatomi Campground near Kankakee State Park in Illinois."

I know where you're talking about, by Warner Bridge and Rock Creek.

"Exactly. It's a beautiful place."

Working as a server?

"I've actually made waitressing a career; I love it. I worked at the Paragon Restaurant in Schererville for 14 years; when the restaurant changed hands I was let go. After a little time off, I went to work for Gus Karalis and his family at the Aspen Cafe. They're very good to me there.

I've worked for Greek people most of my life.

"I have a following; I took all my groups with me: My NIPSCO boys, the Methodist Church ladies in Dyer, my Tri-Town Pastors Association... . All these people followed me to the Aspen Cafe."

That's really something, kid.

"I have an amazing memory. If I ran into you at the grocery, my husband might say, 'Who is that?' I'll tell Marc, 'I don't know, but he likes two eggs over easy with sausage.'"

Tell me about your surprise party business.

"Surprise Parties is a company that was created for women in 1998."

Oh, I thought this was something you came up with on your own.

"I'm an independent contractor. We have reps all over the country and in Canada. Surprise Parties' products are excellent."

Products?

"It's very professional; no men or children. It's a chance for women to get out and enjoy themselves with their girlfriends. I provide a shopping experience at a private setting."

Shopping experience?

"Women can pick things out for themselves in a discreet atmosphere. Everyone comes out with the same brown paper bag."

Brenda, I'm getting this funny feeling that you don't oversee, say, a woman throwing a 50th birthday party for an ironworker named Steve.

"Oh, no. It's an adult party. I offer lingerie, books on how to do things like sexual positions, and toys."

Toys?

"It's done in a very professional manner. We bash men a little bit. I have a lot of one-liners like, 'We have a cream that can make him go from a three-minute man to a five-minute man.'

"A lot of women don't like to go to stores like the Lion's Den or Cirilla's. Some women are intimidated by that."

Are some of the products for someone who doesn't have a mate or significant other?

"We do sell vibrators; the Silver Bullet is a great seller."

Brenda, I must say, you are one of the most honest, open people I've ever met.

"I can talk to anybody about anything. Some husbands worry they will be replaced by the toy. There is a misconception about what toys actually do. Toys and lotions simply enhance the love making; they don't replace the man. With that said, one of my one-liners is, 'Men are put on the planet because vibrators can't mow the lawn.'"

Yikes.

"I'm a member of the NWI Business Network."

How many parties do you do per year?

"One or two per week; I just do it part-time. I took the kids to Indiana Beach with the profits from a party. My parties average $500. I've done shows in Schererville, Dyer, Crown Point, Hobart, Munster, Lowell, LaPorte, South Bend, Fort Wayne... ."

* * *

Brenda Cole told me she loves being a mom and a grandma and enjoys decorating her home for the holidays.

Doesn't surprise me a bit.

Pete Lange *(June 2014)*

"Our wurst is the best."
– Sign in front of Lange's Old Fashioned Meat Market

With all its unique antiques on display, the Harrison clan of the television show "Pawn Stars" would be in seventh heaven if they walked into Lange's Old Fashioned Meat Market in Michigan City.

A vegan would be traumatized. Also on display are Old World home-created sausages, aged steaks, veal, lamb, smoked chops, hams and snack sticks.

.Pete Lange is quite a character behind the counter. He's somewhat eccentric and extremely intelligent. The guy has a degree in sociology with a minor in accounting.

Lange's Old Fashioned Meat Market reminds of a small town barber shop. Friends stop by to sit and chat. He keeps a keg of beer behind his counter and serves frosty steins filled with the amber brew – gratis. Lange himself does not imbibe, saying he's goofy enough without it.

Lange, a colorful raconteur, had plenty of great stories for me. He's met some famous people through the years. I'd love to retell his hilarious encounters with the likes of business magnate Rupert Murdoch, former President Bill Clinton and a couple of the Chicago Blackhawks, but those juicy tales were off the record.

Lange, 54, lives between Michigan City and LaPorte and has owned and operated his business for 23 years. He was presented the Indiana Hidden Treasure Award by former Gov. Frank O'Bannon, and in 1993, his shop was been featured in the food section of the Los Angeles Times.

* * *

Pete, I'm a human interest columnist, I notice stuff about people. If you don't mind me asking, how big are those things? They look like a pair of gun boats for goodness sakes.

"I wear a size18 shoe," he said. "When I was in ninth grade, I was about a foot shorter and wore a size 16. We'd skip school and go to shoe stores for laughs. The shoe salesmen would touch the end of my toes to make sure I didn't have merchandise hidden in there."

Did you grow up in Northwest Indiana?

"No, I'm from a small town in Michigan called Three Oaks. My first job was at the age of 8. I delivered the South Bend Tribune. When I turned 15, I started picking apples and peaches at an orchard. At 18, I worked at a Checker gas station."

Gale Sayers used to do their commercials on television – "That Checker, it's a gas." Now they're known as Speedway.

"I wanted to be an FBI agent, but ended up working for a steel company for nine years. I saw the handwriting on the wall and got out before the place went out of business. During that time period, I was in Michigan City and noticed the huge house that was originally on this property. It was in sad shape. There were 175 tires in the basement. I had the house torn down and had this place built.

"The first two weeks I was here, all I sold was hotdogs, bratwurst and liver sausage. I had a woman come in one day ask for two T-bone steaks. I told her that I didn't sell steaks."

But the woman planted a seed.

"I went out and bought a saw. I'd gone to college with a guy whose dad was in the meat business in Indianapolis. I met with the guy and he set me up. I started selling prime steaks in here. It took off."

Are you a self-taught butcher?

"Pretty much. I got my first taste of butchering when a good friend of mine brought in three elk and laid them on my table."

What are some of your best selling items?

"Beef jerky, turkey jerky, chicken jerky, honey jerky... ."

You're reminding of the character Bubba in "Forrest Gump" with all the varieties of shrimp – pineapple shrimp, lemon shrimp, coconut shrimp, shrimp soup, shrimp burger, shrimp Jell-O... .

"The honey jerky is made with ground sirloin, honey and wine. We marinade it for three days and smoke it for 24 hours. Then we have the snack sticks which are mild and medium; we do a teriyaki that's a big seller. We also do a hot sausage and one that's very hot.

"We smoke our own pork chops and hams. When you bite into one of our hot dogs you don't have to worry about anything looking back at you. You know what I mean? We do ribs here on the weekend. Around the holidays we ship hams and turkeys to all 50 states and into Canada."

Impressive. I bet a good portion of your business is word of mouth.

"I was in Orlando, Fla. about three years ago and a woman asked me: 'How's the meat business in Michigan City? I love your store.' She was from Tulsa, but had stopped by our store while visiting her parents. I don't advertise at all."

Pete, whether at home or at a restaurant, how do you like your steaks cooked?

"I want it so a good vet can bring it back to life. Prime New York Strip – two minutes per side and your done."

Where do you get your meat?

"Out of Indianapolis."

I've been watching you deal with customers, you're a people person.

"Many years ago, a very dear friend of mine told me if you want to learn something about somebody, just cut their meat a little bit slower. By the time first-time customers leave here, I usually know where they're from, how they found me, and what they do for a living. I'm not being nosy. That's who I am. I simply find people interesting."

We're birds of a feather in that respect.

"My goal is to make sure that people who walk into my store taste everything we offer whether they purchase anything or not. My other goal is to make sure they feel better about themselves than when they walked in."

* * *

Since interviewing Lange, I've tried his beefy jerky. It's like no jerky I've eaten. It was at least an inch thick. I sliced off chunks of it and nuked it like Lange recommended. It melted in mouth. His Prime New York Strip? To die for.

Do yourself a favor, stop in and have a beer on the vivacious entrepreneur with the sociology degree and the size 18s.

The funny and friendly German will most likely cut your meat just a tad slow.

Caregivers & Do-gooders

Tevin Gardner *(Jan. 2010)*

"I set goals, take control, drink out of my own bottle
I make mistakes, but I learn from every one
And when it's said and done
I bet this brother be a better one
If I upset you don't stress
Never forget, that God isn't finished with me yet."
– Tupac Shakur

Tevin Gardner has been diagnosed with an enlarged heart; he had a stroke in 2003. He is currently unemployed, but volunteers as a mentor and is the director of activities for Highly Flavored, Inc., a Gary-based group concerned with leadership development of children and teens.

Gardner, 30, lives in Gary with wife, Tyaisha; they have three children ages 10, 7, and 5.

Although Gardner played defensive end for Lew Wallace High School's football team and wrestled, he admits he pretty much was a thug throughout his teens.

* * *

"I grew up at 40th (Avenue) and Jackson (Street) in Glen Park," Gardner began. "Now that I've turned 30, I'd like to go to school for business management. I didn't think I'd live to see 30."

Because of your health issues?

"Because I've done a lot and seen a lot. By the grace of God, I'm still here."

Expound, please.

"Growing up, there were a lot of things to get into, and I found a way to them. I'm not saying my mother or father weren't there, because they were. I chose to do the things I did and, because of that, I lost friends."

Lost friends?

"There were six of us in the crew I hung out with; there's only two of us left. Every summer, for four summers in a row, one of us was dying."

What happened to them?

"All four died from gunshot wounds. The fifth guy moved away. The last time I saw him was at the funeral of the fourth guy who was killed. He told me, 'I'm leaving Gary; I don't want to be next.'"

Were you guys involved in criminal activities?

"The strange thing about people who are involved in criminal activities is, they're not all bad. I see good in everybody. Some of the most mathematically intelligent people I've ever known were dope dealers – cooking and cutting dope to the gram. Can you imagine how successful they could've been if they took that same knowledge and applied it to any other aspect of life?"

Were drugs the extent of it for you?

"One of my friends had a cousin who was in the military; he'd come home and buy us guns to resell on the street."

What kind of guns were you running?

"Police issue 9 millimeters, mostly. That was one of the ways we made money. And that was a really stupid thing for us to do.

"Back then, we trusted the older guys in the neighborhood. Now, being older, I know that it would have been nothing for them to kill us.

"I learned the street had no loyalty. The street is loyal to the street. There's a whole different code. It's crazy. Guys who grew up together, went to elementary (school) together, would kill one another. It's hard to believe that guys who grew up calling one anothers' mothers, 'Mom' could kill one another over a dollar or a harsh word. But it happened."

But you've changed. What happened?

"No matter what I was doing in those days, I always new to pray before I went to bed. As a kid, I attended Pilgrim Rest Missionary Baptist Church. Today, I'm an associate minister there.

"Jeff, it's obvious there's a reason for me to still be here. If my voice can help somebody else see there's another way, so be it. I'm comfortable with the way my life is now. I like the way things are going right now."

Tell me about being a mentor.

"Sometimes, it can be frustrating. I'm a little hard on the youths I mentor,
but it's only because I see what they don't see. I've been to places that most of them haven't. I've lived around the guns and drugs; I've been shot at. It's not a glamorous life. I want them to know that I love them enough to make them angry enough to not want to do those kind of things."

How do they react?

"Some of them don't want to be like me, which is fine. You have to realize that a lot of these kids have been let down by those who were supposed to be looking after them. A lot of people have said one thing to them, then done another. They're running their own lives. In a lot of ways, people like me are the only discipline they know or see."

Your hometown?

"Driving through Gary, you'll see this is not a place that promotes happiness, higher education or positive living. There are some parts of Gary that look like no one has been there in 30 or 40 years.

"We don't have anything for our youth to do. When they do get into trouble, you want to plaster them on the news or in the paper. You want to send them away. To me, that's not the answer."

Your family.

"I might not have the finances other people have who are doing some crooked things. I might not be able to give my children all the things they want, but I give them the most important thing – sound advice on how to live.

"I tell my son, if you're going to be a man, be a man. If you say you're going do something, do it. Stand by what you say."

Your future.

"Sometimes my dreams kind of get pushed out of the way. I watched a documentary by Chris Rock called 'Good Hair.' It was about the hair industry. I really want to open a beauty supply and barber shop. I'd like to employ as many of the area youths as possible. In the neighborhood, if you can cut hair, you can make a decent living.

"Other than being married and being called to preach, I know that working with teens is what God wants me to do. Everything is fueled by helping the youth.

"If what I'm doing as a mentor can help just a couple of people, then maybe they can help someone else someday."

You're doin' alright, Tevin.

"My biggest fear in life was for people to see me coming and hate to see me, that people would leave because I showed up. In contrast, today, it's like, things will get done right because Tevin's here.

"I want to uplift our youth and let them know that somebody loves 'em. I guess that's just me in a nutshell. I'm really not that interesting of a guy. I'm just an ordinary man who was called to do extraordinary things."

Anything else?

"Jeff, I dare not leave the impression that my surroundings dictated my actions when I was younger. I knew right from wrong; I chose to do what I did. I justify nothing.

"It is was it is."

* * *

Four young men died in the streets of Gary, one got the hell out, and one chose to mentor teens. The one who stayed is a survivor, trying to help others do the same.

Sister Brigid *(Dec. 2014)*

"Hearing nuns' confessions is like being stoned to death with popcorn."
– Fulton J. Sheen

My interview with Sister Brigid Fasiang took place at a bake sale held at St. Andrew the Apostle Catholic Church in Merrillville. She was hawking her wares there.

Sister Brigid, 86, has been a nun for 61 years and resides at the Andrean Convent.

* * *

What kind of name is Fasiang?

"Slovak through and through," she said. "My parents were born there."

Where did you grow up?

"Whiting. I went to St. John's grade school and then (Hammond) Clark High School. I say I'm from Whiting because the mail went through the Whiting post office."

Childhood memories?

"When I was in the second grade the priest came to talk to the students. He asked how many boys and girls – when they grow up – will be priests or nuns. I remember putting my hand up. The priest said that he was going to ask us the same question when we were in the eighth grade. I thought to myself, 'My hand's still going up.'

"My mother didn't want me to be a nun because I was the only girl. I had three brothers. She asked me why I wanted to be a nun. I said, 'Ma, I asked you for a baby sister and you gave me a baby brother. I'm fixin' it for myself. I'm gonna have all the sisters I want.'"

From the mouths of babes.

"After several years, my mother thought it over and said to me,

'You know, you made the best decision. This cousin is divorced, this cousin is having problems and you've got it the best of all.' I said, 'You got that right, Mom.'"

What did your father do for a living?
"He was a bricklayer. It was hard work."
Did you make all the goodies on this particular table?
"Yes, the homemade breads and the nut and poppy seed rolls."
Was your mother a good cook?
"Oh, yes. She was famous for her pierogi and golumbki."
Did you knit those doily things?
"No, I crocheted those pot scrappers."
I knew that. What's with the towels?
"At St. Benedict's the laundry staff would throw all their old towels in the garbage bin. I told them, 'Don't you dare. I'll make cleaning rags out of them.' Towels make the best cleaning rags."
Tell me about your career.
"I was at the Mother House for the first 18 years. Then I worked for 20 years at Villa St. Cyril in Highland Park, (Ill). We had a nursing home there, but they closed down. Then we were transferred to St. Benedict Nursing and Rehab Center in Niles, Illinois. I worked there for 20 years. I was 81 when I retired from job."
Where was the Mother House located?
"In Danville, Pennsylvania. I was 22 when I entered. I loved our Mother House; we had a beautiful grounds."
Today, you're actually semi-retired.
"Yes, they needed help at Andrean High School because there are only four sisters there. The convent was built for 26 nuns."
The nuns don't serve as schoolteachers anymore, right?
"Yes, they do. Sister Carol Ann teaches theology and Sister Mary Paul works at the library for half a day. She taught Latin there for 41 years."
What are some of things you do at the convent?
"Whatever needs to be done. I'm the handy lady."
Can you tell me what name you were born with?
"Martha. I've been Brigid longer than I was Martha."
How long does it take to be married to Christ?
"After about five years, you make your final profession. We had 12 in our group. Before you knew it, five were left."

Would you like to see one of your great-nieces become a nun?

"Not unless the Lord called her."

Memorable occurrences on the job through the years?

"I had a 98-year old woman named Dora who said to me, 'I guess I'll never go back to Ireland.' I said, 'Why not?' She said, 'Because no one will go with me.' I told her,'I'll go with you.'"

And?

"I went to Ireland with her. A few years later, I brought her back to Ireland to see her family for her 100th birthday. She lived to 104."

I can't help but envision the conclusion of "Going My Way" when Barry Fitzgerald's character, who was about 98, was visited by his mother all the way from the Emerald Isle. Too-ra-loo-ra-loo-ral.

"Don't quit your day job."

Ahem.

"I've also been to Slovakia, Mexico, Hawaii and the Holy Land."

What do you think of the current pope?

"He's doin' O.K. Somebody's always gonna – you're never gonna be perfect in everybody's eyes. You just have to take each day as they come and pray to do God's will."

Words of wisdom. I see the loaves of bread are $5. How much do you want for one of those nut rolls?

"Those are $10."

That's kinda salty, ain't it Sister?

"Have you seen the price of nuts lately? They're $9 per pound! Don't forget to buy some cookies on the back table."

* * *

It was a pleasure meeting Sister Brigid.

As for her homemade nut roll?

If that moist and scrumptious creation was any better, it would be almost, well, sinful.

Nell Foster *(May 2010)*

*"What a friend we have in Jesus,
All our sins and griefs to bear!
What a privilege to carry
Everything to God in prayer!"
– Joseph M. Scriven, 1855*

Nell Foster's delightful smile features a gold tooth that sparkles like her loving chestnut eyes.

Foster moved into her house in the Tarrytown section of Gary the year I was born – 1957. But the first 21 years of her life were spent in the Mississippi Delta.

She was born Nellie Wright, 78 years ago today.

* * *

"My mother lived to be 92," Foster began. "I'm grateful to be 78 because I've lost two kids who didn't see 50. I had six children; I have 10 grandchildren and 14 great-grandchildren."

Where were you born?

"Durant, Miss., but my parents moved to Ruleville, Miss., before I was a year old. Ruleville is part of the Mississippi Delta in Sunflower County. The Delta is the flat land of Northwest Mississippi; it doesn't have the hills like the southern part of the state around Jackson."

Ruleville during the 1930s and '40s.

"It was segregated; we weren't farmers, but we did pick cotton for pay. My mother would buy baby chicks by the hundreds and raise them to sell."

What did your father do for a living?

"He was a carpenter."

School days?

"Basketball was my sport; we won the county tournament in '49.

They still have our picture hanging up in the new high school."

What was the name of the high school when you played basketball?

"Ruleville Colored School. Civil rights activist Fannie Lou Hamer (nee Townsend) is from my hometown and James Meredith was my classmate when I was in the 11th grade.

He was the first African-American to attend Ole Miss (University of Mississippi).

"Yes; here's a photograph of James and his wife with my husband and me. June Meredith was from Gary."

Fannie Lou Hamer and James Meredith made history. Any other famous people from that vicinity?

"B.B. King is from Sunflower County."

Are you a fan of the blues?

"Not really; I'm more partial to gospel music."

Favorite hymn?

"What a Friend We Have in Jesus."

Ruleville today?

"My first cousin was the first black principal after the schools desegregated. He has since moved up to superintendent of the entire county's school system.

"I have another cousin who is serving her fourth term as mayor of Ruleville."

Tarrytown in the 1950s?

"A lot of black veterans and their families migrated to Tarrytown from Chicago or the Deep South. This side of 21st Avenue is considered old Tarrytown. The south side of the street was called new Tarrytown because the houses were built a few years later."

What has changed in the neighborhood in the past 50 years?

"When the steel mills started going down in the 1980s, a lot of the people lost their jobs and their homes. You can see the deterioration; all you have to do is ride around. The house next door to me is empty. There is so much vacant property."

Today's economy isn't helping matters much.

"This recession doesn't bother me; I've been budgeting all my life."

Hobbies?

"I enjoy sewing, but I call it botching; I'm not very good at it. I botch bedspreads and curtains. I also like arts and crafts – cooking, too."

So you can "put on some pots?"

"All my friends like my pineapple and coconut cakes. I make a good peach cobbler. My dressing is pretty good."

Back in the early '90s, I raised a couple acres of organically grown vegetables and would sell them in the parking lot of Tri City Plaza here in Gary. At certain times of the season, my customers would wipe me out of items like cabbage, bell peppers, onions and green tomatoes. They were putting up (canning) a kind of spread or relish called... .

"Chow-chow; I've made it."

Nellie, I love old family photos. You have quite an assortment hanging from these walls. Who are the folks in these two photographs?

"That's my mother; the one to the left is my grandmother."

Beautiful. Are these your sons?

"Yes; all four of my boys were in the service; two in the Air Force and two in the Army."

Is this the basketball team you played for?

"Yes it is; can you guess which one is me?"

Front row, far right.

"No, but she was my best friend."

In your wildest dreams, while growing up in Mississippi, did you think it possible a black man could be elected president of the United States?

"No; I never dreamed Ruleville Colored School would become desegregated. I was living up here when that happened."

It appears you've been awarded numerous plaques and certificates through the years.

"The one I cherish the most was from the kids of Tarrytown when I was a job developer. Last Saturday, I went to a funeral and a girl came up to me and said how much she appreciated what I had done for her. She'd been on the job I got for her for 35 years."

House of worship?

"I'm a member of Pilgrim Rest Missionary Baptist Church. I served 39 1/2 years as either superintendent or assistant superintendent of the Sunday school. And I'm part of the mother's ministry at Pilgrim Rest; it's for the older ladies.

"The young ladies of the church all like me and I really love them. They call me Mother Foster."

* * *

    Although she's a senior citizen, Foster drove to Ruleville eight times in one year to visit her mother. Times had changed since Nellie Wright played forward for Ruleville's Blue Demons.

    And it took an act of Congress to abolish the blatant segregation that took place in areas like Northwest Mississippi.

Larry Klein *(Apr. 2014)*

*"Well I was born in a small town
And I can breathe in a small town
Gonna die in a small town
Ah, that's prob'ly where they'll bury me"
– John Mellencamp*

Within the green-colored Victorian home of Larry and Karen Klein is a post office. Karen is the postmaster of Leroy.

Larry Klein is a diehard Chicago White Sox fan and executive director of the Lake Heritage Parks Foundation. He recently retired as COO of Lake County Parks and Recreation Department.

Klein, 63, grew up in Shelby, attended Lowell High School and graduated from Ball State University's school of architecture and planning with an undergraduate in city planning. Later, he earned his master's degree in public administration from Indiana University Northwest.

On his last day of work with the parks department, he was presented with the Sagamore of the Wabash award, one of the highest honors someone from the Hoosier State can receive.

* * *

Childhood memories of growing up in Shelby?

"Shelby was a great place. One of the first really vivid memories is of the ice jams in the (Kankakee) River," he said. "That ice would literally pull the trees out of the ground as it moved downstream. You can try to describe that to people, but until you've heard and seen it... ."

Continue, please.

"Soon after I was born, they picked up my parents' home in Shady Shores (subdivision) and took it across the railroad tracks in what was known as Water Valley. When I was about 12, we moved north of the tracks right across from White Advertising and next to Manno's Grocery Store."

Old-timers often confuse my grandfather, Vito Manes, with Vito Manno.

"Vito and Vinnie Manno were the sons of Frank Manno who had the dance hall in Shelby before my time."

Our dads grew up as neighbors in Lake Village. Shelby and Lake Village shared the same priest back in the late '50s.

"Father John Woods. He used to tell me, 'Son, I'm from Kerry, Ireland where men are men and mules have flat feet.'"

I don't get it.

"I didn't either, but it was a very impressive saying to a kid. I was Father Woods' altar boy."

Lowell High School had a good basketball team when you were there.

"Yep, we got beat in the final game of the regional by Gary Roosevelt. They went on to win state. We came the closest to beating Roosevelt. That was my junior year."

Were you on that team?

"No, I played football – a Les Klein requirement."

Your uncle was the coach.

"Both Uncle Les and Uncle Clayton were Little All-Americans at St. (Joseph College in Rensselaer)."

What year did you move to Leroy?

"In 1988."

How many people live in Leroy?

"About 250. Leroy is one of those small towns that you find sprinkled around Indiana. The idea of looking out for your neighbor and getting help without asking for it are just a couple of things that make small town living worthwhile. Life seems more simple and less hurried.

"Knowing everyone is a real benefit. Everyone knows Karen because she's the town's postmaster. I'm known as Karen's husband, which is just fine by me."

The Lake Heritage Parks Foundation?

"As a retiree, I can devote more time to the foundation. The LHPF is a pretty august group right now. It's comprised of some good people who have a lot of responsibilities."

Receiving the Sagamore of the Wabash award from Gov. Pence? Tell me about some of the good things you've done to be nominated. Tell me about volunteering your services for the good of the community. Tell me –

"Jeff, the things that I've done with my life, I've tried to keep to myself. Let's just say I try to give back to others."

* * *

Lawrence John Klein really didn't want to be interviewed. He's not one to toot his own horn. With a chuckle, the good-natured soul told me he just wants to go quietly into the night.

With that said, the term "sagamore" was used by Algonquian-speaking American Indian tribes to describe a lesser chief or great man among the tribe to whom the true chief would look for wisdom and advice. Among those who have received Sagamores have been astronauts, ambassadors, artists, musicians, politicians... .

And one heckuva a nice guy who grew up along the bayous of the Kankakee River in Shelby, before settling in Liliputian Leroy.

Jonathan Wilson *(Aug. 2010)*

"If you're not ready to die for it, put the word 'freedom' out of your vocabulary."
– Malcolm X

Jonathan Wilson lives in Merrillville with Ruth, Stella and Cleo. Ruth Wilson is his mom. Stella and Cleo are cats. Gary, the city, is directly across the street from their apartment.

Wilson, 19, is the youngest of six children and is a graduate of Calumet High School. He is a member of Trinity United Church of Christ in Gary who plans on having a family someday. He's also a Chicago Bulls fan who likes to write rap lyrics and poetry.

And the young man is quite the community activist, too.

* * *

"We moved to Indiana from Chicago when I was 10," Wilson began. "I love Gary and Chicago."

What part of Chicago?

"Stoney Island."

Disappointed the Bulls didn't land (free agent) LeBron James?

"Not really. Guys like LeBron can mess up team chemistry."

Da Bulls. Michael Jordan, Scottie Pippen, double three-peats. Wasn't that a time?

"Yeah, um, I kinda remember all the hype about it... ."

Kinda remember? How could you forget?

"I was born in 1991."

Oh, yeah. Forgot about that.

"Thank goodness I've been able to see Kobe (Bryant) play; he's the closest thing to Michael."

Kid, I have some old VCR tapes of Jordan playing for the Bulls back when you were still riding your Big Wheel. I'll lend them to you. Kobe Bryant is the junior varsity compared to MJ. But I digress. Are you going to college?

"Yes, I finished up my first year at Indiana University Northwest, but I'm in the process of transferring to Purdue Calumet. I'm majoring in political science."

That's cool. Did you like that stuff in high school?

"Actually, I was always more into history. Why are things the way they are now? I think I might minor in history. I loved my government and history classes. Then I got into politics, but I don't want to be politician."

Are you working while going to school?

"Yes, I work for the Central District Organizing Project. I'm a field organizer; my job is to get power back to the residents in Gary, whether it be by petitions or call-ins. It's their city, not the politicians'. The people of Gary elected the politicians to serve them. I believe some city officials have a disrespect for the residents when they attend city council meetings."

You don't say.

"We have community meetings for residents to help them come up with different strategies on how to make the city better. Nothing can get done unless the community gets involved."

When and where are these meetings?

"Every Monday at 5:30 p.m. at 2452 Massachusetts Street. Whether it's activism or social work, you have to love it because you're not going to get paid much, if at all."

I know you're involved with the Gary Freedom School, tell me about that.

"Well, first I have to give you some background. The Freedom Schools started in the '40s and '50s in the South. They were created to teach young African-Americans to fight for justice – how to fight for change, how to do the sit-ins and the boycotts and all of that stuff.

"There are Freedom Schools all around the country now. Last year, I had to go to Chicago's Freedom School event. But, I kept thinking, 'Gary needs a Freedom School.' And lo and behold, Gary got a Freedom School. I jumped at the chance to be a part of it. Fortunately, I was able to be an instructor."

Where and when?

"We meet at Ivy Tech. I'm part of the summer project which is about to end this month, but there will be a fall and spring project. On Mondays and Wednesdays, they have leadership development class and political and social awareness class. On Tuesdays and Thursdays, I teach the grassroots organizing class. The students also have a diversity and arts class on Thursday. Friday is the Freedom Institute which can be anything; participants can pass out fliers, clean up parks, etc."

How many students in the class?

"Ten."

Ages?

"From 14 to 17. They're mostly ninth- and 10th-graders. Most are from charter schools; a few from West Side. I get excited just thinking about my class. It's filled with brilliant young people. I'm glad they're the ones coming up."

Tell me about your grassroots organizing class.

"To make any type of change you have to have the grassroots (support). The first day, I explained what grassroots organizing is; we also talked about identity – how who you are fits into the community.

"The next day, I talked about oppression. I got into the 'isms' – racism, sexism. We even talked about how music can be used to oppress people. Yesterday, the class was on social movements like the civil rights movement, the black power movement, women's movement and the anti-war movement."

Good job, Jon.

"I'm hoping the kids I teach eventually become teachers."

You mentioned that music can be oppressive. Do you mean like gangsta rap compared to maybe something spiritual like gospel music?

"Some gangsta rap isn't oppressive. Tupac (Shakur), Ice Cube and NWA.'s music challenged the system. Their approach to it and their deliveries might be considered kind of standoffish to some people, but their messages were still cool, like taking a stance against police brutality."

Jon, where do you draw the line?

"To me, artists like Waka Flocka (Flame) and Lil Wayne are oppressive because they glorify selling drugs, carrying guns and talking bad about women. They're bad examples for the next generation to follow. And when young people try to emulate them, we take a step back."

Heroes?

"Malcolm X. There was a time when I was going down the wrong path, but after reading his book, and seeing how he turned his life around, I was very inspired."

Anyone else?

"Tupac, Bob Marley, Dr. (Martin Luther) King and Jesus. Whether a person is a Christian or not, Jesus' life is worth studying; how he loved people was amazing."

With the exception of Marley, who died at age 36, the others were killed.

"When you decide to take a stand in this world, that's something that could happen."

Gary's future?

"Maybe we can have a beautiful downtown again. Gary has so much potential; there are so many wonderful people who live here. I think the people of Gary, as a whole, get a bad reputation. I love the people here; they've been nothing but kind to me."

* * *

Gary's future?

Jonathan Wilson and others like him are Gary's future.

Mary Joan Dickson *(Oct. 2005)*

"Thinking good thoughts is not enough, doing good deeds is not enough, seeing others follow your good examples is enough."
- Douglas Horton

As I approach booths of craftsmen and artisans at Cedar Lake's Hometown Fest, I spot her. Mary Joan Dickson. She is the town's parks director and she's a dynamo. Born in Chicago, Mary Joan comes from three generations of Irish Catholic firefighters. She 'walks' me to the parks building where it's quiet. I have to jog to keep up with her. In the privacy of her office, she opens up to me.

* * *

"My family came down here on the weekends just like everybody else," Dickson began. "We had a cottage on Coffin's Shady Beach. We spent two summers in tents. Then, the next summer, my dad bought us a motor home up on the hill back in the late '60s. There were four of us children then; I was the oldest. My dad would commute to work from Cedar Lake, and my mom would spend all day with us fishing and boating. We loved it. Dad eventually found a house on the lake. My parents still live there. We moved out here permanently in '71 when I was in eighth grade. I graduated from Hanover Central."

Tell me a little more about your dad.

"My father is on oxygen now. Emphysema. He worked as an electrician on his off days. You know how fireman work, 24 (hours) on and 48 off. He put us all through Catholic grade schools. He wanted us to have more than he had – and he did."

Remembrances of Chicago?

"We lived on the Southeast side, right by Lake Michigan. We've always lived by the water. It was mostly Polish back then. I thought every dad was supposed to be named Stash or Casimir. They used to call us the Torrenskis so we wouldn't feel different. Cleanest people I've ever met, the Polish. They would scrub their stoops. They'd hose down their sidewalk and berm. I grew up with all those kids. I believe the different ethnic groups all brought a lot of good things to the table in this country."

When did you get interested in the parks department?

"I went to my first park board meeting when I was 17. They established the park board in 1975. I kept sitting in on the meetings. Because of financial reasons, I had to start out at Purdue (University Calumet), but finished up my recreational degree at Indiana University. When I came back here, I was on a grant for two years, a grant that paid for my salary. Then I went down to Lowell and got a job with their parks department. I worked there from '81 through '86. I worked with the Boys and Girls Clubs here in Cedar Lake for five years as well. But then I got divorced and had to take a job at Walmart. I had to look out for my daughter. From there, I started substitute teaching. And then back to the parks department in Cedar Lake in 1990."

You love this burg, don't you.

"My husband mentions that he'd kind of like to move to Flagstaff, Ariz. when he retires. I told him I'm not going anywhere."

I know he's your second husband, when did you and Gordon get married?

"In 1991. We've had two sons together. Tim is 12 and Matt is 7. I was 43 when I had Matt. Kelly is my oldest; she's 22 now. My first husband's mother died of cancer a year before we got married. I raised four of his siblings. They were 12, 13, 14, and 17. I was 22 – Kelly's age. At 22, I thought I could do anything. Now that they've grown and have children of their own, they'll call me up and say, 'What were you thinking back then?' What else was I going to do? I couldn't walk away from them.

"It was a very crucial time for them to lose their mother, then go through high school. I was at the store the other day with my Keystone Club, and Dan, one of the ones I took in, was there. He told those boys, 'You be good to her. She's my mother'. I said, 'No, I'm like a mother.' He said, 'No. You were my mother when I needed a mother.'"

The Stars and Stripes Race that you put on is a beautiful run around the lake, but you need more help.

"Jeff, I need more volunteers in about everything I do."

What's your favorite activity that you put on as parks director?

"Summerfest. It's been around for 25 years now. I love it. The fireworks and all. It's like throwin' a party and not payin' for it.

"If I see teens walking down the street smoking, I'll pull over and say, '*What* are you doing?' My father is at home on oxygen and I don't want to see them end up the same way. I just don't see how smoking can even be a choice for a kid nowadays.

"I watched some youngsters buy a big box of Reese's Cups and then just toss the empty box out in the street. Again, I pull over and ask, 'What did you just do?' One girl got a little short with me. Her friend said, 'Hey, that's Mrs. Dickson. Don't talk to her like that.' She picked it up and threw it away. We have to do this together. Take pride in your community's appearance. And they have to learn it at a young age."

How was substitute teaching?

"I subbed for 15 years. I preferred high school. Of the 15 years, five-and-a-half were in-school suspension. When I started out, I'd get six, eight, a day. The last year, I was lucky if I got two or three a week. I worked myself out of a job, you know. I don't think they liked being in there with me. I'd make them own up to what they did: 'Mr. Fetty sent me here. I didn't do anything.' I'd say, 'Timeout. This is the jail. I'm the jail keeper. Do the time - you own the crime.' I'd make them shelve books in the library. I used to give out certificates to students if they weren't sent to in-school suspension for six weeks. The principal thought it was corny. But you know what, I went to a graduation party once and that's all the kid got. He was never acknowledged for anything else in school, but there were those silly certificates I made. And he had two of them. He became a fantastic young man."

Continue, please.

"Some children just aren't book kids. They weren't meant to sit in a classroom. You give them some kind of technology, or woodworking, or whatever, and they'll knock your socks off. The Sanchez boy, he was in-school suspension a few times. He went off to the service. He's back now. A very intelligent kid. I asked him, 'You're not going to school?' 'Oh yeah, Mrs. Dickson, I'm going to school. I just have to get a job first. So I can afford a place to hang my hat.'

Jesse Sanchez? The Marine from Cedar Lake who appeared in that famous newspaper photo, holding a rifle on Saddam Hussein?

"Yes."

Favorite part of the park director job?

"Being with the kids. We have Easter egg hunts, craft classes, cooking classes. I just love watching them learn."

You're also involved with the Kiwanis.

"I take great pride in the Key Club and Kiwanis. I should wear hats. So people know whether I'm parks department or a Kiwanian. Sometimes, I'll juggle the two simultaneously. Today, at Hometown Fest, my Key Club kids manned the moonwalk and had an auction to benefit the Katrina victims. I try to get the children to participate in the community. I want them to invest in it. Next weekend they're going to sleep in cardboard boxes. They'll raise money for St. Judes in Crown Point. They've done that for almost four years now. They raise a pretty good penny.

"Right here in this town, you have upper-middle class, but you also have a lot of poor children. Years ago, when I was with the Boys and Girls Club, we made peanut butter cookies to go with Christmas baskets. That evening I went up to the house of one of the boys who helped me make the cookies. He said, 'We don't get a basket Mrs. Dickson.' I said, 'Yeah, you do.' He pleaded, 'No we don't...' I could see it in his eyes, what he was thinking: 'Mary Joan, I'm poor. You know I'm poor. You don't have to knock on my door and tell me I'm poor.' I saw that in his eyes. I'm thinking, 'What am I going to do? His mother needs this food for the family. I can't leave it out in here in the snow.' I had my brother go back later and deliver it. Today, I see to it that people get the baskets. I'm there for them. But I'll never go to a house again. I can't do that. I didn't realize... That same young man has come back numerous times and helped with Christmas baskets. We don't talk about what happened that day. He has three sons of his own now – they help me out, too."

Mary Joan...

"Hey, I had a young fellow from a low-income family come up to me, he's going to the prom with a bunch of his friends, right? The other kids all have money. They're all going in on a Limo. It costs like 13 bucks each. He says, 'Mary Joan, what am I going to do? I don't have $13 for something like that.' I'm a single mom at the time. Kelly is like 7 years old. What am I going to do? I go straight home to my vacation jar. I'd save up pennies – 15 bucks. Kelly says, 'Mom, what are you going to do?' I said,

'It's an emergency.' You know, that boy paid me back – with interest.

"I have a plan. I want to build this pool. Here at the lake. For the children. With big slides. Some people think I'm nuts. Never in my life have I asked Cedar Lake for anything. I'm askin' now. I'm askin' for the kids."

Final thoughts?

"People ask me, 'Why do you do these things?' I can't explain it. It's something that can't be taken away from me. I call them heart prints. We need more of that in this country."

Mrs. Dickson?

"Yeah?"

What am I gonna do?

"Huh?"

You've left me, a writer, without words.

Daisy Tidwell *(May 2014)*

"...Nobody ever helps me into carriages, or over mud-puddles, or gives me any best place! And ain't I a woman? Look at me! Look at my arm! I have ploughed and planted, and gathered into barns, and no man could head me! And ain't I a woman? I could work as much and eat as much as a man – when I could get it – and bear the lash as well! And ain't I a woman? I have borne 13 children, and seen most of them sold off to slavery, and when I cried out with my mother's grief, none but Jesus heard me! And ain't I a woman?"

– Sojourner Truth (delivered at a women's convention, Akron, Ohio, 1851)

Daisy Tidwell was a stay-at-home-mom who raised eight children. She buried one of them.

Tidwell, 79, lives in the Tolleston neighborhood of Gary with her husband, Edgar D. Tidwell.

* * *

"I was born in Prescott, Ark.," Tidwell began. "'Tid' was 17 and I was 14 when we got married. We came to Gary in 1955. You couldn't make no money in Arkansas. We moved up here so 'Tid' could get a job at U.S. Steel. In Arkansas, he was a sharecropper."

What part of Arkansas is Prescott?
"About 100 miles south of Little Rock."
Bill Clinton territory.
"Bill Clinton is from Hope, Ark."
Did you and your husband vote for Clinton?
"Oh, yeah. We liked him."
Did your family have a big garden down in Prescott?
"Oh, yeah. We gardened a lot."
Simpler times.
"We didn't have no indoor toilet."

Were there good places to fish?
"My mother, she stayed on the creek."
Can you "put on some pots"?
"I stays in the kitchen."
What are some of your husband's favorites?
"Sweet potato pie, peach cobbler and the cakes I bake with butter icing."
Greens?
"They all love greens. I got a cabbage in the kitchen right now. I mix my mustard and turnip greens together with a ham hock."
Motherhood?
"Mine was good. Me and my children would get together. We just had fun, you know. It's so far back when they was little. I didn't have but three boys, the rest of them was girls."
Five daughters. What's easier to raise, boys or girls?
"I'd rather have the girls. Boys, they go off by themselves. I wouldn't let my girls go off by themselves. No, no, no. Play in the yard."
Has this neighborhood changed since the 1950s and '60s?
"Tolleston, lately, has really done changed. It was more peoples, you know. I got a daughter, she moved to Indianapolis. My oldest boy, he got killed."
Automobile accident?
"Somebody shot him."
Edgar: "We know who shot him. He dead, too."
How many grandchildren do you have?
"I got grandkids and great-grandkids. Oh, Lord. I cain't count 'em. I got some grandkids, they bring in they report cards and say: 'Grandma, I made an A.' It's good to make all them A's. My own kids brought in some good reports, too. It's been so long."
How did you fare in school?
"Mostly, I had to be home. I been cookin' ever since I was 8 years old. I had to be the one doin' the cookin' while they was in the cotton fields. I had to stand up on a chair to stir our food."
Siblings?
"I had five brothers and three sisters."
Did childbirth come easy to you?
"Oh, no. The pain. I went through it eight times, but it were worth it."

Church?
"Pilgrim Rest Baptist Church."
Do you attend Pilgrim Rest every Sunday?
"Ever' Sundy."
What about Edgar?
"No."
Do you own a few fancy Sunday-go-to-meeting-hats?
"No, I just have one hat. It's a white one. Very seldom wear it. I told one of the sisters that I could go a whole week with the money she paid for her hat."

Do you drive?
"I can drive, but the bus always picks me up for church. The reverend drives the bus. One of my daughters sings in the choir. My grandchildren who are here now, they sings in the choir, too. I was in the choir until I had my teeth pulled. You know how the false teeth won't be still. I had to give it up, but I went to the Mothers' Board. That's where I'm at now."

Several years ago, I interviewed a nice lady named Nell Foster who was a member of the Mothers' Board at Pilgrim Rest.
"Nellie! That's my pal!"
One of your favorite hymns?
"'What a Friend We Have in Jesus.'"
Daisy, I remember that song as a little boy, when my mother would take me to church in Lake Village.

* * *

While driving home after my interview with Miss Daisy, fragments of "What a Friend We Have in Jesus" came to mind. Lyrics that made me think of this sweet and humble woman who came up from the cotton fields of Arkansas to raise eight children the best she could in the "Steel City."

"...Are we weak and heavy laden, cumbered with a load of care? Precious Savior, still our refuge; take it to the Lord in prayer."

Amen.

Christy Fisher *(Nov. 2013)*

"Mama, take this badge off of me
I can't use it anymore
It's gettin' dark, too dark to see
I feel I'm knockin' on heaven's door."
– Bob Dylan

I knew her as the bubbly, blonde cheerleader Christy Osburn. Well, I didn't really know her, she was three grades ahead of me in school.

Today, Christy Osburn-Fisher, 59, lives in Wheatfield with Molly and Paddlefoot, a pair of dachshunds. She and her late husband Rick Fisher raised two adult children who graduated from Kankakee Valley High School.

Rick and Christy operated a general store for years, but she sold it in January after her husband's death. Christy is an avid reader who is currently working as an assistant sanitarian for Jasper County.

Our interview marked the first time I'd seen her in 40 years.

* * *

You grew up in Morocco, right?
"Enos," she said.
I'm sure you don't remember me in school.
"Of course I remember you."
Really?
"The funny thing, we sold the Post-Tribune when we had our store and I had been reading your articles for years before I realized it was you. I never looked at the name below the photo."
From what I've been told, the store sounds like it must've been the

epitome of mom-and-pop shops.

"You didn't get far from work because the house was attached. It really wasn't a convenience store; it was more of a general store. We sold worms, freshly made ham salad, pickle loaf and olive loaf sandwiches, beer, shotgun shells, rods and reels, masking tape, fuses for cars, we were a deer and wild turkey check-in station and had gasoline pumps out front. I mean, we turned a little bit of everything. You know? It was a neat place. We also had two six-feet long tables for the coffee guys. It was a bottomless cup – free refills."

Homemade ham salad sandwiches, 20 cups of joe for a buck, nightcrawlers and beer. Dang. What more could a man ask for? "Eat at Fisher's & Get Gas!"

"We opened at 6 a.m. Rick thought we should open at 5 a.m. because the farmers were all there waiting to come in."

Your reply?

"'If we open at 5 a.m. they're still gonna be waiting to come in! They're farmers; that's what they do!' We had one guy who was always sitting out in the lot about quarter after five. I said to him, 'Manley, why do you do this?' He said, 'Why, if I was at home in a chair, I might fall asleep. I don't want to miss anything, so I sleep in my truck until everybody gets here."

Christy, you're killin' me.

"I guess we got known as an easy touch. You know how the hobos would mark houses to let other hobos know which people would give them a handout. We always made sure people down on their luck went away with something."

Some people would consider you and Rick suckers. Some would consider you kind souls.

"Sometimes we'd let them get away from the store, and then we'd pack up a lunch real fast and put 20 or 30 bucks in the bag. Rick would take it to them. We had that a lot. Which was fine.

"I had one guy come up to counter and ask: 'What can I get with this?' He had some change. I made him a sandwich a gave him a cup of coffee. I told him to keep the change. One of our regular coffee customers threw some money down on the counter for the homeless man."

What happened next?

"He said: 'Sir, I'm gonna be honest with you, I'm a smoker. Do you mind if I buy a pack of cigarettes with this money?' Our regular said:

'I gave you that money, you do what you want with it.' Then all my coffee drinkers left. One of them called me on the phone asking if I was O.K. I said, 'Oh, I'm fine. That poor man is harmless.' Well, he was worried for me so he called the police. The police came. I asked the cops, 'What are you going to do with him?' They said they would take him to the county line and tell him to keep on walking."

Like dumping a dog.

"I told the cop, 'You just wait a minute.' I made up a big lunch and put all kinds of stuff in it and money in the bottom of the bag. The cop gave me a dirty look. He came back later and asked why I did what I did."

And?

"I told that officer, 'Why wouldn't I do that? Shame on you for not doing the same.'"

Christy, let's switch gears. How long were you and Rick married?

"Forty years."

How long has it been since he passed?

"It'll be a year on Nov. 23. My father died one week before Rick."

That had to be extremely hard on you. How old was Rick when he died?

"He was 59. Rick had a very bad heart. He lost a leg to diabetes on Nov. 5. The doctors said if they took his leg, they might be able to save his life.

"I think Rick knew he was going to die. We spent Thanksgiving with him. The kids and grand kids were all there. He kept telling the kids: 'You gotta look after your mom now, I can't do it anymore.' When he said grace, he said: 'Lord, you gotta watch out for my family, you know I can't do it anymore.' He died the next day."

* * *

She says her husband had a bad heart. I beg to differ. Sounds to me like Rick and Christy Fisher had big hearts. I regret that I waited all these years to talk to her for the first time. What a good person she is. Losing her father and husband within a week, all the while keeping her faith. Feeding the poor.... . She told me that coast-to-coast bicyclers stopped by her and Rick's store on more than one occasion. She would let these total strangers shower and sleep in their house. One word comes to mind when I think of her – Christlike.

All you have to do is take the "y" off the end of her name.

The Arts

Ismael Muhammad Nieves *(April 2013)*

"Call me Ishmael."
– Herman Melville

Ismael Muhammad Nieves' first name doesn't have an "h" in it, but his friends do call him "Ish."

Names like Ismael Muhammad Nieves delight me. I mean, where but in this great melting pot we call the United States can you flip through the phone book and spot a Luigi O'Hara, Yoko Goldstein or Francois Grabowski?

Nieves, 44, is an incredible artist and an electrical engineer who lives in the Woodmar neighborhood of Hammond with Stephanie, his wife of 20 years.

Nieves has a studio located above the Standard Furniture building just south of the Chicago Avenue on Calumet Avenue in Hammond.

* * *

"I was born in New York and was kinda doin' the Puerto Rican-gypsy thing, bouncing around from city to city for a quite a while," Nieves began. "I went to six different high schools."

What part of New York City?

"Lower East Side, as a kid. We lived in Hoboken (New Jersey) for a while. Hoboken is to New York City what Whiting is to Chicago – right across the Hudson River.

"When I was in elementary school, we moved to Puerto Rico for a few years. We eventually moved to East Chicago. We had family here. Kinda like how everybody ends up in Northwest Indiana. The aspirations of landing a job at the mills."

Memories of Puerto Rico?

" My father was what they called a 'Jibaro' which is Spanish for Puerto Rican hillbilly. We lived just off of the mountains of the rain forest.

That is where my father was born.

"We grew sugar cane, mangoes, coffee, avocados – everything. We'd come into town with100-pound potato sacks filled with all these fruits and vegetables and distribute them among family members. That, and going to the beaches would be my fondest memories of Puerto Rico."

Folks from Puerto Rico come in all shades and colors.

"I have family that are blonde-haired and blue-eyed and some that are purple-black. When I lived in Puerto Rico, everybody was simply Puerto Rican. I didn't know what a white or black person was until I came to Northwest Indiana. Here, you have Mexicans, Puerto Ricans, Polish, the Greek, the black… . I was like, 'Wow.'

"With that said, being a teenager in East Chicago, as far as cultural awareness, we were probably ahead of the overall curve. We had all these different ethnic groups, but for the most part, we got along."

Your middle name?

"For about five or six years, I was real active in the nation of Islam under the minister Louis Farrakhan. I also was a part of the Million Man March. It was one of the best experiences I've ever had. Everybody was just enjoying each other's company."

Did you end up graduating from high school in Northwest Indiana?

"Yeah, I should have been the last class of (East Chicago) Roosevelt High School, but I flunked my senior year, so I was part of the first class of East Chicago Central."

Are you left-handed?

"Yeah. We think differently and have to force ourselves to think right-handed. I think it makes us more creative. In the service, I shot my weapon right-handed. When I'm painting, I use my left eye."

You were in the service?

"Four years in the Army. I was a paratrooper and I'm a Desert Storm veteran."

Then what?

"Then, I earned my bachelor of science degree in electrical engineering at Purdue (Calumet). Purdue is a great school for engineering. For 2 1/2 years, I was president of the Society of Hispanic Professional Engineers. During that time, I really promoted professional development with the students. My professors can attest that everybody who was active in my student organization is now working at either Boeing, Lockheed-

Martin, Ford or Nipsco."

How long have you lived in Hammond?

"Since 2000."

Your art?

"I've been active in the arts since I was a child in New York. I have fond memories of riding in the car with my father through Soho; there was a lot of street art and graffiti.

"I'm still real active in the graffiti writing culture. It's a movement. We don't do it for nobody but ourselves. Commercially, it's an accepted art form. All the major galleries and museums are showing graffiti art in one form or another."

Did you attend art school?

"No, I'm self-taught. Desire feeds the will. I wanted to paint large so I taught myself how to stretch canvases."

Do you wish you could survive solely as an artist?

"I have a friend who is an artist. He couldn't understand why I was going to school for engineering. I would tell him, 'To be a better artist.'"

Explain, please.

"In the engineering field, I can make a livin'. I'm not so worried about selling my art so I can put food on my children's plates.

"Unfortunately, here in Northwest Indiana, we're not appreciated. When you appreciate something, you give it value. It's criminal that we can't make a livin' off our artwork. Northwest Indiana has a big pool of very talented artists who unfortunately have to go to where the market is – Chicago and Indianapolis."

That's a shame.

"This large mural is an acrylic on canvas, I'm painting it for Wishard Hospital in Indianapolis. It could've easily went into a hospital here."

South Shore Arts?

"I've shown my work at South Shore facilities six or eight times. I had the opportunity a couple years ago, thanks to John Cain. He did help me to develop as an artist."

What else do you have going?

"I'm working with the Miller Beach Arts & Creative District on Lake Street. From June 14 through the 16th we're doing a summer kickoff block party outdoor graffiti exhibition. We're going to have 30 to 40 graffiti writers from Indiana and Chicago gather on Lake Street near the

Miller Bakery-Cafe – that whole block."

Any final thoughts?

"East Chicago is in the history books. It's one of the founding cities of the graffiti writing movement. There's a 400-page book called 'The History of American Graffiti' by Roger Gastman which has a section about East Chicago in it. I was interviewed for the book and gave them a little history.

"We had permission when we did our graffiti writing in East Chicago. If we didn't have permission it was because they were what we considered public walls – abandoned buildings and eyesores. The urban decay was not caused by the graffiti writers. What we were bringing was bloom. We were adding color to these walls that were left to rot."

* * *

A talented, colorful and passionate man, Ismael Muhammad Nieves.

Eric Lambert *(Nov. 2006)*

*"Gold will turn to gray
and youth will fade away
They'll never care about you,
call you old and in the way"
-David Grisman*

The first time I met Eric Lambert was about five years ago at the Front Porch. He was hosting open mic night. Outnumbered by musicians, I cast fate to the wind and read to the eclectic crowd. They were kind. Eric was a gracious host.

Then, to cap things off, the bearded gnome perched himself upon a stool in that Valparaiso coffee house. And with a voice as soothing as a mountain stream of wild honey, Eric Lambert made beguiling and beautiful music with his acoustic guitar.

The native Chicagoan has toured all over North America. For the past year, Lambert has pulled up stakes in Lowell, about 30 seconds from my apartment – by foot. I did not realize this fact until a few weeks ago. Birds of a feather perhaps. He lives by himself in a large house. Pictures of a grizzled Jerry Garcia and a youthful Bob Dylan adorn his walls.

* * *

Eric, we'll probably skip around some. Somehow it comes out a story. I can't explain it.

"That's alright. It's all good."

How old are you?

"I'll turn 50 in January."

Me, too. April.

"We survived."

You grew up in Hegewisch neighborhood of Chicago, but attended Mt. Carmel and not the local public school. Were you raised Catholic?

"No. I was raised fast. Actually, I was better off going to Mt. Carmel than the neighborhood high school where I'm sure I would have gotten in a little more mischief than I did."

Did you go to college?

"In theory. Western Illinois University. I ended up playing all over town – festivals, bars, and such. I moved back to this area in the mid '80s."

Eric, when I think of you, I think of singer-songwriter John Prine. He too, was raised in the Chicago area, yet there is a trace of country about him. I believe he has Kentucky roots.

"My parents were originally from North Carolina. Dad ended up at Republic Steel. That was the plan – grow up in Hegewisch, attend Washington High School, work at Republic for 30 years. That's what people did; people who had migrated from the South or Eastern European folks. That's why Hegewisch existed. It was also a neighborhood where a lot of firemen and policemen lived because it was still within the (Chicago) city limits. You either worked for the city or in the mill. I just never bought into that."

You had the music in you.

"I always knew what I was going to do for a living. That was a blessing. It's what I was meant to do, I suppose. I've always had what I needed."

Do you still teach guitar lessons in East Chicago?

"Yes. And you're also sitting in the student's chair. This is my teaching studio here in Lowell. My engineering station is in the other room. That's where I record not only my CD's, but other people's as well. I teach everything there is to teach about guitar. I want to spread the knowledge and the music. Sharing the gift by performing is one thing, people enjoy it, but teaching people how to play allows them to experience it for themselves."

What do you prefer, electric or acoustic?

"Nowadays, acoustic. I haven't made a living on electric guitar for several years. I grew up on Rock-n-Roll – top 40 stuff. I remember sneakin' a transistor radio in bed with me. I think one of the first albums

I bought at Hegewisch Records was 'Cream's Greatest Hits'. The bands of the day got me going, but it was the Allman Brothers Band that affected me more than anybody. Then somebody turned me onto an album called 'Old and in the Way.'"

I have that album!

"Stone bluegrass. Just a couple years ago, I met a friend up in LaCrosse, Wis. We drove across Minnesota and the Dakotas, headed for Jackson Hole, Wyo. for a two-week gig. We traveled through South Dakota where the cell phones don't work and the only lights were the stars in the sky. My friend had an Old and in the Way CD in his hand. He asked me: 'How many times have you listened to this?' 'Millions,' I said. He looked at me and smiled: 'Yeah, at least.' He popped it in and we sang along with that CD all the way across South Dakota and on into whatever is on top of Wyoming. Montana, I believe."

When did you first start playing the guitar?

"My dad was involved in an accident in the mill. His foot was amputated just above the ankle. Ironically, one of his buddies gave him a guitar so he would have something to do during his rehab. He never picked it up – but I did."

Who are you standing next to in that photograph?

"Steve Kaufman. The only thee-time Winfield Flat Pick Champion. I attended his flat picking camp in Kansas. About 200 people from all over attended. They have guest instructors who are former Winfield Champions."

Did you enter the Winfield Championship while you were down there?

"Yes. I finished in the top five. A guy from the state of Washington finished third, a guy from France placed second, and a fella from Indianapolis won it – good guy."

What is this flat picking?

"Flat picking is something you're not gonna learn around here. Flat pickin' is a style. A bluegrass style."

You've got the perfect voice for it, too. Those guys can get up there.

"Yes, they do. That's bluegrass. Men singing at the top of their range. Sometimes squeakin' and sometimes cracklin', not always perfect pitch."

What kind of guitar is that?

"That's a Collins D-2-8. I was fortunate enough to purchase this from a fella down in Florida by the name of Allen Shadd. He had posted it on the Internet. I talked to him over the phone. I've got videotapes of Allen playing. Here I am talking to this world class guitar player that I've always admired – and he's just as nice as can be. I asked him: 'Just tell me one thing, Allen. Is it a player?' He said: 'Oh yeah, buddy. It's a player. It does have some cosmetic challenges on the soundboard.' I said: 'Well, I don't mind that a bit.'"

Is there any instrument you prefer to play?

"I play a lot of mandolin these days. One of my favorites is this Gibson 1918 A4 – but I was born and raised a guitar player. I'll die a guitar player."

1918 Gibson. Is that the year it was made?

"Yes. Listen to this sweet little piece..."

...Eric, remind me to never erase this tape. Have you ever seen a movie called "Matewan"? It's based on a true story. Matewan is a town in West Virginia. There's this scene where these striking coal miners are sitting around three segregated campfires. At the native West Virginians' campsite, a man starts playing the fiddle. Then an African-American begins to play the harmonica from his campsite. Finally, an Italian immigrant joins in on the mandolin from their respective campfire.

"That's how American music was born. When all these people became ingredients in the melting pot. That's how the music was made by my ancestors in those mountains."

Was that the birth of bluegrass?

"No. Bluegrass was invented by Bill Monroe who was raised on Old Timey music. When I play out with The Tar Heels, we'll play some of those songs that predate bluegrass. Songs like 'Lazy John', 'Soldier's Joy', 'Flop Eared Mule'..."

You mentioned your ancestors. Where did they come from?

"I'm part Scotch, Irish, French, English, and Cherokee. If I had four legs, I'd have a tail. I'm a mutt."

Brother, you're as American as apple pie. Bluegrass isn't simple music is it?

"The musicality, precision, and technique that it takes to play bluegrass equates with classical music and jazz. Earl Scruggs didn't create a three-finger style of bluegrass banjo that no one had ever heard of by pressing a button on a keyboard. I tell my students: 'Playing this guitar is not a hard thing to do, but it requires attention every day.'"

You've never stopped learning, have you?

"How could I ever stop learning? How could I put restrictions on what I can play? I believe that I should try to learn everything I can learn. People ask me, 'What kind of music do you play?' I ask them: 'How much time do you have?'

"I still perform approximately 180 nights per year. I spent three years – five nights a week – in a country bar playing with a fantastic country band. Those guys taught me all about the depth of a Merle Haggard or a Marty Robbins. They taught me how to pick. How to sing in harmony. I learned on the stage with those guys. I toured with Big Shoulders for a couple of years. We were playin' that rootsy-bluesy-Americana-New Orleans-Cajun-rumba kind of music, you know. Those cats put me to task, man. They were heavily steeped in tradition. They taught me a lot about rhythm and groove. They were out of Chicago. Got their name from Sandburg's poem."

Stormy, husky, brawling, city of the big shoulders... Eric, it's been a pleasure.

"Here's my latest CD, you're welcome to it. It was released on the Internet in September. It's called 'Doin' Alright.'"

Thanks! Eric, you wrote a tune called House on the Moon. You sing that baby with attitude. Could you, maybe –

"...One of these days I'm gonna build me a house on the moon. And one of these days, I'm gonna build me a house on the moon. Not too big, not too small, ten million miles from a shoppin' mall. One of these days..."

* * *

What can I say? I'm a fan. It's alright.

And my neighbor, Eric Lambert?

He's doin' alright, too.

Wiley E. Dummich *(May 2013)*

"A ship is always referred to as 'she' because it costs so much to keep her in paint and powder."
– Fleet Admiral Charles W. Nimitz

My friend Mary McClelland of South Shore Arts tipped me off about abstract artist Wiley E. Dummich of Cedar Lake. McClelland told me that Dummich, 83, is an inspiration and probably the smartest person she'd ever met.

Whatever.

Upon entering Dummich's home atop a hill overlooking the lake, it wasn't acrylic abstract paintings I was shown, but a stack of large black-and-white photographs he'd taken of dilapidated barns and houses. They were of a quality that would make Ansel Adams or Walker Evans blush.

* * *

Married?

"Yes, to Carol," he said. "Between us we have four daughters and nine grandchildren."

Born and raised in Cedar Lake?

"I was born in Attica, but we moved to Indianapolis when I was about 2 because there was work there for my father."

What did your father do for a living?

"He was a wood pattern maker. Years after he retired, I told him: 'Dad, I hate to tell you this, but they don't have wooden pattern makers any more.' He couldn't believe it. Dad did everything by hand."

A true artisan. Was your mother an artistic type as well?

"My mother was an invalid, but I'd rather not talk about that."

Childhood memories of growing up in Indianapolis?

"We lived behind the women's prison on the east side of Indy. I used to climb over the back wall of the prison and pick apples in the orchard there."

Early memories of drawing or painting?

"There was a comic strip called 'Lil' Abner' by Al Capp. I learned to sketch all of his characters when I was 8. I received a minor scholarship from the John Herron Art Institute out of Indianapolis when I was 13."

At what high school did you attend?

"Howe High School, but I dropped out and spent five years in the Navy. Once I got out of the Navy, I thought I better go back to school. I showed some papers to a Dr. Maxim at Butler University. He asked me if I'd taken any tests in the Navy and I told him that I'd taken lots of tests in the Navy. Maxim asked me if I knew what GED meant, I told him I did not. I studied journalism for two years at Butler without a high school diploma."

Then what?

"I became a sketch maker at a forging company while attending Purdue University (West Lafayette) where I studied mechanical engineering."

Then what?

"I got into marketing. I wanted to be the best ball bearing and roller bearing salesman you could ever be. The problem was, the company told me they were going to transfer me to Cleveland. I told my wife at the time about Cleveland and she said, 'Well, goodbye.' So, I was let go because I refused to go to Cleveland."

Then what?

"I moved to Chicago to work for Aircraft Gear Corp. in Bedford Park. I became vice-president of marketing. I had 35 years in the aerospace business and had air force secret clearance and what is called Level L clearance."

Really?

"Really. I spent some time with Gordie Cooper; there were certain things we couldn't say."

Are you referring to the late astronaut Gordon Cooper?

"Yes, the man who rounded the Earth. I saw him on television several years ago. He was no longer with the government and he admitted that he looked out the window of his spacecraft and saw UFOs following him. He wasn't allowed to talk about that before."

Interesting.

"The government wouldn't allow me to say things such as S8G or A1W. I was involved with the nuclear reactor on the aircraft carrier

Chester W. Nimitz. My thumb print is on that reactor."

Like you, Chester Nimitz quit high school to join the Navy. It wasn't until years later, after he became Fleet Admiral, that he was awarded a high school diploma. Please, continue.

"I was on several missions during the Korean Conflict. Eventually, I was transferred to the carrier Tripoli. We went from New York to the Panama Canal to pick up some aircraft for MacArthur's invasion of Inchon. I was newspaper editor of the ship. We called the paper 'The Tripolitan.'"

Wiley, you're an eclectic cuss.

"I've been in every jet airplane and helicopter plant in the country. When I got of the marketing field, I started my own consulting business called Coyote Engineering. I did that for several years."

Other unique experiences?

"In the '70s, a cousin of mine who was a television stuntman in Hollywood approached me about marketing a hang-glider."

And?

"I designed and built a hang-glider I called the Dyna-Soar. We produced them in Carmel. Our hang-glider appeared in a television episode of 'Planet of the Apes' and an episode of the 'The Magician' starring Bill Bixby."

Cool. Can I have the dime tour of your art studio downstairs?

"Sure. This painting is a favorite with the kids, it's called 'Blue Spiderman.' This one has never been shown to the public, it's called 'Love Dancer.' Do you see how she has her hand holding a bouquet behind her back? She's facing away from him while he is doing the love dance."

Very nice.

"This is a self-portrait I took from a Leonardo Da Vinci sketch."

Amazing. This acrylic painting has an Ancient Latin title.

"Yes, 'Ex nihilo' – out of nothing or how the Earth was created. Book of Genesis."

I really like this one called "The Actress."

"You can buy it for $2,500."

Wiley, that's $2,490 more than I have on me right now.

"This one, 'Hermes and The Three Graces,' will be shown at Butler University soon."

I must confess that I kinda got faked out on this interview. When I entered your front door, I was expecting to see some guy wearing a beret and a pencil mustache. I figured we'd talk about your painting for an hour. Mary McClelland didn't tell me all that you've done in your life.

"I've never told her. Art is really the smallest part of my life. People around here know me as an artist and a photographer, but they don't know much about my personal life."

Wiley?

"Yes?"

They will now.

* * *

Wiley E. Dummich is not only a friendly man and a tremendous artist.

He's probably the smartest person I've ever met.

Trilly Cole *(Aug. 2010)*

"Corn won't grow at all on rocky top,
Dirt's too rocky by far.
That's why all the folks on rocky top,
Get their corn from a jar."
– Boudleaux and Felice Bryant

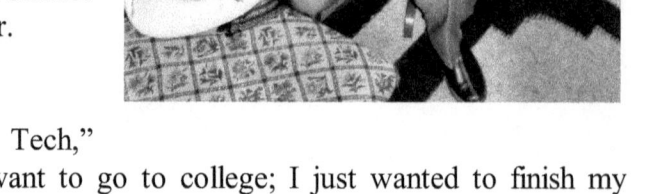

The first time I met Trilly Cole, she was strumming her banjo and singing to the crowd at Aukiki River Festival in Kouts.

Cole, 59, has been entertaining audiences with her music since she was 6. She was born and raised in Hammond, but now lives in Kouts with a delightful mongrel she named Founder because she found her.

* * *

High school?

"Hammond Tech," she said. "I didn't want to go to college; I just wanted to finish my schooling and go on the road. And that's what I did. I never looked back."

Were either of your parents musicians or singers?

"No, but they wanted all three of us kids to take lessons at Judy's Music Studio on State Line Avenue which, back then, was really big. Are you familiar with Uncle Len?"

When I interviewed Indiana 105 DJ Mac MacLeod for this column, Mac told me Len Ellis is a member of the Country Music DJ Hall of Fame.

"When Uncle Len was at (Hammond radio station) WJOB, I first appeared on his show at age 6. I sang 'Sugartime.' Uncle Len probably wouldn't remember me, but I'd love to meet with him."

Have you ever been married?

"Yes, my legal name is Walsh. I've always used my maiden name, Trilly Cole, for my stage name. My husband is deceased, but he was my manager since I was a little girl. He was 25 years older than me.

"By the time I was 8, I was working Calumet City, Ill., because you could go into the bars of Cal City as a kid, as long as you had a sponsor or a parent."

Did you ever perform at the Hammond Civic Center?

"Oh, yeah; I sang with Red Foley at the Civic Center. I've done everything I wanted to do in life except perform in front of a president of the United States."

Tell me about your career once you graduated from high school.

"My first real job on the road was in 1970 in Cedar Rapids, Iowa. After four years on the road, I went to Nashville and worked at the Captain's Table in Printer's Alley. I did three shows a night, six nights a week for 15 years. I have the record for the longest running nightclub act in Nashville. It only seated 85 people; we turned it."

Turned it?

"The first show started at 7 p.m., the next show at 8:30 and the last one at 10. We moved them in and herded them out like cattle."

Grand Ole Opry?

"I was never asked to perform; that's invitation only. Of course, when you're a Yankee... ."

Did you perform with or open for any stars other than Red Foley?

"I fronted for Tammy Wynette, Waylon Jennings, Bobby Bare, Mickey Gilley, Kenny Rogers, Boots Randolph, Kitty Wells, Burl Ives... . Phil Harris was a good friend of mine; he also was from Indiana."

One of your most requested covers?

"'Rocky Top.' I did that song three shows a night at the Captain's Table. People would come into Nashville by the busloads to hear 'Rocky Top.' It's like when you go to Philadelphia, what are you going to order?"

A Philly cheesesteak sandwich.

"You got it."

Name a few of your more prestigious appearances?

"Well, I'm showing my age, but I was on 'Ted Mack & The Original Amateur Hour.' I also was on 'Hee Haw.'"

Trilly, as a teenager, I'd watch "Hee Haw" because of the bevy of scantily-dressed country girls that were featured. My dad was a big fan, too.

"I was invited to go on 'Hee Haw' because of that reason, but I wouldn't put on what the other women were wearing. I didn't want to exploit myself that way."

You're absolutely right; ahem, that part of the show was shamelessly sexist. What I really enjoyed was "Hee Haw's" highbrow humor – pure comedic genius. What instruments do you play?

"Banjo, guitar, harmonica, piano, mandolin, dulcimer and fiddle. I'm self-taught on all of them. I've never read music. I basically got nurtured at Judy's Music Studio. He taught me by ear because he couldn't read music either."

He?

"Harold Judy; he hand-made this double-neck guitar back in the 1950s. When I was on the road, I was endorsed by Gibson Guitar Co.; I want to show you something. Do you know what that is?"

An electric guitar.

"Take a closer look."

Oh, my gosh; the shell of it is made from a bedpan!

"Gibson gave me that. They once said, 'Trilly, if we'd put strings on a bedpan, you could play it.' It's porcelain; they had to use a diamond drill bit to get everything in there so it wouldn't shatter. You've heard of Willie Nelson's 'On the Road Again.'"

Sure.

"I wrote 'On the Commode Again.'"

One of your toughest gigs.

"Bud & Swede's in Watseka, Ill.; I was about 12. I'll never forget going on stage that evening."

Why's that?

"President (John F.) Kennedy was assassinated earlier that day."

Odd gigs?

"Twice, I've played 'Here Comes the Bride' on the harmonica at outdoor weddings."

Favorite instrument?

"Banjo; it's happy."

Life after Nashville?

"I was in (Las) Vegas for 10 years. When my husband passed away, it was kind of like, 'I'm done.' He'd been with me since I was like 10. I came back home to Indiana in 2000."

How did you find Kouts?

"My mother's side of the family was from Kouts. We spent all the holidays here."

You've come out of retirement.

"That's right. And I'm picking up more nursing homes and festivals all the time."

* * *

Trilly still has a ton of pizzazz. She's a professional entertainer and a crowd pleaser whose only regret is that she never performed for a president of the United States. But maybe she has and doesn't realize it.

Envision little Trilly Cole of Hammond belting out "I'll Fly Away" at Bud & Swede's on the evening of Nov. 22, 1963.

Corey Hagelberg *(July 2013)*

"...Last night me and Kate we laid in bed talking about getting out
Packing up our bags maybe heading south
I'm thirty-five we got a boy of our own now
Last night I sat him up behind the wheel and said son take a good look around
This is your hometown"
– Bruce Springsteen

As part of the Study Abroad Program, Corey Hagelberg traveled to Italy in 2004. Later that year, he co-organized a volunteer effort to help rebuild Bosarge Park in Bayou La Batre, Ala. after Hurricane Katrina had destroyed it. In 2006, he earned his BFA in sculpture at Ball State University. In 2011, he received his masters of art in printmaking at BSU.

But Hagelberg's hometown is Miller and he plans on sticking around. He just turned 30 on June 30 and lives on top of a dune overlooking Lake Michigan with Kate Land, two cats and a black lab pup named Rita.

I had to ascend 86 steps to get to the two houses Hagelberg purchased about a year-and-a-half ago for a total of $24,000. Every step of the way was a joy. The property is an ecological wonder.

* * *

High School?

"Andrean," he said. "After earning my bachelor's at Ball State, I took four or five years off to build commercial playgrounds for my dad. I worked in about 30 different states, spending almost all my time on the road.

"Our three- or four-person crews spent a lot of time in Louisiana, Alabama Texas, New York.... I worked on many Indian reservations. A lot of poor areas where we would kind of get the sense of community development happening as we were building a playground. You could see the energy that surrounded it. People wanted to talk to us. For the first time, I got a feel for working in a community and understanding what certain actions could do."

It all ties into what is going on in Miller right now.

"Yes, we're hoping the community develops around the art gallery we built on Lake Street. We're beginning to see how people use those places that we've created to start conversations about the community, which is really what it's all about."

Tell me more.

"I get a good sense the people in Miller that are kind of running the arts and creative district are looking for youth to come in and join them. There's a diversity in this area. Not only bio-diversity, but a cultural diversity as well, that is really unique, I think."

These houses you've purchased?

"They're both nice houses and you can tell they were extremely nice houses in their day. They were built for entertaining and they're isolated. They were abandoned for five years. The people living here suddenly moved out leaving almost all their possessions including a lot of antiques.

"During the five years they were abandoned, the houses were basically torn apart. Almost all the antiques were stolen. We did find a couple of really amazing objects. All the copper was taken out. The walls were tore out. There was a fire set in this house. All the windows were boarded up. I had to redo all the plumbing and heating systems."

What were some of the treasures you did find on the property?

"A little creamer from the Hotel Gary, old sewing machines, silver.... The entire library was left untouched. This book is called 'Cradled in the Dune Lands' written and signed by Jeanette Vaughn Konley. She was the Indiana Poet Laureate from 1958 to 1959."

Does the Miller Historical Society have its own museum?

"Not yet. There is talk of redoing the Miller Town Hall into a museum. They do have a collection of historical artifacts and documents."

That really piques my interest about the original owners. I wonder what happened to them?

"Well, it was two gay guys and one of them eventually died. Then, I believe the other got sick and had to find another place to live. Those guys really cultivated this property. Everything was elegantly gardened. As we remove all the invasive plants, we find beautiful hostas, daylilies, flowering trees.. ."

Are you going to rent out the other house?

"Kate and I have made it into an artist's residency. We feel that we were very lucky to get these houses. We feel that we should share them. We want to help artists and the community."

Very nice. You know, Corey, writers are artists, too.

"The last two people who stayed here were writers. One of them is a poet and the other a writer of fiction. So far, we've had two writers and three painters stay here."

How much does it cost to live here for a week or a month?

"At this point, there's no charge. Some of the artists help us with our gardens. What we have here is a lifetime project."

This place is an Eden, and you got it for a song, but you've put a lot of work into it.

"Our friends and family were generally very supportive when we took this project on. Our neighbors were ecstatic. Some of Kate's friends from other parts of Indiana were very skeptical when she told them she was moving to Gary to buy and rebuild a couple of abandoned houses. But when they came to visit, they were shocked by how beautiful it is here and how amazing all the people are."

You mentioned your neighbors.

"Right below me is a young artist named Cullen B. Daniel; you'll have to meet Cullen. He runs the Miller Beach Historical Society. (Environmental activist) Lee Botts is one of my neighbors. That wooded area you see out the window is all Shirley Heinze (Land Trust). Green Heron Pond sits over there.

"A couple of years ago, there were quite a few abandoned houses around here. But in the last year or so, people are moving back in. People who have a passion for gardening and for focusing on the appearances of their houses. There's a lot of good energy happening in this neighborhood right now. Artists have the ability to see possibilities that others sometimes can't."

Your art?

"Do you know the process of wood cut? What I do is carve these blocks, then roll ink on the surface and then put the paper down and rub the back. It's kind of like a big stamp. Most of my work intertwines industry and the Dunes. This specific wood cut book shows the Calumet River which starts in Marquette Park."

Wow, a 12-feet long, hand-carved book. Read it to me.

"Sure: 'The headwaters of the Grand Calumet River originate from a small lagoon in the pristine dunes near the southern shore of Lake Michigan. The word Calumet means pipe, and refers to the one the Ilihiwek Indians smoked with the French missionary Father Marquette as a universal sign of peace. Today, near the site of this historic ceremony, where the river enters into an area of heavy industry, the Grand Calumet River disappears into a pipe.'"

Elegance in simplicity. Corey, your book tells quite a story.

* * *

While touring the property, we munched on a few daylily blossoms as we meandered through lush ferns just below a canopy of pines and oaks. My mind drifted. And in my reverie, I thought about how lucky we all are to live in Northwest Indiana where what's left of the Dunes and Grand Kankakee Marsh are but 40 minutes apart.

And it was good to feel the energy exude from young Kate Land and Corey Hagelberg.

Mike Poore *(April 2009)*

"You dislike the Emancipation Proclamation and, perhaps, would have it retracted. You say it is unconstitutional; I think differently."

– Abraham Lincoln, from a letter written to his longtime friend, James Conkling, Aug. 26, 1863

Mike Poore is a native Ohioan who lives in Indiana and works in Illinois. We sometimes debate whether John Chapman, better known as Johnny Appleseed, was from Ohio or Indiana.

Neither of has researched the truth because both of us know we're right. Besides, we enjoy arguing with each other.

Poore, 42, lives with his three mix-breed dogs in Hobart and teaches seventh-grade social studies at McKinley Junior High School in South Holland, Ill., and also is a gifted author whose short fiction has been published in numerous literary magazines throughout the United States.

* * *

"I'm from Wright brothers territory," Poore began. "Troy, Ohio, is my hometown; it's a little bit north of Dayton. Troy used to be the biggest airplane producer in the world through World War I."

Childhood?

"Well, my mom and dad and step dad were always straight up with me about the fact that I was adopted. I've never really researched who my biological parents are. So, I can be from royalty if I want. But I was conceived in 1967; I figure I'm the offspring of flower children."

Mike, I've run two marathons in Ohio. Coincidentally, one was near Dayton and the other in Athens, Ohio, where you went to college (Ohio University). When I talked to folks from Dayton, they sounded similar to people from Northwest Indiana. The folks from Athens had strong southern accents. It was like two different states. Athens was breathtakingly beautiful, by the way.

"Ohio University is called the 'Harvard on the Hocking (River).' Troy is located in the plains. The Athens area is like a little piece of West Virginia; it's very Appalachian. Most of the people lead lives close to the bone. You drive just five minutes out of Athens and you'll see little cracker-box houses with 15 people living in them and the parents probably don't send their children to school.

"It's like Peabody Coal came into some of those little towns, took everything, and then left. A generation later, people still live there, but there is nothing there.

"I drove a taxi while living in a set of apartments located in Athens; they were kind of like the projects for Appalachia."

Did you go to college to become a teacher?

"No, I majored in journalism. I had a really good time in college for about two years. After two years, Ohio University invited me to take some time off."

Huh?

"I flunked out. I went back to Troy where I worked as a waiter and at a bookstore. I went back to college at about the age of 22 and got a degree in education."

What changed your mind?

"I talked to people who had gone to work for newspapers, and most of them liked their jobs, but it didn't sound like what I wanted to do. I thought about all the fantastic teachers I had in Troy. They always looked like they were having a good time."

Social studies in South Holland?

"I focus on early American history up to the Civil War and I also teach the U.S. Constitution. We take the kids to Springfield (Ill.) for a field trip; they really enjoy the Abraham Lincoln Presidential Library and Museum."

Mike, let's switch to your writing career; you've had short stories published in Northwest Review, Greensboro Review, Southern Review, Baltimore Review, Pacific Review, North Dakota Quarterly, Carolina Quarterly, Story Quarterly, Glimmer Train, Asimov's, Second Writes, Fiction, The McGuffin and Talebones – just to name a few.

You've been featured on Chicago Public Radio and received Honorable Mentions in Year's Best Fantasy and for a 2006 Fountain Award.

"Did I tell you I was arrested for grave robbing in Louisiana?"

Those are some prestigious literary magazines on you're resume. Glimmer Train, for example, receives thousands of submissions per month and might accept two.

"There was a time when I was having trouble getting published. This is kind of terrible, but I got to thinking, 'What if I tried to publish my story about the guy who got hit by lightning 600 times under a minority pen name?'"

Yeah?

"Carolina Quarterly bought it right up."

And your pseudonym was?

"Arlo Ramirez."

Your writing style sometimes reminds me of T. C. Boyle. One of my favorites is your story about the alligator that gets inside of a Wal-Mart.

"If it hadn't been for a few writers like T. C. Boyle, the short story would have went the way of the dodo bird."

Short stories were the television shows of the 1930s.

"As late as the 1950s, Kurt Vonnegut would sell a short story for $5,000. And that's when you could make it on a salary of $15,000 a year."

If you could survive as a writer, would you give up teaching?

"John Grisham can make his living off of writing; the rest of us probably have something else going. Jeff, you're the only person I know who has had the courage to do that."

Yeah, John's made a few bucks. But he's pretty good, huh?

"Frankly, if I gave up teaching, I would miss my kids. On one hand, I don't have children. On the other hand, I have 150 kids in South Holland."

You're working on a novel called "Up Jumps the Devil."

"Yes, I have a feeling about this one. It's basically a biography of the devil as an American folk character. It goes back through American history. It looks at instances where people might ask, 'What if the devil had tempted Abraham Lincoln as a young man?' or 'Would the devil have been involved as a radical character during the music scene of the psychedelic sixties?' 'What would the devil think of today's society where everybody seems hypnotized by their televisions, all the while the government, big business and banking are getting away with murder behind our backs because we no longer know how to protest?'

"In the prologue, the devil has a reality TV show where he tempts ordinary people to do terrible things they wouldn't normally do. He has this huge bank account."

Like Boyle often does, you've incorporated some famous people from our past.

"Bluesmen Robert Johnson and Lead Belly appear in the story. Richard Nixon appears. The devil gets inside of President John F. Kennedy and lives his lifestyle for a few years – has the time of his life. And then he's surprised to find himself assassinated.

"He also gets involved with George Washington and sort of helps the American Revolution happen. The Ku Klux Klan is very much in it; the devil is a very big supporter of the Klan, of course."

History is a perfect fit for you to write about.

"A lot of people don't know about the period right after the Civil War; it was almost as violent as the war itself. Terrorism was committed on African-Americans in the South. There were wholesale massacres and murders – you know, the part of history our 'white-bread' schoolbooks don't like to talk about."

Are any of your students African-American?

"Ninety-eight percent of them."

Two of your favorite authors?

"Ted Kosmatka, who is an up-an- coming science fiction writer, and Kurt Vonnegut."

A pair of Hoosiers.

"What about you?"

Toni Morrison, Ambrose Bierce and Sherwood Anderson come to mind.

"Three Buckeyes."

Mike, I beg to differ. Anderson was born and raised here in the Calumet Region. He wrote a book of short stories about his hometown called, "Whiting, Indiana."

* * *

Mike Poore is my kind of guy – a left-handed, red-haired stepchild who sometimes can be found out in left field.

John Chapman was born in Massachusetts on Sept. 26, 1775. He died in 1845 and is buried along the St. Joseph River near Fort Wayne.

In between, "Johnny Appleseed" spent much of his life in Ohio.

Charlie Capek *(Sept. 2013)*

Scotty Lundegaard: (finishing supper) *"May I be excused?"*
Jerry Lundegaard: *"Ya done, there?"*
Scotty Lundegaard: *"Yah. Can I go out?"*
Jean Lundegaard: *"Where ya goin'?"*
Scotty Lundegaard: *"Just to McDonalds."*
Jerry Lundegaard: *"Be back at 9:30."*
Wade Gustafson: *"He just ate – he didn't even finish! He's goin' to McDonalds instead of finishin' here."*
Jean Lundegaard: *"He sees his friends there. It's OK."*
Wade Gustafson: *"It's OK, MAC–Donalds. Heh. Whaddya think they do there? They don't drink milkshakes, I assure you."*
– from the 1996 film "Fargo"

Charlie Capek lives in Schererville and teaches the laboratory part of a food microbiology course at Purdue Calumet in Hammond.

Capek also is a tremendous artist who enjoys ballroom dancing. Being ambidextrous, he can paint, write or throw a baseball with either hand.

Our interview took place at the Lake County Library on U.S. 30.

* * *

"I come from a rural area in southeastern Minnesota," Capek began. "When I left, there were only four stop lights in Filmore County."

Did you have scads of Scandinavian folks for neighbors in Filmore County?

"Yes; Swedes, Germans, Norwegians…. In Filmore County we still celebrate Syttende Mai (May 17) which is Norway's Constitution Day. During the festivities, ethnic dishes such as lutefisk are served. Our Old

Order Amish are also a significant part of the population and valued craftsmen."

Lutefisk?

"Lutefisk is cod that is 'cooked' by soaking it in lye or sodium hydroxide. Molecularly, it changes the proteins. After the cod has been soaked in lye, you rinse it. My aunt had a good phrase after she tried lutefisk for the first time."

What was that?

"'It tasted just as bad coming up as it did going down.'"

What ethnicity is Capek?

"Czechoslovakian. The surname Capek is about as common in the Czech Republic as Smith or Jones is here."

Other memories of Minnesota?

"My brother and I used to spend the summers working on my uncle's dairy farm. What a blast we had when we were kids. The river fishing in Filmore County is phenomenal. It's known for its trout. We enjoyed inner tubing in the Root River. There were underground caves where you could go spelunking."

High school?

"I went to a couple of different high schools. I won't mention their names, but one of them is one of the recognized 'hockey factories.' Here in Indiana, it's all about the high school basketball tournaments. Let me tell you, come to Minnesota during the state hockey tournaments. It's Hoosier Hysteria on steroids."

Your parents?

"My mom was a research assistant at the Mayo Clinic in Rochester and a long-time librarian. My dad was a professor in linguistics and taught courses such as Old English and Old High Dutch.

"With our parents' encouragement of reading, my brother and I boosted the book circulation significantly at every library we used. One of the things I really appreciate about this area is the terrific libraries."

College?

"My undergraduate degree is from the University of Minnesota. I have my master's from Purdue Cal. I majored in biology."

Your art?

"The art is something I have been doing since I was 11. I do some portraiture, but the majority of my work is landscapes. This particular painting is a combination of woodcut printing and watercolor painting. I've incorporated the wood grain pattern as part of the overall painting design, and have the woodcut layers as a skeleton. The watercolor 'fleshes out' the rest of the painting. The contrast between the opacity and bare-bones effect of the woodcut layers, and the brilliance of the watercolor, which can range from transparent to near-opaque, really adds to the painting's three-dimensional effect."

I've never seen anything like that.

"I may have invented a new art form by incorporating the wood grain pattern into a watercolor painting.

"My portrait of horses, 'Brown-Collar Workers," will be exhibited in the 64 Arts National Exhibition at the Buchanan Center for the Arts in Monmouth, Ill. this month. 'Heartland Evening' will be in the Faber Birren National Color Award Show at the Stamford Art Association in Connecticut. 'Wild Child,' my portrait of a young girl with her pet rooster, won Best of Show in a national exhibition at the Salmagundi Club in New York several years ago."

Very impressive. Ballroom dancing?

"I started ballroom dancing about 10 years ago and I wish I would've started 10 years before that. One of the great things about Northwest Indiana is the number of really good dance studios and ballroom dance teachers. Tim Dustin teaches classes at the Lincoln Center in Highland. Even if you think you have two left feet, Tim is a great teacher and it's marvelous fun."

Food microbiology?

"It's a really well-designed class. Each week, we go through a particular exercise. We actually have the students go out and find examples of fresh, perishable foods that they can test for particular pathogens as well as spoilage microorganisms. By the end of the course, the students are able to do their own mini scientific Consumer Reports testing of food samples."

What kinds of jobs would your students get in that particular field?

"Anything to do with quality control, health departments, testing laboratories.... We want our food to be safe. You're familiar with the term 'shelf life.' That's very important to a lot of the testing we do.

"You remember the case a couple of years ago where the Peanut Corporation of America had areas where birds could get inside the roofs. The facility wasn't sealed off properly from the outdoors. It turned out that they shipped out a lot of peanut butter that contained salmonella. A lot of peanut butter paste went into products that were shipped to schools and nursing homes. Deaths occurred."

Pigeon poop in your Peter Pan will do that.

"Exactly."

Charlie, on the other hand, when I first started hearing adults use the word "Sal Monella," I figured they were referring to a member of the Italian side of my family. I mean, my brother and I were known to eat Easter eggs after they'd sat next to the heat register for two weeks. We never got sick.

When I was in grade school, I remember one kid who had something called asthma. Nowadays, every kid has asthma. It's my hypothesis that today's youth don't spend enough time outdoors building up immunities.

"That's been documented to be true. As far as building up a healthy immune system, yes indeed, early exposure to dirt is a good thing."

* * *

An interesting and talented man, Charlie Capek.

Rosemary Gard *(Sept. 2013)*

"Tko istina gudi, dobije gudalom po prstima."
(All truths are not to be told.)
– Croatian proverb

During Gary's Golden Jubilee in 1956, Rosemary Babich rode on a float and in the back of convertible along Broadway in downtown Gary. Croatian Queens do that sort of thing at parades.

Today, she goes by Rosemary Gard and has written and published a pair of novels that are heavily linked to her ancestors. She is currently working on a third book to complete the trilogy.

Gard lives with husband Bob in Crown Point; they have raised two adult children.

* * *

Age? I have to ask, it's a part of my job I really hate.

"I'm 75," she said. "My plan is not to die in a nursing home, but in my young lover's arms in the south of France."

Oui, oui Madame.

"I was born in Gary, Indiana at 2645 Van Buren. My mother, from the Old Country, delivered me herself. That area was once known as 'The Patch.' My brothers were 20 years older than I. It was like growing up with three dads."

That would mean your siblings were born before 1920. That poverty-stricken area was probably still referred to as "The Patch" when they were children.

"They resented being Slavic, I'm sure. They were called garlic eaters and hunkies. My brothers attended Froebel High School. I graduated from Lew Wallace. It was a great school and I loved all my teachers.

"But my parents were immigrants and they didn't want me to go to college. I was supposed to get married, have children and clean the house. One of the counselors at Lew Wallace, Violet Street, cried. I believe Violet lived in the Gary Hotel back then."

A different era.

"My father was Croatian and my mother was Czechoslovakian. Mother learned to read English; my father never did learn to read or write English – he could sign his name. Dad came to this country at 13 by himself using a 75-year old man's passport. They looked the other way."

When did Bob enter your life?

"I dated Bob when I was 12. I lied and said I was 16. He eventually found out how old I really was, but came back when I was of age because I was so fascinating."

This has the makings of a novel in itself. Tell me more, please.

"When my parents realized that I was serious about him, my mother asked: 'What is he?' I said: 'English, Irish, French, German... .'"

Mama's reply?

"'Oh my God, a hillbilly.' They sent me to Yugoslavia for three months."

I'm tellin' you, this has the makings of a real page-turner.

"I slept on a straw bed, dirt floor, cooked on a clay stove... . But all the men were in love with me. Our house was above the barn. When I came out on the stairway, it was like looking off of a balcony. I was serenaded. They brought me gifts. You want to know what my sex appeal was?"

Your drop-dead gorgeous looks and voluptuous figure?

"They knew if they married me they were automatically an American citizen. There went my sex appeal."

What about Bob?

"I married him. He got drafted a few months later and was sent to Italy. I went with Bob; that year in Italy was the happiest year of my life. It was our honeymoon.

"I watched a movie the other day and I yelled from downstairs up to Bob, 'I'm being nostalgic and I'm crying.' He says: 'Oh, God you're watching an Italian movie.'"

Life after Italy?

"We moved to Glen Park. When we were in California visiting one of my brothers, Bob saw a truck at a dealership. People were buying lunches from it. Bob said: 'I think I want to do that in Gary.'

"When we got back home, Bob lined up all the dealerships and businesses before we ever bought the truck. Then we drove back to California, bought the custom-made truck, and went into business. That was in the early '60s."

This truck must have been what we called a roach coach during the '70s and '80s in the steel mill.

"'Bob's Mobile Lunch and Coffee Wagon' was the best business we ever had. I prepared all the food. Bob would buy doughnuts from the Tolleston Bakery owned by Mr. Angotti. He paid 60 cents per dozen for them fresh out of the oven. Bob also would go to the Peerless factory in Tolleston and buy potato chips hot off of the assembly line."

How long was "Bob's Mobile" in existence?

"About 10 years. While we were doing that, we opened up the art gallery in Miller. I slept like three hours per day back then. We had a coffee house below the art gallery. There was a $1 cover charge after 8 p.m. because we had folk singers. We sold juicy t-bone steaks for $3."

What happens next on Bob and Rosemary's excellent adventure?

"We moved to Crown Point in the early '70s where we sold antiques and jewelry. I made necklaces from antique jewelry. Our store was in back of the old jail. Bob has sold antiques in several locations in Crown Point through the years."

Have either of you held 9 to 5 jobs since you've been married?
"Never."

Your writing career?

"I started out writing feature articles for the Glen Park Herald, kind of like you do, but not as good."

The "Destiny" series?

"Katya, the heroine, is partly based on my mother. 'Destiny's Dowry' is the first book. Katya is born in 1892 as was my father. It takes place in Yugoslavia. It's a mystery with a history. Fact-based fiction. My mother was a healer, so Katya is a witch who can cure people."

Tell me more.

Katya is born in a convent and is eventually raised in a village where she does not belong. When she is 15, she is sold to a Turk. She escapes from the Turk and meets a band of gypsies who help her find where she really belongs.

"'Destiny Denied' is a continuation. The final book of the trilogy will be when Katya emigrates to Gary."

You were turned down by several publishers.

"Yes, they wanted a sexy cover and they wanted sex inside the book. Well, of course my mother had sex, but I didn't want to dwell on that kind of thing. So, after seven or nine of them turned me down, I said to hell with them and I self-published."

How has that worked out?

"I won a Finalist Award in the Reader's Favorite category for 'Destiny's Dowry' and a five-star review with a Gold Medal for 'Destiny Denied.'"

Do you have a title picked out for book three?

"'Destiny's Dance'" because that's what life is – a dance. We go in circles."

Final thoughts?

"Jeff, I was the only Croatian-American to show up at (Indiana University Northwest) when they had International Day. I was invited and told to bring my books. There were all these Serbian groups there and no one to speak for the Croatians.

"Here I am at the microphone in front of this sea of Serbs and I'm thinking they're not going to like or care about what I have to say. But I went ahead and read an excerpt from 'Destiny's Dowry.'"

And?

"I sold books to Serbian-Americans."

I think that's great.

"You see, it's yet another generation. Most of the hardcore old-timers are gone."

* * *

In 1913, under the same circumstances, the character Katya probably wouldn't have received the warm reception Rosemary Babich Gard received at IUN.

It's our destiny; we go in circles.

Dave Mueller *(Dec. 2013)*

"From the shards and midden heaps of the past, you can find nuggets that will tell you what life was really like."
– Jean Shepherd

To me, Dave Mueller has the looks and voice of Kris Kristofferson. He is the owner-operator of Paul Henry's Art Gallery located next door to the Towle Theatre at Hohman Avenue and Sibley Street.

The gallery also is a hardware store which was started by Dave's great-grandfather, P.H. Mueller. With its wooden floors, ancient cash register and antique glass display cases, it's one of the most nostalgic buildings in Northwest Indiana. If you don't buy a painting from Mueller, he will be glad to sell you a hacksaw, fan belt, putty knife or padlock.

Mueller, 67, lives in Hammond with his wife, Rita. He is a graduate of Hammond High School and Knox College where he earned a degree in environmental biology.

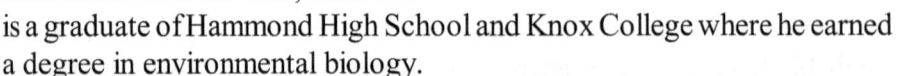

* * *

"My great-grandfather started this place in 1887," Mueller began. "Then it came down to my grandfather and his brother. They had the place until the early '60s. Then, it was passed to my dad and his brother, and then me."

Was the business strictly a hardware store?

"Along with the hardware store, it also was a sheet metal shop. That was this room; 17 guys worked back here when it was going good in the '20s. That went on until 1939.

"My grandfather and his brother weren't making it during the Great Depression; they were losing money every year. In '39, they closed down the sheet metal shop and became a Dupont jobber – selling automotive paint. As you can see by all the colors of spilt paint on the floor, this was our mixing room."

How did that work out?

"It kept us going for 65 more years. I got out of the automotive paint business in '06."

Do you still have customers as far as the hardware business?

"Once in a while, somebody stumbles off the street looking for some crazy thing I might have. I'll sell a bolt, or a screw or a key from time to time. My focus now is the art gallery. I've kept the store in tact because it is a point of interest – people like it."

Was P.H. Mueller an immigrant?

"Yes, they came from Germany to Fond du Lac, Wis. When Chicago burned down, they went to Chicago. After all, they had to rebuild Chicago and P.H. was a tradesman. The family stayed in Chicago for about 15 years, then they came here in 1887."

In its day, Hammond was a shopping Mecca.

"Three things killed it. It was rust belt syndrome. It was a lot of the money moving south of the Little Cal. And then, you had the development of the shopping centers. Everybody points their finger: 'It was the trains.' No, it wasn't the trains. This place thrived many, many decades with trains."

Woodmar and River Oaks were probably telltale signs of things to come.

"That was the beginning of the end. By '75, downtown Hammond was a shell of its former self. Downtown Hammond was way bigger than Southlake Mall. You had Penney's, Woolworth's, Goldblatt's, Minas and hundreds of other storefronts."

Jean Shepherd?

"A lot of people from this area had great careers in all different walks of life: athletics, business, science, music, the arts.... Jean Shepherd, is somewhere near the top of that. Not only was he a brilliant writer, but he managed to capture our personality second to none.

"Some people resented the way Shepherd portrayed us. It's like looking in the mirror and not liking what you see. He would come back and speak at IUN and people in the audience would heckle him. His humor was very dry and sardonic – Jean Shepherd was one of us."

What made you decide to make an art gallery out of this place?

"When we were getting out of the paint business, my wife and I wanted something that wasn't accounts receivable. We had to have something that didn't necessitate a great amount of investment. When I was in the automotive paint business, I had to have at least $200,000 worth of inventory."

How long has the art gallery been in business?

"Five years; we're still building up our customer base."

Tell me about Thursday nights here at Paul Henry's Art Gallery.

"That's Acoustic Night. Four hours of live music and a potluck dinner for five bucks. It's the best deal in town. I set up about 50 chairs and we get crowds of about 60 to 90 people every Thursday. It starts at 7 p.m."

Dave, you display some very unique and fascinating pieces of work here.

"These walls showcase creative efforts by more than 170 artists. They are individual pieces of beauty assembled together within the building. All this creative energy concentrated together has an impact on people when they come here. I've watched people come in here for the first time who were awestruck as if they were inside a cathedral or something."

I really like this artsy enclave with the Towle Theatre, Paul Henry's Art Gallery and the sculpture across the street.

"It has potential. One of the really driving calls that I have is to see downtown Hammond begin to flourish as far as redevelopment. I'd like to see a viable and commercial neighborhood like we once knew. We'll never achieve the levels of the glory days. However, there is a lot of room to push forward and expand as a business district. Who knows? In another five years, you might see crowded sidewalks again."

* * *

Everyone needs to visit Paul Henry's Art Gallery at least once. It's really something to see. If you attend Acoustic Night and bring a side dish or play an instrument, it's $2 off the $5 cover charge.

And where did Mueller get the name Paul Henry's Art Gallery? Those were his great-grandfather's first and middle names.

The Good Earth

Terry McCloskey *(Nov. 2011)*

"I believe in the aims and purposes of the Izaak Walton League of America, and pledge my aid and support in the protection and restoration of America's soil, woods, waters, wildlife and wetlands..."
– Izaak Walton pledge

Terry McCloskey has been married to Elizabeth, a biologist with the U.S. Fish & Wildlife Service, for 28 years. The McCloskeys live in a very cool house that was built in 1874 in LaPorte.

McCloskey, 65, has helped save Gibson Woods as a nature preserve, was a badge-carrying warden for The Nature Conservancy and has been very active with Save the Dunes and the Shirley Heinze Land Trust in the past. He joined the Izaak Walton League of American in 1978 and has served as Indiana's IWLA president, and is currently treasurer of the Porter County chapter.

McCloskey is an esophageal cancer survivor who never smoked; his voice comes and goes.

* * *

"I was raised in Lansing, Ill.," McCloskey began. "I graduated from Thornton Fractional South High School. My dad had a gas station in the Hessville section of Hammond since 1938.

"In 1971, I opened up my own auto parts store. It went so well that, in 1973, we built onto my dad's gas station. We were there until 2000. We were on the west end of Gibson Woods."

Did you eventually move from Lansing to Hammond?

"Yes, I lived in Hammond for about 10 years. Liz and I moved here in 1984."

This place has a lot of character, and that's quite a "shack" across the street.

"It's called the Ruth Sabin Home. Her husband was with Gen. Sherman during the Civil War. Their only son was killed at Chickamauga.

"The Sabins owned an entire block here; they created a working farm. It was kind of like communism. Everyone worked according to their own ability and needs. The Sabins had a tremendous reputation in LaPorte."

When did LaPorte become a town or city?

"Legally, in 1832. Anybody who settled here before that was a claim jumper."

A squatter?

"Yes, there's a plaque near the Kentucky Fried Chicken that dedicates the Indian boundary line. Chesterton also has an Indian boundary. The Potawatomi were pretty good business people.

"When the Indians were moved west, the Potawatomi around here were allowed to stay because they never caused problems and a good number of them were merchants. The Indians were a very necessary transition for the white people who were coming here.

"The first ferry to cross the Kankakee River in LaPorte County was run by an Indian."

Tell me about your conservation efforts.

"My dad used to kid me about being a land conservationist."

Why's that?

"Because my grandfather, Raymond McCloskey, Sr., was superintendent of construction at Inland Steel Co. When he started working there in 1912, they were basically on the beach. I have photos of my grandfather's crews moving the beach houses away so they could build a new mill. Grandfather helped fill in six square miles of Lake Michigan."

The Kankakee River divides LaPorte and Starke counties.

"I've been very active on the Kankakee River Basin Commission. They invented the Wide Levee Land Utilization Committee back in 1982. I was the Izaak Walton representative on that committee.

"You see, there is a three-county drainage board which consists of LaPorte, St Joseph and Starke. They've become very proactive for conservation – silt traps, soil stabilization, planting trees... . We're trying do whatever we have to do to stop the sand from going into Illinois."

Good for you.

"We had been hitting a political wall on the Kankakee River up until two years ago, when a young man named Tony Hendricks was elected LaPorte County surveyor. He was able to work with the LaPorte County Drainage Board.

"One of the first things Hendricks did as a surveyor was study how well does the Kankakee River drain; he did flow studies. He found that the river drains too fast. So, flooding is not going to be solved by the old farmers saying, 'We have to dredge it.'

"The old-fashioned way of dredging was you wipe out one side so the equipment can get in, dig everything out, put it in a spoils bank and that's a dredge. That idea is now dead."

What methods are now being utilized?

"Bank stabilization; we remove trees that are about to fall into the river and use them as silt barriers. We'll take the logs to a place where there is a lot of erosion. We also plant native vegetation."

Tell me more.

"During the late 1990s, the (Army) Corps of Engineers gave the KRBC permission to construct about eight silt traps, which they did. But they never cleaned them. A 20,000-yard silt trap will fill up in six weeks."

But there's a new sheriff in town.

"When Hendricks got involved, he went back to basics. He figured if we're going to use silt traps, let's keep them cleaned out. That has now been agreed upon.

"At one time, recently, Starke County commissioners passed a resolution not to support selling any land in Starke County for conservation. They were that much opposed to the wide levee; they were that much opposed to anything else other than dredge, dredge, dredge. They didn't give a shit about sending their sand to Illinois."

Is the Yellow River, a tributary of the Kankakee, the culprit?

"One of the projects Hendricks is working on is a permanent silt trap and a pump on the Yellow River somewhere adjacent to the Kankakee Fish & Wildlife Area. Then, the sand can be placed on the Fish & Wildlife Area in such a way as to create dunes and swales."

Interesting.

"It would be great for shore birds and waterfowl. We're also working upstream with private landowners to stop erosion in the tributaries.

"One of the biggest landowners is the Pokagon Band of

Potawatomi. They currently have a restoration of about 1,200 acres near the St. Joe-LaPorte county line. It's actually the old Kankakee River channel."

It's in North Liberty. I've met with a direct descendant of Leopold Pokagon who is involved with that restoration project. Those wetlands actually reduce flooding in the area because water is retained on the band's property.

"Jeff, I'm a big believer in private land ownership. I would rather approach a man and his wife and talk to them about trying to protect their land with a conservation easement."

* * *

Before there was a Sierra Club, TNC, or Save the Dunes, there was an IWLA. Back in the 1930s and '40s, the "Ikes" were fighting for the restoration of the Grand Kankakee Marsh. For nearly 34 years, Terry McCloskey also has fought the good fight.

And it's good to know my Potawatomi friend, Mike Zimmerman, and his people, are reintroducing wild rice near the banks of the upper Kankakee.

Leopold Pokagon would be proud.

John Bryant *(Feb. 2010)*

"There's no farmer songs on that car radio
Just cowboys, truck drivers and pain
Well, this is my way to say thanks for the meal
And I hope there's no shortage of rain"
- Murray Mclauchlan

John Bryant, 68, married an "older woman." It wasn't until two weeks after he attended his future bride's first-year playpen birthday party, that he turned 1 year old.

John and Kathy Bryant graduated from Hebron High School in 1959. They have a Hebron address, but live on the Lake County side of County Line Road, making them Lowellians. They've raised three children.

John graduated from Purdue University with a degree in agribusiness management. He's a farmer.

* * *

"This farm has been in the family since 1854," John began. "We have just under 1,000 acres. It started out six 40-acre parcels. One of my ancestors paid the state of Indiana $1.25 an acre for it. It was part of the Arkansas Swampland Grant Act.

"The federal government gave the land to the states; the states were to sell the land and use the proceeds to pay for drainage. Well, Indiana sold the lands, but the money got embezzled and it was never used for drainage."

Wasn't Hebron known as the dredge capital of the world back in the 1870s?

"Yes; my ancestors on my mother's side worked on the dredges. During the 1920s and '30s, Kathy's grandfather, Olo Nichols, helped build seven of the bridges over the Kankakee River."

Tell me more about your ancestors.

"I have letters that my great-great-grandmother wrote to her son who was attending Indiana University during the early 1870s.

"In one particular letter, she wrote how the marsh portion of our property had caught fire; it was drier than hell that year. Most of it was meadow with haystacks; we didn't have tilled fields here then.

"More than 100 men from Hebron hauled barrels of water to the farm to fight the fire. One of them mentioned that he'd just heard all of Chicago had burned the same day."

Your thoughts on draining the Grand Kankakee Marsh.

"People had to eat. Back then, we didn't raise as much per acre as we do now. By the 1850s, one farmer – raising wheat, corn, beef, hogs and chickens --could feed 10 people, maybe. Over half the population was involved in agriculture in one way or another.

"Then, with mechanization, more people moved to the cities, but they still needed to be fed. Farmers in this area looked at the flooded marshlands as a good way to get fertility, and they didn't have to clear many trees."

How many people can a farmer feed today?

"Probably close to 100."

What do you grow today?

"Just corn and soy beans."

How many hired men?

"None."

John, you're pushing 70; you farm 1,000 acres by yourself?

"Yip."

Yikes.

"As a hobby, I've been remodeling a house that was built in the 1840s. It was owned by a broom maker before my family bought it in 1911. They moved it to a wooded four-acre site that was never really part of the main part of the farm.

"When they were digging the basement for the soon-to-be relocated house, they came across a skeleton."

Human?

"Yes, we have two sites on the property where we find a lot of artifacts, they're 5,000 and 6,000 years old. I plowed up two charcoal pits on a sand hill several years ago."

Once that house was relocated, who lived in it first?

"I had four unmarried great-aunts who were from Hebron; they used it for a summer place.

"When my dad and uncle were making homebrew during

Prohibition, and they heard the old maids were coming out to inspect the farm, they'd have to hide their stills.

"My dad and uncle also hired a herdsman named George Washington who lived here on the farm. George also was a bootlegger in Chicago, and, at one time, was a Pullman cook."

That's fascinating. There probably weren't too many people of color living in this neck of the woods during Prohibition. I mean, there aren't many in 2010.

"My uncle would ride up to Chicago with George when he'd check on his stills. My uncle hated the (Ku Klux) Klan."

And he loved homebrew. John, let's switch gears. You were an auctioneer for a while.

"Yes; I sold wrecked vehicles in Chicago. I remember selling 484 cars in four hours one morning."

Can you still "make that music," Col. John?

"One bid 50, 75, will you go two, will you go two, will you go two, now a quarter, 75, will you go 50, now 75, will you go three, will you go three, three? Three? Sold!"

Thanks, I needed that.

* * *

John was a key player in the group SCROD (South County Residents Opposing Dumps) during a seven-year fight against a proposed landfill that would have been placed near the Bryant farm.

Kathy was the first-grade teacher of one of my twin daughters. When I entered the Bryant home, she gave me a photo of my daughter that she'd saved for 20 years.

The twins were held back that year. A meeting was scheduled with Mrs. Bryant and her colleague, Mrs. Frank.

With a quivering voice, my wife said, "But, we're saving so Natale and Nicole can go to college."

Kathy replied: "You keep saving; the Manes twins will go to college and earn degrees."

Her words rang true.

For a guy like me, the story of the Bryant Family is a paradox. They were part of the draining and dredging of one of the grandest freshwater wetland ecosystems in the world.

The Bryants also did their parts helping to feed and educate my children.

Mary Catterlin & Amy Lukas *(Feb. 2013)*

"We said there warn't no home like a raft, after all. Other places do seem so cramped and smothery, but a raft don't. You feel mighty free and easy and comfortable on a raft."
– Mark Twain

During the 1860s, Huckleberry Finn and runaway slave Jim poled their way down the "Big Muddy."

In the 21st-Century, Mary Catterlin and Amy Lukas paddled their way around the "Big Lake."

While a college freshman, Catterlin had the trunk of a huge cottonwood hauled to her parents' backyard. Four years later, she and Lukas would paddle and sail all around Lake Michigan in that tree.

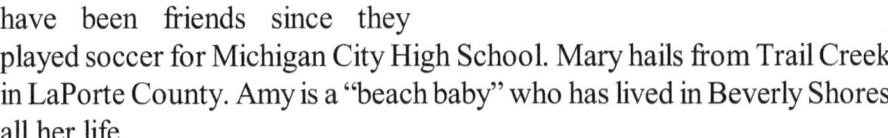

Catterlin and Lukas, 24, have been friends since they played soccer for Michigan City High School. Mary hails from Trail Creek in LaPorte County. Amy is a "beach baby" who has lived in Beverly Shores all her life.

Lukas attended MCHS, but could have gone to Chesterton High School because she lives in Porter County. Mary earned a degree in fine art at Indiana University. Amy earned a degree in biochemistry at Valparaiso University.

I recently met these adventuresome young ladies at the Hammond Marina where they were named "Paddlers of the Year" by the Northwest Indiana Paddlers Association.

* * *

"Amy and I both graduated from college in 2011," Catterlin began. "We took a year off and got ready for the trip last summer in 2012. Some people go backpacking around Europe after they graduate college; we circumnavigated Lake Michigan."

When did you have this epiphany?

Catterlin: "We were sitting around a bonfire one night talking about the boat and I said, 'We should go around Lake Michigan.' I was completely serious; Amy thought I was kidding, but I was serious from the very beginning."

When did that conservation take place.

Catterlin: "About a year into making the boat."

How long did it take to complete the boat?

Catterlin: "It took me four years; I was going to IU at the same time, so I'd work on it during my summer vacations and winter breaks."

You became quite adept with a chainsaw.

Catterlin: "For some of the major chainsaw work, I had a friend or family member who helped me, but pretty much, I just went into it head first. I did some research and made a few models, learning as I went along. Most of the work was done with an adze. The outriggers and two pontoons are fiberglass-foam. They were lightweight, durable and gave more stability to the boat. It was a sailboat as well."

But mostly you paddled.

Lukas: "Yes, we got a deal on some handmade, lightweight paddles. The brand name is Bending Branches. We got a few sponsorships for items such as life jackets, a water filter, water purifier, energy bars.... We also had friends and family contribute.

Catterlin: "I made topographical maps of Lake Michigan for people who gave to us. There is an example hanging on the wall."

Oh, my. You wood-burned that?

Catterlin: "Laser-etched."

Lukas: "Most of the maps say, 'Two girls and a tree named Makeba; thank you.'"

Makeba?

Catterlin: "The canoe is named after the calypso singer Miriam Makeba and Jacques Cousteau's boat 'Calypso.' It's a link to both of them."

What month did your journey begin?

Lukas: "July 1. We were guessing that it would take about three months."

How close was your prognostication?

Lukas: "We made it back to Beverly Shores 93 days later on Oct 1."

Amazing. You two are like modern-day versions of Meriwether Lewis and William Clark.

Lukas: "The last comparison someone gave us was Tom Sawyer and Huck Finn."

Catterlin: "We like Lewis and Clark better."

Lake Michigan is not to be taken lightly.

Lukas: "Growing up on the lake, we were aware of its potentials. It can throw up waves at any moment. We used a marine radio every day. We checked (the National Oceanic and Atmospheric Administration) for wave heights and direction."

Catterlin: "We always wore our life jackets and were very familiar with wave patterns and what our limitations were. Neither one of us were afraid to talk to the other person, like, 'I'm uncomfortable with this.'"

Lukas: "We're not thrill-seeking daredevils. We made intelligent decisions together. We also knew the capabilities of the boat we were in. Because Makeba is an open boat, we knew we couldn't be on the water if there were crashing waves."

How many days were you land lubbers?

Catterlin: "About 30. Kayakers could be out on the water where we couldn't."

Lukas: "On one of our weather days, we discovered a Scandinavian festival on Washington Island near Wisconsin."

Catterlin: "And there was a yacht club's annual beach party in South Milwaukee."

Your trek was taken in a clockwise direction.

Catterlin: "Yes, we started at Beverly Shores and headed toward the steel mills. Then, we went up through Door Peninsula and island-hopped to the (Upper Peninsula) cutting off Green Bay. That was about 16 miles of open water; we did that in one day."

Then what?

Lukas: "We followed along the U.P. We tried paddling underneath the Mackinac Bridge, but the current was a bit strong. We met a friend in the U.P. who trailered our boat over the bridge. Then we followed around to Little Traverse Bay."

Catterlin: "When we got to Grand Traverse Bay, it was really foggy so we had to go into the bay like 17 miles to the finger, which is called Old Mission. We camped at Old Mission in our tent and cut across the next day."

Day 93?
Lukas: "From Warren Dunes to Beverly Shores, about 21 miles."
What was your longest day?
Catterlin: "About 43 miles."
Paddling versus sailing?
Catterlin: "About two-thirds paddling and one-third sailing. We averaged 2 to 3 mph paddling; when we were sailing, maybe 4 mph, 5 was pushing it. The slowest we ever went was like 1 mph – seven miles in seven hours."
Lukas: "We usually did eight- to 12-hour days."
Food?
Lukas: "We ate donated energy bars every day. Luckily, they gave us seven or eight flavors so we didn't get sick of them."
Catterlin: "We mailed some of our food to ourselves."
Explain, please.
Lukas: "We had chosen like 13 different post offices around the lake which were within walking distances. We'd mail like a week's worth of food to ourselves via general delivery. Mary's parents mailed them for us."
How big is Makeba?
Catterlin: "Almost 11 feet long; she weighs 300 pounds."
Mechanical problems?
Amy: "We had a few leaks, but we brought marine caulk and epoxy with us."
What's next?
Both: "We'll think of something."

* * *

Some folks have dreams and bucket lists that never are fulfilled. For 93 days, Mary Catterlin and Amy Lukas lived theirs. You feel mighty free and easy paddling a dugout canoe.

Sandy O'Brien *(Apr. 2013)*

"Never doubt that a small group of thoughtfully committed citizens can change the world. Indeed, it's the only thing that ever has."
– Margaret Mead

As the crow flies, Sandy O'Brien's home is maybe a mile from the bustling intersection of I-65 and 61st Avenue in Hobart. The house isn't visible from Liverpool Road and I didn't spot her mail box when I pulled into the driveway. I did spot an automobile with an Obama bumper sticker and an environmental license plate, a flat of native plants, and a three-acre pond teeming with pied-billed grebes, hooded mergansers, mallards, ring-neck ducks and a blue-winged teal. The terrain surrounding the far side of the pond had recently been burned.

I knew I was in the right place.

O'Brien, a conservationist with a degree in biology, is a shy, humble and unassuming person. But when it comes to battling invasive species, the 54-year-old mother of three is a warrior queen.

* * *

Born and raised in Hobart?

"No, I lived in the Aetna neighborhood of Gary until eighth grade," she said.

I recently interviewed former Chicago White Sox slugger Ron Kittle for this column; he was from the Aetna area.

"Ron was in some of my classes; I haven't seen him since he became a major league baseball player."

Did you graduate from Hobart High School?

"Yes, then Purdue (University Calumet in Hammond)."

I realize girls athletics hadn't quite taken off in the early and mid-'70s, but did you play any sports for the Brickies?

"No, I was the kind of person who made bad grades in gym."

Nice spread you have here. How many acres?

"About 15, the pond is 25 feet deep. When it was dug, the clay went to the Gary landfill to provide daily cover between the layers."

Are you an angler?

"My husband and I don't fish much. We let the diving ducks do the fishing and once a year the osprey stop by. We also have kingfishers, green herons, blue herons and egrets that frequent the place – lots of wildlife.

"We're part of Hobart Marsh which is 1,000 acres of protected land. It's a lot of wetlands interspersed with dry ground."

Hobart Prairie Grove?

"I helped get it into the Indiana Dunes National Lake Shore expansion bill that passed in 1992."

Name a few of America's most unwanted invasive species.

"In the wetlands, it's definitely phragmites. You can probably add hybrid cattail right after that. In the woods, garlic mustard is one of the worst."

Now that you've burned near your pond, what will pop up this spring?

"Prairie grasses, wild white indigo, wild bergamot, yellow coneflower, lead plant, beard tongue, prairie dock, compass plant, resin weed... ."

You have clients who want their private lands managed.

"Yes, I do burns and take care of their invasive species problems. Then, I plant native species. Native landscaping is getting to be more popular these days. People are realizing how important it is to support our native insects because our alien landscaping doesn't. The native insects are what supports the native birds."

Sandy, on our way home from Bloomington after doing a presentation of the documentary "Everglades of the North: The Story of the Grand Kankakee Marsh," my co-producer Patty Wisniewski and I discussed the fact that unless a person is an American Indian living in this country, they are an invasive species.

"True. Humans have had an incredible impact on the planet to the point that we've almost ruined it."

The Potawatomi and Miami lived in harmony with Mother Nature along the Grand Kankakee Marsh.

"Yes, and there wasn't that many of them either."

While researching for our film, I read where one of the first school teachers in Porter County was told by an elderly American Indian that they didn't mind when a few whites moved to the area because they could trade with them and they could serve as interpreters. The aged Potawatomi also added: "But when the Europeans really commenced to coming, they came like the (passenger) pigeons."

"The Native Americans set up the ecology of this area by annual fire. The native flora, and to some extent fauna, depend on that fire because that's what we've always had here in Northwest Indiana. It's a fire-dependent ecosystem – the prairies, savannas and the wetlands. They all burned unless they were underwater or sheltered by water."

I'm sure you're familiar with The Nature Conservancy's Pembroke Savanna across the state line from Willow Slough. It is considered the best example of black oak savanna in the world. Sadly, only one-tenth of one percent of our black oak savanna survives on this entire planet. Why do you think it has thrived in Pembroke Township or Hopkins Park, Ill.?

"I don't know, but I've always wondered why all that good stuff is still there."

That area doesn't have a fire department; it's one of the most impoverished rural communities in the United States. Those folks burn their own garbage. Because of that, Pembroke Township has had accidental wildfires through the years.

"That's why! It makes so much sense. It hasn't changed since the Indians burned there. Wow."

Urban sprawl?

"The sprawl cycle is very bad for nature because you keep developing further out while further in, it's empty. At this point, 150,000 people have left the urban core and the first ring suburbs."

First ring suburbs?

"The communities that are closest to Gary, East Chicago and Hammond. Highland, Griffith, Lake Station and New Chicago all have lost people. Hobart probably would've lost people, but we've got the new development going in the south part of town which kind of makes up for the old northern part of the city.

"It's a bad cycle because you're depopulating and not investing in the northern communities while spending tax money on new roads that wouldn't be needed if the urban core communities were proper places to live. If people didn't need to run away from the urban core communities and the first ring suburbs we wouldn't need to be spending money on new infrastructure."

Is anything being done about this dilemma?

"(The Northwestern Indiana Regional Planning Commission) has a recent long-range plan, finally. One of the priorities is restoring the urban core communities. Michigan City is one of those urban core communities that is taking advantage of the plan."

I'd sure hate to see the area around the Kankakee River get swallowed up by sprawl.

"It could happen, and believe me, that Illiana Expressway is all about sprawl."

Hopes for the future?

"I hope we can restore both our natural areas and our communities."

Who could argue with that?

"The developers have been pretty much in charge of things, but they are starting to see opportunities in the urban core."

* * *

Most of the natural areas she takes care of are done on a shoestring budget because they aren't funded. But that doesn't deter Sandy O'Brien and her small group of thoughtfully committed citizens. Folks who roll up their sleeves, walk the walk, and celebrate Earth Day 365 times a year.

Bud Koeppen *(Aug. 2011)*

"The head is of monstrous size. The neck is short and strong, with a great hump between the shoulders; the legs are big and short, covered with very long wool.

"Upon the shoulders and around the neck and horns, there is a great black mane, falling over the eyes, and giving them a terrible appearance. ...The flesh of these beasts is very relishing and full of juice."

– Father Louis Hennepin

The above description of the American bison was written by Robert de LaSalle's diarist as the band of voyageurs canoed down the Kankakee River in December 1679.

Bernard Koeppen goes by Bud; I wish he'd go by Buffalo Bud. Along with his wife, Ruth, and brother, Wally, they operate Broken Wagon Bison. Their farm is located in Porter County, but has a Hobart address.

Koeppen, 59, graduated from the old Wheeler High School.

* * *

"My brother, Wally, and I are the third generation to farm this ground," Koeppen began.

Were you and Wally the first generation to raise bison?

"Yes, we started talking about it in 2002. In 2003, we purchased 10 on Thanksgiving weekend. There were seven bred cows, two heifer calves and one 18-month breed bull; his name is Big Bad John.

"Big Bad John is still here; I don't think we'll ever butcher him. He's our largest animal and probably the most cordial. When we bought him he weighed a little over 900 pounds."

How much does Ol' John weigh today?

"A little over a ton."

When you purchased the original 10 head, was it for monetary gain or simply a novelty.

"We planned on making money at it; we weren't making a great deal of money at the time because grain prices were so low for so many years. We were lucky to break even. We figured if we were going to lose money, we might as well make it interesting."

Is there a difference between a buffalo and a bison?

"No, the term buffalo is a nickname; they are technically an American bison. There are no American buffaloes. Bison aren't related to, say, a cape buffalo in Africa. It's kind of like prairie dogs; they're not a canine, they're in the squirrel family."

Tell me more about Broken Wagon Bison.

"We sell meat, hides, skulls, gifts and give tours."

I've eaten a buffalo burger or two. What cuts of meat do you sell?

"Our bison steaks are Swiss, sirloin, New York strip, tenderloin and rib-eye. We also sell arm, chuck, rump, round or sirloin tip. And we have ground bison, ground bison patties, bison brats, bison hot dogs, bison stew meat, bison short ribs, bison roast, bison lunch meat, canned bison meat, bison jerky... ."

"Buffalo Bud," I can't help but think of the shrimp fisherman, Bubba, in the film "Forrest Gump." I think he even mentioned shrimp Jell-O. Is buffalo meat healthy?

"A 3.5 ounce serving of cooked Bison meat has less fat, more protein, less calories, less cholesterol, more iron and more vitamin B12 than a similar-sized serving of beef, pork, chicken or sockeye salmon."

You wouldn't buffalo me, would you?

"At Broken Wagon Bison, we use no growth hormones or stimulants in raising our herd, and strongly oppose the use of these substances in the production of bison for meat."

Is this your retail shop?

"Yes, these are bison leather purses, handbags and clutches homemade by my wife. She also makes pillows, fur vests, hats, lampshades, wallets, jewelry... ."

Those are some mighty stout fence posts you have out there.

"The more remote you are, the less fencing you can get away with. We don't want our buffalo walking down the main drag of Wheeler. That would be a bad thing. A buffalo can jump six feet."

How fast can they run?

"A select animal can top out at about 50 mph. A whole herd can do about 35 mph. The old saying goes, 'Breakfast in Texas, lunch in Oklahoma and dinner in Kansas.' A herd of buffalo can cover some ground when they want to."

How big is your herd today?

"We have 83 buffaloes."

The American bison was all but wiped out.

"Supposedly the last free-roaming buffalo to be killed in Indiana was in 1830. The American Bison were saved by a few ranchers like Charles Goodnight. At the urging of his wife, he went out and captured calves and started his own herd."

* * *

The Indians of the Great Plains consumed the buffalo's flesh and also used the animals' bones, hide, hair, tail, sinew, dung, hooves, fat, ribs, bladder, beard, horns, brains, skull and teeth.

The market hunter only was interested in the hide. The carcass was left to rot.

As late as the 1850s, there were approximately 100 million American bison in North America. By the mid-1880s, their population was down to a few hundred.

The American bison is North America's largest native land mammal.

Other than humans, its only predators are grizzly bears and wolves.

Today, there are approximately 500,000 bison in both public and private herds in North America; there are about 15,000 animals that are considered free-ranging wild bison.

Bud and Wally Koeppen are members of the National Bison Association and have won conservation awards for their methods of pasture rotation at Broken Wagon Bison.

Joy Bower *(April 2010)*

*"...Though her words are simple and few,
Listen, listen; she's calling to you:
'Feed the birds, tuppence a bag,
Tuppence, tuppence, tuppence a bag.'"
– "Feed the Birds," performed by Julie Andrews
from the film "Mary Poppins."*

The Gibson Woods Environmental Awareness Center, in the Hessville section of Hammond, resembles a miniature Field Museum with stuffed waterfowl, fur bearers and fish mounted to the walls. It also features the remains of a 10,000-year-old mastodon found in Lake County.

The 131-acre Gibson Woods Nature Preserve, one of the Lake County parks, is a living museum showcasing rare flora and fauna. It also is the work place of Joy Bower. Before I could interview her, she had more important matters to address.

Joy Bower fed the birds.

* * *

"The juncos and tree sparrows enjoy the millet," Bower began. "The blue jays love the peanuts. We'll sit behind the one-way glass for the interview so we can watch the birds; the room also is wired for sound, so we can hear them, too."

Wow, this is nice, rocker-recliners.

"A gentlemen who worked at the La-Z-Boy warehouse donated them."

Joy, have you lived in Hessville your entire life?

"No, I graduated from Highland High School in '68. My husband, Dick, and I moved to Hessville in 1974."

You were associated with Gibson Woods before it became a park.

"Yes, I'm an avid birder; I have been since I was about 9 years old.

I'd ride my bike here in the summer and see all these really neat birds. Then, in the spring, I noticed plants that I hadn't seen before and I realized this wasn't just an empty lot; there was something different about Gibson Woods."

Who was Gibson?

"David Gibson was an early settler who ran an inn just west of the preserve in the mid-1800s. The inn accommodated travelers who went from Michigan to Chicago along one of the higher dune ridges; it probably was an old Indian trail at one time.

"Back then, most of the travel was done east and west. You couldn't go north and south because of all the water. Think about it, Ridge Road and old Route 30 were all east-west high-ground travel created after ancient Lake Chicago, the forerunner of Lake Michigan, retreated.

"The Michigan Central Railroad purchased the inn from Gibson in 1852 and used it as a station; it was the first railroad in Lake County and was built along the same high ridge where Gibson settled."

Looking through this glass wall gives one a bird's eye view of a very unique landscape.

"It's dune and swale. That's a swale right in front of us. Just beyond it, on that little ridge, is a dune. Just beyond that is another swale. Farther to the north there's a really large swale with bridges over it. It's like 130 acres of up and down, pretty much like it was 4,000 years ago. The topography is almost all sand deposits; there are only a couple inches of topsoil. The ecosystem here is considered a black oak savanna.

"This region was probably full of areas like Gibson, but most were obliterated. Everything in Lake County seems to get bulldozed down sooner or later.

"I think what prompted me to action was when I rode by here in the late '70s and saw a big 'For Sale' sign. I called Lake County Parks and they put me in touch with some people who they knew also cared about conservation. I'm an amateur photographer, so I just started taking pictures and gave slide show presentations to civic groups and anybody who would listen."

You eventually became a full-time employee.

"Yes; since '96."

Joy, you're a perfect example of a grassroots activist. Who else helped Gibson Woods survive?

"Initially, I was unaware there was a federal survey being done at that time. They were attempting to find out all the remaining natural places within the Lake Michigan Basin. Gibson Woods was rated very high.

"You might not think it, but some of the most significant areas were right in the Hammond, Gary and East Chicago, areas that had been bought up by various companies, but were never used; those areas were inadvertently preserved.

"The state also was looking at this property because they recognized the significance of it."

Name a few sand-loving native wildflowers and grasses that thrive here.

"Yellow coneflower, lady's slipper orchids, prairie cordgrass, and big and little bluestem. Over 300 species of plants have been identified in this preserve and more than 160 species of birds."

Threatened fauna sighted at Gibson?

"Franklin's ground squirrel and Blanding's turtle. The Karner blue butterfly is a federally endangered species. They like open areas where lupines can grow; that's all they feed on."

Like Monarch butterfly larvae feed only on milkweed.

"Yes; some species don't adapt well once we've destroyed their habitat. Without help, they're... ."

Doomed like the passenger pigeon?

"Yes. They were actually the most common bird in the world."

Who initially purchased the land from the railroad?

"The Nature Conservancy; they were willing to buy it in 1980 and hold onto it for a year."

Then what?

"The Lake County Parks and Recreation Department purchased the tract from TNC and it was dedicated by the state of Indiana as a nature preserve in November of '81."

Maintenance?

"We usually do a spring and fall controlled burn. Hopefully, that will bring back some of our wildflowers that have been lying dormant."

The city kids?

"This place is very eye-opening to them. Most of their 'woodland experiences' consist of what they've seen on television. They're fearful that an alligator is going to emerge from one of the swales."

Lions and tigers and bears, oh my!

"Once they realize they're not going to get devoured, they really get into it.

Another program we have is 'Mighty Acorns' where we get about a 100 fifth-graders from Morton Elementary to come out here three times a year; we're partnering with the Dunes Environmental Learning Center. The kids do two activities with their staff and then do a stewardship program with us."

Trails?

"We have a 1/2-mile loop, a 1-mile and a 2-mile. When I get a little frazzled, and I'm on my lunch break, I'll say, 'I gotta go take a walk in the real world.' Gibson Woods can be very soothing. Studies have been done on the subject; people need some kind of connection with nature.

"There is no fee to come to Gibson Woods. I hope more people continue to discover and explore us. We're still an unknown to some people right here in the neighborhood."

* * *

At about 1 p.m., on Sept 1, 1914, Martha was laid to rest in Cincinnati at the age of 29; she wore a handsome slate-gray blazer over a wine-colored sweater covering her ample breast. She was the last passenger pigeon on the face of the Earth.

Seeing Bower sprinkle millet and fill feeders with gray squirrels at her feet and finches inches from her face was like watching a latter-day St. Francis of Assisi. She was doing her part as a rare turtle sunned itself near a swale or a Franklin's ground squirrel scampered through the black oaks.

And the Karner blue clung to lupine for dear life.

Ed Gustafson *(Aug. 2013)*

"Borta bra men hemma bast."
("There's no place like home" – more or less.)
– Swedish proverb

Ed Gustafson, 83, is a lifelong bachelor who lives in Chesterton. He's also a Korean War veteran and a retired steel worker with a college degree who is a self-taught expert in geomorphology.

* * *

"I was born at St Margaret's Hospital in Hammond, but my parents were living with my dad's brother Axel in Lansing, Ill.," Gustafson began. "Later, we moved to Gary because Dad worked in the engineering department at U.S. Steel."

In what part of Gary did you live?

"We lived on Jackson Street. The same street that Michael Jackson's family lived on."

That means you lived in Midtown.

"No, not that part of Jackson Street. I lived in the white area. The Jackson family lived in the colored section. I remember taking a bus to kindergarten. Do you know what that word means?"

I know the Germans came up with the concept.

"Kinder means children and garten means garden. We moved to Chesterton after kindergarten. I graduated from Chesterton High School in 1948. We had 57 students in our class and 23 were Swedish. This was a very Swedish area. I'm named after my grandfather, Karl Edvard Gustafson – Edvard with a 'v.'"

Like the insane artist Edvard Munch who created the painting "Scream."

"Yes, and the great composer Edvard Grieg. But they were Norwegians."

Have you ever seen the classic film "I Remember Mama"?

"They also were Norwegians."

C'mon, Ed. Swedes, Norwegians, Danes, Finns, Swiss, Germans, Dutch – what's the difference?

"'I Remember Mama' was heartwarming, but I couldn't believe how the Norwegians talked about the Swedes in that movie. They were rivals, but they're actually closely related. About 1,000 years ago, Sweden, Norway, Denmark and Iceland all spoke the same language which was known as Old Norse."

Did you remember going to church with your mama as a boy?

"She made me. My father didn't go to church. I remember mama, ahem, I remember my mother liked a church in Porter that is now Methodist. It was Evangelical when it was built it in 1942."

When you wore a younger man's klader (clothes) were you a towhead?

"Oh, yes. Blond hair, blue eyes."

College?

"I attended Valparaiso University for five years; I wanted to be a history teacher. After two years of college, I decided I was too shy to be a teacher. I went to a very interesting place on the north side of Chicago called the Human Engineering Laboratory. I took six hours of intensive aptitude tests."

The results?

"They decided I should major in business and minor in music."

Your first job?

"When I was in eighth grade, I mowed lawns all summer. In high school, I worked at the A&P store in Chesterton. The Great Atlantic and Pacific Tea Company. There aren't many A&P stores around anymore. The one in Chesterton was built in 1921 and was in operation for 50 years. I loved working there.

"My maternal grandfather had a shop in downtown Chesterton. He re-upholstered furniture. Teagarden is not the original spelling of his surname; it was Americanized. Grandfather Teagarden was Pennsylvania Dutch which is actually German not Dutch. One of our ancestors – Abraham Teagarden – came over on the same boat as Jonathan Hager who settled Hagerstown, Md. I believe that was in 1740."

The Gustafsons?

"My paternal grandparents came from Sweden in 1882. They

settled near Attica, Ind. There's an old Swedish church they built down there. Back then, they had the services in the Swedish language."

The war?

"I graduated from Valparaiso University on May 31, 1953 and was drafted on June 11. I was in the signal corps, but was deferred for two years because I was in college. There was another young man from Chesterton named Bill who also was drafted. We went to Indianapolis for our physicals at the same time."

And?

"He was killed in Korea while I was in college. He was married to a Swedish girl and they had a baby. Bill is buried in the Catholic cemetery; he was Irish. I've visited his grave. His last name escapes me."

Life after your time in the service?

"My dad helped me get a job at U.S. Steel. I became a weigh master in the open hearth. It was shift work. I had to weigh the material that went into the furnaces. I also had to figure the percentage of yield of each heat. We had two sheets for each heat. One showed all the stuff they put in the heat, the other sheet showed all the stuff that came out of the heat. Usually about 87 percent of what they put in became steel. I worked at U.S. Steel for 30 years and retired."

Geomorphology?

"Yes, the study of the surface of the earth. I've been interested in hills, valleys and rivers since I was 10. I read a lot about it in the library in Gary. Did you know that anybody can take books out of the library at (Indiana University Northwest) if you have an Indiana driver's license? I think that's wonderful.

"I have 27 topographical maps. Here is the Chesterton quadrangle. The Valparaiso Moraine goes from 650 to 850 feet above sea level. Here are the kettle lakes."

Kettle lakes?

"The Chain of Lakes north of Valparaiso would be an example. Mink, Loomis, Wauhob and Long Lakes were formed when huge pieces of ice fell off the glacier. There are a lot of kettle lakes near LaPorte as well. That area also is at the top of the moraine which goes into Michigan.

"The St Lawrence River drains out the Great Lakes. Lake Erie flows into Lake Ontario, Lake Huron flows into Lake Erie, Lake Superior flows in Lake Huron. Lake Michigan and Lake Huron are the same lake. They are always at the same the level because they are the same lake. They didn't realize that when they named them."

You're a member of the Porter County chapter of the Izaak Walton League.

"Yes, it's a fine organization. Our president is married to a Swede."

* * *

Gustafson is a lifetime bibliophile who is currently rereading James Joyce's "Finnegan's Wake." As I interviewed him, I couldn't help but envision him playing the part of the hermit grandfather in the 1937 classic "Heidi."

But I didn't mention it because I know he would have admonished me, saying: "They were Swiss!"

Marty Lucas *(Sept. 2009)*

"There ain't any finer folks living than a Republican that votes the Democratic ticket."
– Will Rogers

I've always been perplexed by dirt-poor Republicans and well-to-do Democrats. But Will Rogers would have made a darn good interview for this column. And, I believe I've met a few folks who met his description in the quote about.

Martin Robert Lucas is a doctor of jurisprudence; he attended the Indiana University Maurer School of Law in Bloomington. He's also is a musician and environmentalist.

Lucas and his wife, Corinne, live in a century-old Victorian within the town limits of North Judson. His family has been in Starke County since the 1800s. Lucas also owns 580 acres just outside of North Judson that he calls Big Eastern.

* * *

How old are you?

"I don't give out my exact age," Lucas began. "That's just another thing identity thieves can use against you. As a lawyer, I suggest people lie about their age, keep 'em guessing."

That's interesting. What year did you graduate from North Judson High School?

"1973."

Marty, I'm more familiar with Lake, Porter, Newton, Jasper and LaPorte counties than I am with Starke. You were elected Starke County attorney. Do you mind stating what –

"Everybody knows I'm a Democrat."

This is probably a conservative area, right?

"Barack Obama won Starke County."

Really?

"I was raised as a Republican and was even a public party official in my time. But the Republican party has gone out of the nation. I do know some old-fashioned Republicans for whom I have a lot of respect. We have a senator in Indiana who is more conservative than I am, but I have a ton of respect for him. Dick Lugar is a fine statesman; I wish there were more Republicans like him."

Give me the dime tour of North Judson.

"North Judson's history is different than most small towns in Indiana. It had a lot of ethnic diversity that other places didn't have. There were a lot of Italian and Polish immigrants who settled here.

When I interviewed Verna Schrombeck, who was raised near here, she mentioned a couple of farm families that have for several generations raised truck crops. The surnames were Sakaguchi and Gumz.

"Yes, the Sakaguchi family raises delicious Asian vegetables and the Gumz family grew mint and a lot of potatoes and onions."

You mentioned North Judson having a diverse population, it sounds like area soil has the ability to produce a wide range of produce, including soybeans and field corn.

"Jeff, I think it's sad that English Lake is gone because I'm a big environmentalist, but I must confess, the farm ground around here is really prime. Now, I don't know if that is true in the area where Beaver Lake used to be, south of Lake Village. From what I've seen, it's kind of barren and sandy.

"You have to wonder if the land would have been worth more as a lake, given the fact that real estate on lakes in Indiana is the most valuable real estate there is – not farmland. Back in the 1850s, there was a different sentiment."

Marty, I grew up near the Kankakee River close to the state line. Tell me more about the Starke County portion of the Grand Kankakee Marsh.

"People always point to the economic development regarding the draining of the wetlands. And that's true. Certainly at the time, it stimulated the economy. But now, when you look at today's economy, you have to wonder. Look at Culver; they're not there to look at corn."

The progress of man.

"The legend that everybody was in favor of draining the marshes at the time is simply not true. I've looked back at the records from that time period; there were letters written by people saying exactly the same things environmentalists are saying today.

"The idea that people were ignorant savages back then is not true, either. In fact, on the average, people were more eloquent in their writing then they are today, because that's how people communicated – by writing letters. The skill of writing has actually declined since the 19th century."

C'mon, Doc. U gotta B yankin' my chain. LOL.

"Our family farm is a little southeast of North Judson; it's called Big Eastern."

Why Big Eastern?

"It was named after a marsh; the marshes in this area all had names. Out on Indiana 39, south of North Judson, is the Blue Sea. I believe it got its name because it looked like the sea when the blue flag irises were in full bloom.

"The creek running through the Big Eastern was largely artificially dug to drain the Big Eastern. We're on the Bogus Run about six miles upstream of the Kankakee River.

Bogus Run? I've heard fascinating stories about counterfeiters using Bogus Island as a hideout in Newton County, but I'm not familiar with Bogus Run.

"The Bogus Run is kind of like a mini-Kankakee River. It has a wetland area around it like the 20-mile-wide marsh the Kankakee had at English Lake. The Bogus Run was a stream that was channelized; it wasn't artificially created.

"There is no connection between the Bogus Marsh and Bogus Island except that counterfeiters made fake coins at both locations. Here in Starke County, there's a place they called 'The Cave,' which was basically a dug-out spot in the bank that served as a hideout. I recently found documents naming the people who were arrested by federal marshals."

I realize that Beaver Lake, which surrounded Bogus Island, was the biggest lake in Indiana before it was drained. How big was English Lake?

"Not as big as Beaver, but close. English Lake was actually a wide part of the Kankakee River. Only one of the tributaries between English Lake and the Kankakee River had a clear mouth into the lake – the Yellow River. The other tributaries, like the Bogus Run, would just kind of lose themselves in the swamps."

Where do the Yellow River and Kankakee River join?

"In the tiny town of English Lake. There's a very interesting book; it's actually a collection of articles from several newspapers through the years, entitled, 'Who Pulled the Plug on English Lake?'

"The Kankakee Fish and Wildlife Area is what's left of English Lake; that would have been the deepest part of English Lake. The area east of English Lake was more of a marshy prairie. West of English Lake to the state line was a wooded swamp.

"There are only 50 acres of traditional row crops on Big Eastern. Some of the land is used for reforesting, primarily native species. We have tree plantations, too. I've also planted native prairie species. And part of it, we just let go wild."

* * *

I chose to talk a little politics and lot on blue flag irises and long-lost lakes with Lucas. Space does not permit me to include the vast amount of interests and talents this man has.

His undergraduate degree is in anthropology and archaeology – namely, salvage archaeology. He worked on finding sites before they were flooded, like Patoka Lake near French Lick. He produced the first online audio program on the Internet called "Geek of the Week."

Lucas doesn't consider himself another Ansel Adams, but if you go to his very cool website: bigeastern.com, you'll see he is an accomplished photographer.

Lucas does consider himself a musician and recently wrote the music for a children's program that will air on Nickelodeon. While in high school, he played a number of brass instruments. After high school, he became a keyboardist for a rock-'n'-roll band. But it was by being a sound man for other bands that really helped pay his way through college.

Lucas plays mostly acoustic guitar these days. A beautiful instrumental called "Sand Bar" is just one of many songs he's written.

When I asked him to name a couple of his favorite musicians, bands or singers, he mentioned: Radiohead, The Who, John Coltrane, Iron & Wine, Miles Davis, Amy Mann, Hoagy Carmichael, The Rolling Stones, Beethoven, Bob Dylan and Death Cab For Cutie.

Like the ecosystem of Big Eastern, Marty Lucas is diverse.

Jack Weinberg *(Aug. 2013)*

"...Well, they passed a law in '64
To give those who ain't got, a little more
But it only goes so far
'Cause the law don't change another's mind
When all it sees at the hiring time
Is the line on the color bar..."
– Bruce Hornsby

Jack Weinberg lives with his wife of 36 years, Valerie Denney, on the east side of Gary's Miller neighborhood near the county line about a beach ball's toss from Lake Michigan.

Weinberg was 24 and attending the University of California, Berkeley when he told a reporter, "Don't trust anyone over 30." That quote soon made the headlines of most major newspapers throughout the country. Today, at 73, he assured me he does trust himself.

* * *

Where were you born?

"Buffalo, N.Y.," he said. "I lived a very sheltered life as a boy growing up in the 1950s."

Are you Jewish?

"Yes, but not religious. That's my ethnicity, at least. I grew up in a religious, Jewish immigrant family. They were Polish Jews. Fortunately, my immediate family came to the United States before Hitler. We have no relatives left."

Berkeley in 1964?

"I studied abstract mathematics at that time. Berkeley was probably the top school in the world in mathematics. Then, I got caught up in the civil rights movement. From there, the free speech movement.

"I was the chairman of the campus chapter of the Congress on Racial Equality Corps for the Civil Rights organization. We were involved in demonstrations around the San Francisco Bay area over discrimination against African-Americans."

The beginning of a volatile period in U.S. history.

"I had already been active and was involved in demonstrations and arrested a number of times at sit-ins. The summer of '64 was called Freedom Summer. Many of the students went to the Deep South. That's when (James Earl) Chaney, (Andrew) Goodman and (Michael) Schwerner were murdered. They were there to register voters."

"Mississippi Burning."

"Correct. Our campus was very active. During the fall semester, the university announced new regulations saying that you were no longer allowed to pass out leaflets or do anything that advocated any type of activity that was
social or political in nature.

"Some of the businesses that we had been targeting for discrimination told the university, 'You must stop the students from attacking us.' So the university announced rules that would prohibit students from protesting and demonstrating on or off campus."

And?

"The student groups got together and said, 'We're not going to obey these rules. We'll try to negotiate with you, but we have a right to free speech – we're citizens.' So, we started systematically violating those rules.

"I was arrested and put in a police car which immediately was surrounded by students."

Thousands of students.

"Yes; I sat in that police car for 32 hours. I was eventually released after I was booked. The charges were dropped. That's when real negotiations began. After four months, the negotiations broke down and the university started expelling students. We had a sit-in at the administration building where 800 students got arrested. It was the largest mass-arrest in California history."

Then what?

"The students went on strike. That's when the faculty voted to support the students' demands. It became an international story. Many people consider that the starting point of the activist '60s. Vietnam escalated right after that."

You hung around Berkeley until the end of the '60s. Then what?

"I took an interest in unions. In '69, I worked on the assembly line for (General Motors) in Los Angeles. I was very interested in the history of the (United Auto Workers). I moved to Detroit and lived there from '70 to '77. I worked for a number of auto plants, mainly Chrysler. I got involved in some activities and was fired during a wildcat strike at Chrysler."

How long have you lived in Miller?

"Well, we first moved to Miller in 1977 when Valerie and I worked at U.S. Sheet & Tin. Valerie was a millwright and I was in quality control. We worked there for about eight years. We were members of Local 1066. I was an assistant griever for a while.

"Things got bad in the early '80s and we moved to Chicago and pursued other careers. About 10 years ago, we missed Miller so we bought this place. We also have a condo in Chicago, but we spend most of our time in Miller. Living in Miller is what made us become environmentalists."

Not a lot of rank and file Steelworkers from Northwest Indiana are Berkeley grads.

"While I was a member of 1066, they were building a nuclear power plant right next to Bethlehem Steel. I was one of the key organizers of what was called the Bailly Alliance that was in opposition of building the plant. After five years, NIPSCO pulled the plug.

"We started that in 1977, which was before Three Mile Island. People didn't know that much about nuclear power plants back then. That all changed after Three Mile Island."

Where did you work after U.S. Steel?

"I was fortunate enough to get a job with Greenpeace International. I worked for Greenpeace for 10 years. I started out working with chemical pollution in the Great Lakes. I coordinated a program that was international because it included Canada.

"After that assignment, I began working on a global treaty which dealt with a class of chemicals known as persistent organic pollutants. The same chemicals that were affecting the Great Lakes had become an international concern.

"In 2001, the treaty was adopted. Today, it's called the Stockholm Convention of Persistent Organic Pollutants. About 130 countries ratified that treaty."

When did you leave Greenpeace?

"In 2000. Then, I went to work for another organization that basically just gave me a paycheck, a credit card, gave me office space and let me go wherever I wanted to go in the world to promote the implantation of this treaty and to build this network.

"In 2008, I retired but kept volunteering and consulting. The last couple years, I've gotten really involved again. That conference call I was on when I let you into the house was somebody in Geneva (Switzerland) from the United Nations Environmental Program and some people from California. We were negotiating funding for a project in Africa. In the last six months, I've been to Asia four times."

Final thoughts?

"In 2014, it will be the 50th anniversary of the free speech movement. It was a landmark event.

"I think back to when I was 24 and about the things that happened 50 years before that. And I realize how ancient 50 years ago is. With that said, I've done all the things I've wanted to do and I've been all over the world. I was active in the civil rights movement, the free speech movement and was involved in the anti-war movement, unions and I'm still involved in environmental health."

Jack, you're a warrior who has had a multifaceted career to say the least.

"I couldn't have dreamt of a more fulfilling set of experiences in life."

* * *

The freedom of speech, the freedom of the press, and the right of people peaceably to assemble... .

Lest we forget.

Gina Darnell *(Jan. 2014)*

"There can be nothing in the world more beautiful than the Yosemite, the groves of the giant sequoias and redwoods, the Canyon of the Colorado, the Canyon of the Yellowstone, the Three Tetons; and our people should see to it that they are preserved for their children and their children's children forever, with their majestic beauty unmarred."
– Theodore Roosevelt

My buddy Jim Sweeney tipped me off about Gina Darnell. He said Darnell, a professional forester, would make a good interview. Sweeney added that Darnell is a Republican and a self-professed "tree hugger with a chainsaw." I assured Sweeney that I was not alarmed being as "I'm a Democrat with an electric Mr. Twister fillet knife."

Darnell, 59, lives in Chesterton with her husband Craig, a captain with American Airlines. The Darnells have raised two adult sons and a pair of Gordon setters.

Darnell grew up in Beverly Shores and attended both Michigan City Elston and Michigan City Rogers High Schools.

Our interview took place at the Third Coast Cafe in Chesterton. .

* * *

Beverly Shores?

"When I grew up in Beverly Shores there was the Red Lantern Inn," she said. "It was one of the only places with a big, beautiful view of Lake Michigan. Beverly Shores has always been a very eclectic community."

Your maiden name?

"Arbas, which is short for Arbaciaskas. I'm first generation Lithuanian and speak the language fluently. If ever you've seen the dunes of the Baltic coast, they look the same as the Beverly Shores area. That's why a lot of Lithuanian immigrants settled there."

College?

"I graduated from Purdue in West Lafayette with a bachelor's degree in forest management."

The name of your company?

"Forest Resource Planning. Mostly, my niche is in urban forestry. I work with cities and towns on their tree care programs. That involves measuring all the street trees in town, computerizing them and analyzing them to see what maintenance needs they have. I also help with the tree planting programs."

What about tree removal?

"Yes, we're dealing with the emerald ash borer that's killing all the ash trees. If you don't treat the trees, they're dead. Every ash tree in Porter and Lake counties has it. A Purdue entomologist came up and did a talk to the town of Munster. He said the emerald ash borer dwarfs the number of trees killed by Dutch elm disease. The beetle eats on the leaves of the ash tree, and that's not too bad. But then it lays eggs and the eggs get under the bark and eat all winter.

"I have a job at Wicker Park where there are at least 500 ash trees and they are dying, if they aren't dead already. We have to do something about that. It's going to drastically affect the looks of the golf course. It's going to be a massive die-back. And, unfortunately, it going to be a massive clear-cut. But, we're getting funds to replant."

A tree hugger with a chainsaw?

"I love trees. There are trees that are beautiful, but dangerous because they could fall on a house. They have to be cut down.

"I worked for a company for 10 years where I'd grow trees to make paper. We need paper. God forbid we run out of toilet paper. Back in 1976, I was actually the first female forester to work in the South. The tree huggers to the far left side, don't want anything cut down: 'Oh, the poor tree, it's alive.' At the other end of the spectrum, you have people who desecrate natural resources and ruin the environment."

You're a member of the Northwest Indiana Paddling Association.

"Yes, I'm the Blueways stewardship chair. All of my friends in the group are Democrats. I like to remind them quite often that I'm a Republican and that a Republican can be an environmentalist – look at Teddy Roosevelt. Many of the individuals I know who are Republicans love nature, hunting and fishing and the parks. There's just this bad corporate image."

Gina, let's switch gears a bit. Jasper County's surveyor applied for a permit to improve drainage along the Kankakee River starting at

U.S. Highway 231 and ending at Indiana State Road 49 – a distance of nearly 10 miles.

Work will consist of clearing of trees, logjams and brush from the south bank. The river side slope of the levee will be armored with limestone rip-rap to create a 1:1 slope on the bank. The Department of Natural Resources' Division of Water has recently approved the permit. Your thoughts?

"There is an obligation by the drainage board to keep the river open. Part of that obligation is that there has to be an access road on the top of the levee where equipment could be brought in to remove any obstructions or repair a break in the levee.

"With that said, why do the entire levee by blatantly cutting everything all the way down? When I first saw the pictures of what was done on the Porter County side of the river, I thought, 'Oh, we shouldn't cut any of it; it's terrible.' But then, I thought about the drainage board's responsibilities to the cities and towns that might get flooded. Just do it in the most environmentally friendly way."

Supposedly, no trees suitable for Indiana bat roosting will be cut down, and if any archaeological artifacts or human remains are uncovered during construction, state law requires that the discovery must be reported to the DNR within two business days.

"We shall see."

It seems the powers that be want to move the water out of there as fast as possible.

"Why? The thing you want to do is store the water upstream. You want to have places where the water can go rather than flushing everything downstream. There has been a lack of insight about the quickness of the water going downstream stream and the sand accumulating across the Illinois state line where the river remains in its natural state."

Limestone rip-rap?

"I'm not crazy about that idea. I believe re-vegetating the slopes is the better way to go. Normally, trees are the best thing you can have along a river – unless you have a levee. When a large tree gives way, its root ball can actually cause a levee break. It is good to have shrubs along the banks. The shrubbery actually slows the velocity of water."

* * *

Gina Darnell will be speaking at the Porter County Expo Center on Jan. 25. Her topic will be planting trees for your urban site.

Lloyd and Regina Bohl *(Oct. 2014)*

"...There's no farmer songs on that car radio
Just cowboys, truck drivers and pain
Well this is my way to say thanks for the meal
And I hope there's no shortage of rain..."
– Murray McLauchlan

Lloyd Bohl raises black angus beef cattle naturally on his 400-acre farm in Grant Park, Illinois. No antibiotics, no hormones, no steroids. He grows corn, soybeans, alfalfa hay and a little wheat, too.

He's a big man of German ancestry with a right hand the size of a ham. His left hand comprises of a little finger, a thumb and less than half of an index finger. When I questioned him about that, he answered: "Auger."

"Nuff" said.

Bohl's business card reads: "Fatherfarms, conserving our land for future generations." Under his name it reads "Land Steward."

I like that.

Bohl lives with Regina, his wife of 16 years, and their 14-year old son, Hank, who does his part on the farm. Regina attended Moody Bible Institute in Chicago. The Bohls attend the First Regular Baptist Church in Grant Park.

My interview began at 6 p.m. with Regina who had been mowing grass on a John Deere lawn tractor. There was still some daylight left and Lloyd had chores to do.

* * *

Where we sit is considered Grant Park?

Regina: "Correct. This little section is Yellowhead Township. Yellow Head was an Indian who had yellow hair. This area was basically settled by German farmers and was known as Petersburg."

I'm familiar with Yellow Head. He was a Potawatomi warrior who had a knife fight with fur trader Gurdon Hubbard who eventually became a founding father of Chicago. The trail – Hubbard's Trace – that went from Chicago to Vincennes is known as Dixie Highway today.

Regina: "Minne Monesse golf course is named after Yellow Head's daughter."

I figured Minne Monesse was a Native American word or phrase, but I didn't know that it was the name of Yellow Head's daughter. You learn something every day. Your role on the farm?

Regina: "I'm chief cook and bottle washer."

Fill me in on Fatherfarms until Lloyd gets here.

Regina: "Well, we receive a premium for our non-Roundup ready soybeans. We try to do everything as healthfully as we can. Lloyd's home now."

How yuh doin', buddy?

Lloyd: "Lloyd."

Jeff. Jeff Manes. How's the price of corn and soybeans today?

Lloyd: "Hittin' the skids hard. Corn is under $3 (a bushel) and beans are barely $9."

How many head of cattle do you have on the farm?

Lloyd: "Probably 300. Primarily Angus. I've got some crossbreeds with Herefords in them so we get some black baldies"

Lloyd, bear with me. I'm the son of a steel worker. In 4-H, I took entomology while the farm boys showed swine and cattle. What's a black baldy?

Lloyd: "It's a black-hided, white-faced animal."

Are the cattle born here?

Lloyd: "Yep. Everything is born on the farm and raised all the way up – from birth to butcher."

At what age are the moo-moos slaughtered?

Lloyd: "About 18 to 20 months old. The majority are sold for freezer beef."

Regina: "We sell through the Butcher Block in Lowell."

Lloyd: "We bring the customer list in and the Butcher Block processes it to the customer's desire. The customer orders the beef from us."

Do you know how to butcher a cow?

Lloyd: "I did it growin' up. I can't do it commercially because I'm not inspected and licensed. My parents both grew up on farms. My father cut two beef up every winter. And a hog or two, most years. My mother raised chickens, ducks, geese and a large garden."

They were self-sustaining.

Lloyd: "Yep."

Regina: "The Butcher Block lets the beef hang for 14 days. We sell 1/8ths, quarters, halves and wholes."

Lloyd: "We use a bovine nutritionist; he has a PhD in animal nutrition. He visits our farm about every two weeks. He tweaks their rations. We use probably 15 different rations throughout the year. The calves are born on a dirt pasture. They can go where they want to. We use a rotational grazing program. We have several different types of clover and grasses. We have chicory."

A lot of work maintaining a farm.

Lloyd: "We keep busy about 20 hours a day."

Regina: "That's no joke."

Lloyd: "People tell me: 'I had 60 hours in last week.' I ask them: 'What did you do after Wednesday?' It's a hard life, but it's a rewarding life. The animals need to be cared for properly."

How many breeding bulls do you have?

Lloyd: "Seven."

Regina: "They're brought in from different farms."

Why is that?

Lloyd: "Otherwise, you'd have inbred cattle."

Earlier, you mentioned your nutritionist, what about a veterinarian?

Lloyd: "We use Dr. Rodawald, his office is only a couple miles from our farm. His wife has a small animal practice in the clinic and he has a large animal practice on the road. We use a very intensive vaccination program."

Have you had any trouble with coyotes?

Regina: "Oh, yeah."

Lloyd: "If a coyote kills a calf and drags it out of the field, I won't necessarily know what happened to it. But coyotes are present. You have to be vigilant. A good mama cow will protect her calves."

Favorite cut of meat?

Regina: "Hands down, mine's a tenderloin. I like them cut thin and served cold with horseradish."

Lloyd: "Mine's a hamburger on the grill. My wife makes some fantastic burgers on the grill. I eat a pound of beef to a meal. I need meat – protein – to work. If I run short, I fade."

From where do your customers hail?

Lloyd: "From Rockford, Illinois to Lafayette and all points in between. Word of mouth, mostly."

Final thoughts?

Regina: "My husband takes this very seriously. It's kinda like a ministry to him. He wants what he provides to people to be of good value and good for their bodies and wholesome. He's one of the hardest workin' men I've met in my life."

* * *

After our interview, Lloyd took me for the grand tour of his cattle farm. With his blue healer, Rodeo, at his side, he spoke of his place with pride.

Meanwhile, back at the ranch, Regina got back on that John Deere to finish what she started.

Salt of the earth, Lloyd and Regina Bohl.

Thanks for the meal.

Bonnie Swarner *(Oct. 2013)*

"I do not want to talk about what you understand about the world. I want to know what you will do about it. I do not want to know what you hope. I want to know what you will work for. I do not want your sympathy for the needs of humanity. I want your muscle."
– Robert Fulghum

I had thoughts of interviewing the mother-daughter team of Bonnie and Susan Swarner and making one column out of it. After glancing at their impressive resumes, I opted to interview mom only and save Susan for another occasion.

Bonnie lives on beautiful Long Lake in Valparaiso. Susan, a bearded dragon as stoic a sphinx and a loquacious African grey parrot sat in our chat.

Swarner, 63, is a former animal rehabber who manages several extensive woodlands. She also is a member of Wahoub Lake Association, Northwoods Parks Improvement Association, Hoosier Environmental Council and is currently involved in a federal program to remove invasive species.

But what has she done for the environment lately?

* * *

"I was born in Fort Wayne," Swarner began. "When I was 6, we moved to Bluffton near Oubache State Park. Oubache is a Native American word; its translation is Wabash. We went to Oubache every Sunday after church."

Like public libraries, parks are wonderful things for people of all walks of life.

"Back then, people didn't have much money and they didn't want to spend what they did have after enduring the Great Depression."

Education?

"I graduated from Bluffton High School in '68 and then attended Hanover College down on the Ohio River near Madison. I graduated from there and then I went to graduate school at Indiana State University for school psychology. I decided to be a psychologist by the time I was 12."

And you've always had an interest or love of nature.

"Yes. My husband also attended Hanover which is near Clifty Falls State Park. We went there all the time. We've always had a park to go to."

Your husband?

"John was a doctor who was the head of the critical care unit and pulmonary department. He also was director of the nursing home all at the same time. He had a heart blockage which is so ridiculous because that's what he took care of. John died in '99. My husband just didn't take time to care for himself, but he is well-remembered in this community."

Did he smoke? I mean, it amazes me the amount of doctors and nurses I know who smoke?

"No, John wasn't a smoker, but he would tell his patients: 'Go ahead and smoke, you're putting my kids through college.'"

Good one. Let's fast forward. I used to work in the mill with quite a few guys from the Valparaiso area who fished lakes like Flint, Wahoub and Loomis. It seems like they fared well most of the time.

"I used to rent boats, but know I just sell fishing rights. They are only $100 a year and the anglers have unlimited access. By charging, you get serious fishermen. You don't get people who are going to be destructive and leave trash all over."

Environmentally speaking, tell me some of the good things you do.

"We're working to remove invasive plants on my three nature preserves. Susan has helped a lot with that. The one at Wahoub is 65 acres, the one at Loomis is 22 and the one in Suman Valley which is 55. I got a farm grant and we worked for three years removing those unwanted plants."

They're tough to eradicate.

"We're still working on removing invasive plants. Every year they come up with a new one."

Reaching out to kids.

"I'm the education chairman for the Izaak Walton League and Suzie is the youth program coordinator. We've started a program where we go into the schools and have what we call Environmental Family Fun Night.

"We did two last year. We're currently advertising to expand it to all the schools in Porter County. We get outside groups like Porter County Parks, the Recycling District, Dunelands Learning Center, Master Gardeners... . This year, I talked to someone from the Department of Natural Resources about coming to our 'Fun Night.' Jim Sweeney takes care of the water quality station."

A few more examples?

"Susan did a display about the ages of trees. The kids draw 'tree cookies' and then denote a specific event that occurred with each ring in the tree. People like Charlotte Read and Marilyn Spencer participated. They help the kids make wind chimes. Don Frame did soil quality.

"We have lots of live reptiles and amphibians at our 'Fun Nights.' Porter County Wildlife Advisory Board came. We had a man from the south side of Chicago who brought bats. Kids love that; it's like going to the zoo."

I hope you get to as many schools as possible.

"We take care of everything financially and we supply the manpower. The schools don't have to do anything."

Obviously, Environmental Family Fun Nights are after school. How long does an event last?

"A couple of hours, usually from like 6 p.m. to 8 p.m."

* * *

Kudos to all the area folks like Bonnie and Susan Swarner who walk the walk, roll up their sleeves and get things done. Mother Nature is a resilient old dame, but she can always use a helping hand.

George Smolka *(July 2013)*

"...Hey farmer farmer
Put away your D.D.T. now
Give me spots on my apples
But leave me the birds and the bees
Please"
– Joni Mitchell

It was my friend Jim Sweeney who tipped me off a few years ago about environmental activist George Bunce of Griffith. Well, Sweeney has another green Griffith George for me. He says George Smolka is probably the most intelligent man he's ever known.

Smolka, 72, is a Vietnam veteran who has lived in Griffith for 20 years. He has been a small business owner, patent holder and is an expert odonologist (dragonflies and damselflies).

* * *

"I was born in Whitchurch, England," Smolka began. "It dates back to the 900s. I came to the United States in 1950 and lived in Chicago until I was 22."

Education?

"I graduated from Elgin High School. For my undergraduate work I went to Illinois College in central Illinois where I earned a double degree in biology and chemistry. For my graduate work, I attended Iowa State where I received my master's in biochemistry.

"I didn't go directly from Illinois College to Ames (Iowa State) because I got drafted. When I came out I had a disability, which I still have. The G.I. Bill helped pay for my schooling at Iowa State."

What years were you in the service?

"From 1965 through 1967."

How did you become disabled?

"It was a fungus of some kind I picked up in Vietnam. It did a great deal of damage to my lungs. It kept getting worse. Eventually, medicine caught up to my condition. With the advent of certain steroids I am better, but it doesn't go away."

You're also a rabid enviro.

"I've always had an interest in that area. Indiana has one of the worst environmental records around. The damage is outsourced to the public. A significant number of Indiana corporations are doing this and the general public doesn't understand it. We are paying the price for the air and water pollution. It can eventually lead to certain diseases."

Example, please.

"Do you know the percentage of deaths in Indiana from cancer? I'm talking dead people only, not the ones who survive. Forty-eight percent of the people in Indiana die of cancer. It's very suspicious.

"We need to stop trying to cure cancer. We need to start trying to prevent it. The amount of money we are wasting looking for cures is a travesty. In the mid-19th Century in London there were studies done on all sorts of cholera. They discovered it was related to the water. Eventually, they traced it to some wells. Seepage from cisterns and septic tanks and from the river itself were oozing into these wells and contaminating them. Did they try to cure the disease?"

I don't know; tell me.

"They took the sewage and instead of dumping it in the river like they had been, they piped it way out into the estuary which is right next to the channel. By the time any contamination came back, there were only harmless organisms. They solved the problem with an engineering solution, not a medical one. Is that maybe the way we need to go now? What was the guy with the rope? The comedian?"

Will Rogers?

"Thanks; I had a senior moment. Will Rogers said, 'When you find yourself in a hole what is the first thing you must do? Stop digging!'"

George, let's switch gear. You're into dragonflies.

"Yes, I became interested in them in the late '80s."

Do you attempt to net or film them?

"All the time. The adult dragonflies and the nymphs are both carnivores. A large dragonfly can eat as many as 200 mosquitos a day. They go back about 250 million years.

"Dragonflies and damselflies are useful from the standpoint of ecology because they are the top predators as far as insects are concerned. Dragonflies are also food for a lot of other creatures. If dragonflies feed on other flying insects that have fed on polluted substances they in turn cause problems with amphibians and birds. If you study the dragonflies, you get an idea of the rapidity with which some of these pollutants are being distributed in our environment."

So, you're telling me when the blue darner (dragonfly) engulfs pollutant-gorged mayflies or mosquitos and in turn gets slurped up by a bull frog which gets gored and gulped by a blue heron in the bayous of the Kankakee River, said heron is ingesting pollutants many times over.

"Yes."

Disconcerting.

"You mentioned the Kankakee. I don't have to tell you this, but the Grand Kankakee Marsh was one of the premier environments in the entire United States. It was a fabulous resource and everything was destroyed. Here we had a resource – if for no other reason – that would have made tons of money just from the tourist trade. And those idiots couldn't see that far ahead."

Tell me how you really feel.

"The Grand Kankakee Marsh was immense enough to sustain itself. We wouldn't have had to do anything. They have now converted it to pick corn and that's about it. Do you know how many miles of field tile were purchased when they were draining the marsh?"

I have those numbers at home. I know supply couldn't keep up with demand.

"Pardon my French, but it was un-fucking-believable."

Let's switch to overdrive. Genetically modified organisms?

"I have a very low opinion of GMOs. Because of a consequence of the misuse of GMOs, they are no longer working. Take bacillus thuringiensis corn for instance. You're aware of Bt-corn?"

I think so. Not really.

"You're kidding me?"

Sorry.

"It's a genetically modified corn that supposedly makes it resistant to the attack of insects such as corn borers. Aside from the stupidity of that which was done, it has caused all kinds of problems. All of the pests that they were trying to control became resistant. Now they're spraying more insecticides then ever."

* * *

Space does not permit all that Smolka and I discussed including subjects such as community collapse syndrome and genetically modified apples that don't bruise or brown.

And although he's an academic and a scientist and I'm more a blue-collar river rat kind of guy, we concur on at least one thing.

Leave us the birds and bees.

Maggie Byrne *(May 2014)*

"To me, one of the best faces America has ever projected is the face of a Peace Corps volunteer. That face symbolizes this country: young, curious, brimming with idealism and hope – and a real, honest compassion."
– Teresa Heinz

Maggie Byrne is a grant specialist for the Indiana Department of Natural Resources and is on the board of directors of the Northwest Indiana Paddling Association.

Byrne, 39, is single, lives in Griffith and was raised in Lansing, Ill. She graduated from Thornton Fractional South High School. A few years after college, she joined the Peace Corps.

* * *

College?

"Ball State University," she said. "I have a degree in natural resources and environmental management."

You work for the DNR.

"Yes, their Lake Michigan coastal program. I've been there for two years."

Where did you work before that?

"For seven years, I was with The Nature Conservancy. My job title with TNC was conservation coordinator, but I did a lot of wildlife habitat restoration work. I also did some land acquisition projects and was with the Indiana coastal cooperative weed management area for a couple of years."

Phragmites, purple loosestrife and garlic mustard feared you.

"Yes."

Why did you leave TNC?

"It was a great job and I learned a lot. But this job opened up and it was a better opportunity. I get to work with people a lot more now. Today, I'm based at the (Indiana Dunes) State Park and that's really kind of awesome and a dream come true."

Good for you. Tell me about your kayak adventure in Puerto Rico.

"We paddled halfway around the island last summer. We were in Puerto Rico for 16 days, but we actually paddled for 11 of those days. We started in the southeastern corner and went north and west."

Some pretty cool sights?

"Very cool. I got to see manatees, sea turtles and lots of fish, of course. We didn't see any dolphins, but we saw monkeys on an island. They weren't indigenous. It was like a research island where they study monkeys. We tried to land, but there was a DNR officer who wouldn't let us."

You could've told him that you work for the DNR, but he probably wouldn't have believed you.

"Probably not. Plus, my Spanish isn't that good."

Your next excellent adventure?

"In August, I'm going with a group of people up to the Apostle Islands in Lake Superior for about 10 days. "

Aren't you some kind of paddling instructor?

"Yes, I'm certified by the American Canoe Association."

What kind of kayak do you have?

"I actually own four kayaks. Two of them are sea kayaks. None of them are tandems.

"We offer kayak classes through the Northwest Indiana Paddling Association. I wish more people would take advantage of that. Kayaking is one of the fastest growing sports in the country."

The Peace Corps.

"It was the best thing I've ever done in my life, so far. I arrived in Cameroon, Africa on Oct. 31, 2001. We were supposed arrive on Sept. 25, but were delayed because of 9-11."

How long were you in Cameroon?

"For 3 1/2 years. It was challenging every single day, but it was a great experience. The people were so wonderful and friendly and open and giving. They see a white person and they want to know what you are doing there. They're very curious. The Cameroonians assume you have a lot of money so they want you to buy their stuff."

Most young people in the Peace Corps aren't exactly lighting their *cigars with $100 bills.*

"It's funny, it's sorta like you're a celebrity. It's kind of annoying at first, but once you get used to it, it gets to be kind of fun."

How did you help those folks?

"I worked with subsistence farmers as an agri-forestry extension agent. I tried to teach them how to raise nitrogen-fixing trees so they could improve soil fertility, prevent erosion and grow their own firewood. Deforestation was a huge issue where I was posted.

"I speak Pidgin English, by the way. The vocabulary is pretty much the same, but you use the verb tenses differently."

Example?

"For instance, in America, we'd say, 'I came' or 'I went.' In Pidgin English it would be 'I done come.' It's more about the inflection and pronunciation than it is about the actual words. When I speak Pidgin in this country to people from Africa they're shocked at how well I speak it. It's so much fun because they're so excited. 'What is this coming out of you?'"

* * *

Maggie Byrne obviously enjoys the wonders of nature, oftentimes viewed from the seat of a kayak.

And from the coast of Africa to the coast of Lake Michigan, she's been doing her part to preserve natural resources or help heal this planet's ills.

I call that gratitude.

Thomas Frank *(2014)*

"The skies are often dreary
And air is filled with smoke
In Northwest Indiana
From the gas, and coal and coke
But we wouldn't be without it,
For it's just the way we grow
In Northwest Indiana
Where the furnace fires glow"

- Written for the first celebration of
Indiana Day at Indiana Harbor, Dec 11, 1908

After interviewing Thomas Frank, I kept wanting to type his name Frank Thomas because of the former Chicago White Sox slugger and Hall of Famer. I probably would have done the same thing if I'd have interviewed someone by the name of Aaron Henry.

I met with Frank at his home in East Chicago. The house sits across the street from Washington Park and was built three years before the creation of Gary, Indiana – 1903.

Frank, 50, teaches part time at the University of Chicago Laboratory Schools and has lived in East Chicago with his wife Kristin for 17 years. They have two children ages 12 and 10.

* * *

"I was born in Bucktown (neighborhood of Chicago)," Frank began. "Then my family moved to the northwest suburbs. I married into this community. My wife's from East Chicago. She is the daughter of former East Chicago Roosevelt (High School) basketball coach John Todd."

Coach Todd was a legend around these parts. What about your parents?

"My mom is from wealth and establishment. Her great-grandfather was the mayor of Chicago. His name was Roswell B. Mason. He brought the Illinois Central to Chicago and built the first bridge over the Mississippi. He was the mayor prior to the Great Chicago Fire. My dad, on the other hand, grew up in Bucktown and was a street kid. He was the son of a coal shoveler for the railroad.

"That's why I can't solve a problem from one framework. I have to move between different frameworks, from the working class and the educated class."

College?

"I went to the University of Kansas where I studied philosophy, fine arts and painting. Then, I went to The Sorbonne (University) in Paris for a year. I love France. Then, I studied at Indiana University where I earned a master's degree in painting. Once I came here, I tried to re-purpose my skills and went back to school at the (University of Illinois, Chicago) in urban planning."

A diverse education, to say the least.

"I used to be the director of the Indiana Harbor Shipping Canal. That's considered the most polluted body of water in America. Right now, it's being dredged by the Army Corps of Engineers at a cost of $250 million."

Tell me more about your activities here in East Chicago.

"I became the president of redevelopment for about four years. I also chaired a committee that did a comprehensive plan for East Chicago."

Thomas, I was tipped off about you by Dave Mueller, the owner of Paul Henry's Art Gallery in downtown Hammond. I figured we'd talk about oil painting, water colors, pastels and the like. I didn't know about this side of you.

"Right now, if I were to describe myself it would be that I'm an artist-activist. I kind of rub this administration and the previous one a little bit hard. I'm about 1,000 times more transparent than they would be."

Explain, please.

"If something's happening, I'll speak about it. I won't cover it. I think there is a need for the public to know what's going on. I consider this area kind of a giant black hole. We're used to operating without many eyes on us."

Some might consider you a whistle blower, then, again, some might deem you a watchdog.

"Indiana discharges more industrial pollutants in its waterways than any other state in the Union. In fact, we discharge 30 percent more than the second worst offender. When we do something, we really do it bad."

Disconcerting.

"There are 3,140 counties in America. Lake County, in Indiana, usually ranks about No. 10 year after year in how much industrial waste it discharges into our air. My argument is let's try to be average. That has been what's gotten me in trouble in the region."

With industry or politicians?

"Both. When I was director of the Indiana Harbor Shipping Canal, (British Petroleum) announced its project – the largest tar sands refinery in the U.S. The BP project also is the largest private investment in Indiana's history.

"At that time, I decided to voice my opposition of BP's project to my city council. We're one of the poorest communities in the state – and we're Democrat strong – and we awarded one of the wealthiest industries in human history a $164 million tax abatement to move the refining capacity to East Chicago. The mayor, at the time, told me if he didn't vote for it he wouldn't have a political future."

Tell me more about tar sands.

"Tar sands is the most damaging form of fossil fuel. The project area up in Alberta (Canada) is the size of Florida. They're doing mountain top removal. It's in the great Boreal Forest. The Boreal Forest is the largest carbon sink. They're tearing down the Boreal Forest to get to the peat."

Once again, the progress of man.

"For the last 10 years it was the second largest deforestation project on the planet. Now, it's the largest. It's larger than the Amazon."

Let me get this straight, the oil is piped from Canada to Northwest Indiana where it is refined.

"Correct. So we can burn it in our vehicles. This is all very devastating to our climate. Unfortunately, in our region, we went all in.

"James Hanson, the lead scientist for NASA and lead climatologist in the world has said that if we continue to exploit the tar sands it will be game over for the climate. Basically, what he's saying is we're shifting the climate away from the carrying capacity for humans."

What does NASA know? I mean, look at all the "experts" who write into Quickly saying climate change is a bunch of hooey.

"We thought we had 100 years, we thought we had until 2100, but it looks like we don't have much more than a generation. We're cooking ourselves. People can't drink oil."

And the Quickly experts continue to aid and abet Big Industry and its use of fossil fuels by scoffing.

"Jeff, there are 30,000 environmental attorneys in our country. Industry employs 28,000 of them full time. Government agencies employ less than 2,000 environmental attorneys. Non-profits employ about 600 and citizens groups less than 200."

What about that resilient old dame we know as Ma Nature? How many lawyers represent her?

"She doesn't have an attorney."

* * *

Thomas Frank told me it is ironic that East Chicago is the home of world-class integrated steel facilities and a tar sands refinery that generates billions of dollars, yet the community is faltering. He said when you're at the bottom of the food chain – like many of the folks from East Chicago or Gary – you should be the first to be served.

Maybe we can talk art next time.

Rod Smart *(May 2013)*

"Here's to the kids who are different,
The kids who don't always get A's
The kids who have ears twice the size of their peers,
And noses that go on for days...
Here's to the kids who are different,
The kids they call crazy or dumb,
The kids who don't fit, with the guts and the grit,
Who dance to a different drum...
Here's to the kids who are different,
The kids with the mischievous streak,
For when they have grown, as history's shown,
It's their difference that makes them unique."
– Digby Wolfe

Like Claude Monet, Thomas Edison, Jack London and Walt Disney, Rod Smart didn't graduate high school. Years later, he did earn a GED so he could get custody of his son, Tyler.

Smart, 51, has a Lake Village mailing address, but actually lives in an area known as Conrad, a once bustling burg, but now a ghost town. His house is literally a stone's throw from where the town's founder – Jennie Milk Conrad – once lived. Jennie's house is no more.

As a kid, Smart lived mostly in Lake Village and Sumava Resorts. For the past 15 years, he has worked as a hired man for farmer Ron Styck. Rod loves his job and the people he works for.

His paternal grandmother, Edmere Gervais Smart, was of French stock and originally from St. Anne, Ill. Rod and I are not blood kin, but we do share the same Aunt "Sassy."

Smart enjoys oil painting, wood burning, photography and collecting various artifacts. For the past three years, he has traveled to Thailand. Neither of us have hunted warm-blooded creatures for years, but after our interview, we did stalk the elusive and delectable morel mushroom.

We'd tell you exactly where, but then we'd have to kill you.

* * *

Memories of Sumava?

"We lived in the fifth house east of U.S. 41 on the north side of the road," he said. "It was Father Woods' house next to the tavern. My parents purchased it from St. Augusta Catholic Church in Lake Village."

The priest imbibed a bit.

"Restauranteur Jimmy Lukes once told me Father Woods often would knock on the back door at like 3 a.m. wanting more beer. Jimmy would always serve him."

Hey, let's take a look at that arrowhead collection.

"I had an archaeologist tell me this axe head is from 6000 B.C.; it's full-grooved."

That thing is huge. What are those?

"Large chunks of petrified wood I found right here in Newton County."

What else do you have there?

"This is a nickel dated 1874. And this is a 'good for one free drink' trade token. I found these Indian Head pennies where there must've been a house at one time. Same with these clay marbles, mother-of-pearl buttons and porcelain doll parts."

Very cool. What's that?

"It's a stem from a pipe. As you can see, it has 'Montreal' printed on it. They were clay trade pipes. The French traded items like pipes and beads to the Indians in exchange for furs."

When did you really start collecting arrowheads and the like?

"About 20 years ago after I got sober. It gave me something to do. Life has gotten a lot better since I gave up the drink."

Let's switch gears. Thailand?

"There are two types of people. Those who like Thailand and those who love Thailand. I love Thailand. In 2010, I went for two weeks, in 2011 for three weeks and last year I stayed there for two months. Eventually, I want to live there.

The people are very friendly and peaceful. It's like a disgrace to get angry with somebody."

You met someone over there.

"Yes, a very nice lady. I stayed with her last year. We traveled around Thailand together. She's a seamstress."

What's her name?

"Rasi Sanuchit. Her nickname is Nok."

Financially speaking, are people real poor in Thailand?

'They get by. What impresses me about Thailand is it has a very low unemployment rate. Everybody works. Thais are very family-oriented as far as taking care of the elderly. They're very respectful people. I love the culture.

"Another thing that I found impressive is they have a very high import tax. I wish the United States would do that. If another country wants to import something into Thailand, that country is going to pay dearly. That high import tax keeps the manufacturing base in Thailand. Thais produce their own clothing, motorcycles, furniture.... Thailand could get products from nearby China, but they don't do it because of the tax."

Interesting.

"Can you imagine if we had a 1.6 percent unemployment rate in this country? I really don't want to talk politics, but I feel that instead of taxing us working people so highly, how about taxing the heck out of China and all the other countries that are importing goods into the United States."

Tell me about some of the sites you've seen over there.

"I spent about five days in Ayutthaya, which is the ancient capital. The Burmese came in and sacked the area in the 1770s. I also went to the town of Fang where the government had provided mulberry trees to keep the silkworm production in Thailand."

So exotic. What about mysterious Conrad?

"I love Conrad, too. That's another childhood memory I have. When I was a kid, this wasn't on my bus route, but I was going to stay with one of my friends after school. I remember riding his bus through here. We drove across the historic Upside-down Bridge spanning Beaver Ditch. I remember the way the gravel road curved through the woods to where the Sipes lived. Jeff, I also remember thinking to myself, 'What a beautiful place this is.' As a kid you usually don't think about those kind of things. And after all these years, here I am living in Conrad."

* * *

Rod Smart has seen and thoroughly enjoyed Thailand's mysterious temples and ruins. But he'll be the first to tell you Conrad has its ruins, too. And when some of us are among those mighty oaks where wild turkeys scratch, red-headed woodpeckers pound and the sponge mushroom emerges in the spring, we feel as if we're walking through the most magnificent temple ever created.

But then again, maybe we're just different.

Kindred Spirits

Karen & Kelly *(Feb. 2013)*

"I know that God will not give me anything that I can't handle. I just wish He didn't trust me so much."
– Author unknown, from a clipping attached to the refrigerator of Karen Hess Goheen.

Karen Hess Goheen, 55, and Kelly Hess, 47, are sisters who were raised in Lake Village. We met at Karen's house in the Shady Shores subdivision of Shelby. Kelly lives in Niles, Mich.

Karen and I were classmates from first through 12th grade. I don't remember Kelly, but I do remember when Karen and Kelly's mother died.

Karen was 12 and Kelly, 4.

* * *

Karen, I remember attending your birthday party when we were in the fourth grade.

"Yes, you and Jeff Ridgeway were the only boys who showed up."

That's because we were raised to be respectful and our mothers forced us to go to a girl's stupid birthday party.

"Do you remember when I broke both arms on the playground at school?"

Vaguely.

Karen: "Danni Jo Love and I were going up the slide and some ornery boys were pushing us up the ladder, telling us to hurry up. Danni yelled at the ornery boys to stop, but, of course, they didn't. All of a sudden, when I got to the very top, I got pushed off."

It's sort of coming back to me.

"Those ornery boys were you and Jeff Ridgeway."

You were wearing a green dress and white go-go boots. It was the other Jeff who did all the pushing. I swear; ask Danni Jo. Strike that. She'd never get it right.

"It was late October and I didn't get to go trick-or-treating because my arms were in casts."

Alrighty then. Kelly, any pleasant Lake Village memories for you?

"I remember Wiley Stone helping me with my poetry. I loved Mr. Stone. He'd be working in his greenhouse and I'd help him."

I have a signed book of his poetry, "Echoes of Home." Wiley Stone was born in 1900 and died in 2000. Strange how some live such long lives and others are taken so young.

Karen: "I think one of the hardest things for me was watching Mom deteriorate. She wanted to let me know what it was like to have lung cancer. She'd show me where the radiation had burned her so badly. Mom was a two-pack-a-day smoker. She made me promise that I would never smoke."

Anything else about your mother's final days?

Karen: "She'd say, 'I think I could eat this, do you think you could make it if I tell you how?' My dad would position the bed so she could see from the bedroom doorway into the kitchen. I learned to make soups and things she could handle."

Kelly, you were so young, did you know what was going on?

"I knew Mom was sick and couldn't get out of bed. I remember the night she died; they took her out on a gurney. I stood there in my pajamas and watched my mom go away. I can close my eyes and see her face.

"Losing your mother when you're young, and then when you become a mother yourself, it makes you hold on that much tighter and makes you love that much harder."

Karen: "When Kelly was living in Tulsa, she asked me a question about Mom. I thought to myself, 'Oh my God, I never realized, she wouldn't know that.' I decided to write down Mom's favorite flowers, color, songs – her hobbies. Once I finished the list, I called Kelly and we had a great talk. There were a lot of laughs and a lot of tears."

Kelly: "It wasn't like I hadn't asked before. I had asked Dad, my brothers and Grandma Iliff. None of them wanted to talk about Mom. Once she died, Mom was a taboo subject. Dad always said I looked too much like my mother and it brought him too much pain."

Karen, I felt so bad for you, but at age 12, I just couldn't find the words. I remember you began hiccuping uncontrollably soon after your mother's funeral.

Karen: "Those hiccups stopped just a few years ago. The doctors said it was from nerves."

Kelly: "Can you imagine sharing a bedroom with her?"

Karen: "Every substitute teacher would think I was being a smart aleck. They would tell me: 'Once more and you're going to the office.' I was like, 'Sure, make me more nervous.' Off to the office I'd go.

"My home-economics teacher would get furious with me. She made me put a paper bag over my head and hold it around my neck. She made me do that in front of the entire class. She also made me drink dill pickle juice. The craziest thing she made do was to drink a glass of water upside down."

Your brothers, Kenny and Benny, were out of high school when your mother passed.

Kelly: "Karen became a mom to me."

Karen, taking care of your kid sister couldn't have been easy. I mean, you were just a kid.

Karen: "If she had homework, I'd help her with it. Then, I'd do my homework, and cook, and clean. Wherever I went, Kelly went with me. With Kelly on my shoulders, I'd walk from our house in town all the way out to my friend Diane Dexter's house."

That had to have been at least three miles. Karen, I recently was told you've suffered from multiple sclerosis for years.

"Before I realized what I had, I could hardly get my hands off the steering wheel when I came home from work. Doctors told me I was overtired and overworked – stressed.

"I told one doctor, 'I can't be feeling like this, I have to care for my dad and husband who are dealing with grave health issues.' Then, my brother drowned while diving for clams; Dad died five weeks later."

When was that?

Kelly: "In 1993."

Karen: "I was finally diagnosed with MS in '94."

You were widowed early.

Karen: "Joe, my first husband, was diabetic from the time he was in high school. He went for a kidney-pancreas transplant and didn't make it."

Kelly, life after high school?

"Dad and I couldn't seem to see eye-to-eye on anything so I took off. I wound up in California. That's where I met the first of my two abusive ex-husbands."

Karen: "Kelly would call me every week."

Kelly, is it safe to say you became a wild thing?

Karen: "That wouldn't begin to describe her."

Kelly: "Yeah, I was the holy terror of the family."

Any parting thoughts?

Karen: "Kelly was not only my sister, she also was like my child. The townspeople really helped me out a lot with her when she was growing up."

Kelly: "They say it takes a village to raise a child. Well, that's what Lake Village did."

* * *

It was nice meeting Kelly and reuniting with Karen for the first time since the '70s. Like most us, they've endured some rough patches. But they have each other, and it was touching, witnessing these two sisters staring into each others' eyes while holding hands from across the kitchen table – remembering their departed mother.

And, maybe, after all these years, I've found the words.

Nick Parente *(March 2005)*

"...Well, they showed you a statue, told you to pray
They built you temple and locked you away
Aw, but they never told you the price that you pay
For things that you might have done
Only the good die young...
- Billy Joel

It's 9:30 a.m. when Nick Parente makes his way toward my apartment door. It's Friday. Good Friday.

Nick turned 21 last October; he is the possessor of a slight build and stammer. The reedy one has black hair and sports a goatee. He's been bespectacled since grade school, has been a Spiderman fan for years, and loves playing the drums. He's also the owner of the most genuine smile I've ever seen.

Nick is the son of Rick and Nan Parente, both school teachers at Three Creeks Elementary. He has one sibling, younger brother Scott. Nick was named Homecoming King his senior year in 2003. As a junior at Lowell High School, Nick Parente ran cross country for me. As a senior, he became our team's manager.

* * *

"How's it going, Coach?"

All right. You're looking pretty good, kiddo. Come on in. What have you got there?

"I brought you some breakfast. A couple of sweet rolls."

Thanks. How's it going at St. Joe, Nickie?

"I'm just taking one class this year. It's called Feature Writing. We write magazine articles, profiles, we learn about interviewing people. I told my professor, Mrs. Kingman, about this interview. She said to bring her a copy as soon as the paper comes out."

I'll try to watch my double negatives. You're still working at the movie theater, I hear.

"Sometimes, I work the box office now. I also work concessions, clean up, take tickets, but mostly I'm an usher."

Do you have to shush up an occasional obnoxious patron?

"Yeah. And then there's the teeny boppers with their miniature cell phones. They wear them in their ears. Have you seen them?"

Yeah, ah, I think so...

"When they wear hats or hooded sweat shirts you can't even see the things. These people will be looking at me and talking while their standing in line. I say, 'Pardon me?' They'll say, 'Hey, I'm talkin' on the phone.' I tell them, 'Well, be sure and shut that off before entering the theater – please.' Its like they're walking around talking to themselves."

What will they think of next? I don't even have a microwave. Nickie, we're so glad you're still with us. You had me baffled when you were a junior. I knew you had been a good distance runner in middle school and you did well your first two years in high school for Coach Thomas. And then when I got you, as a junior, you'd lost it. I could tell you were trying. You just couldn't go. We all felt so bad, later, when we found out you had leukemia.

"I know. You were never mean to me, Coach. I went to Florida that following year for spring break and didn't want to do anything. Just sleep. Ironically, by getting into the collision with that cow on the 9-mile stretch, I received a blood test; on July 25th of '02, I was diagnosed with chronic myeloid leukemia. Because of Gleevec, a miracle drug, I was doing pretty good for quite a while; I could still skate."

Roller skate?

"Skate boarding, Coach. Then to be prepared for my bone marrow transplant, I went for radiation in Indy. That about killed me. The 11 weeks of Graft vs. Host was the hardest part of the whole ordeal. When I got pneumonia in September of '04, it was touch and go.

"I was on a lot of drugs when I was in the hospital. My parents tell me funny comments I made when I was under heavy medication. Once, when I had just got off the ventilator, I don't remember anything about that, I look up, and all the doctors are wearing lobster suits. I look over to the other side of the room and there's two little gnomes. One is sitting on my window sill laughing and having a good old time. I whispered to my dad, 'Why are the doctors wearing lobster suits?' Dad laughed and assured me we were alone."

I had a similar experience back in the '70s.

"I finally got to go home the day before my 21st birthday. I'd lost all the hair on my head, but not my goatee. I didn't have any strength. I needed a walker and a wheelchair, but luckily I was young enough that my body was strong enough to fight it. Not that there weren't some close calls. It took a lot of therapy to recover. I take fewer pills now. I'm up to 130 pounds. I got down as low as 109. At 6-feet, 1-inch, that's pretty skinny."

Yes, it was Nick. Hey kid, who were some of your favorite teachers back in high school?

"All of my English teachers. Mrs. Iussig. Mr. Schmidt, he was too cool. Miss Casey, she was awesome. My senior year, I had Mrs. Magley; she's been a sweetheart to me. She helped me prepare for my ISTEPs. So did Mrs. Kalvaitis; she was a good teacher, too. She taught US History. I had more in common with those kinds of teachers. The English teachers, they're artsy. They like music and creative stuff. You don't hear much about music when you're sitting in algebra class. It's nice when you have common interests with your teachers. Mr. Mottolese, he was a major influence on me at St. Joe as far as getting into writing. So is Maia Kingman now."

I want to show you something... Here, look at this, it was taken three or four years ago in St. Joe's theater.

"Wow, you and Mr. Mottolese!"

He invited me to read some of the stuff I'd written. His students seemed to enjoy it. You're right, he's really a nice guy. Your favorite drummers?

"Buddy Rich, Gene Krupa, Keith Moon, Tre Cool, Travis Barker, Tommy Lee, John Bonham..."

What do you remember about cross country?

"My freshman year. The coolest kids I've ever met. Like Dustin, Todd, Matt and Adam Willis. I was very intimidated by them. But I knew I was in when Todd called me from his house wanting me to just come over and hang out with him and Dustin and the rest of the team. We were a tight group. I was just this freshman, and it's like, 'What am I doing here?' Nathan Long and I were the only freshmen on the team. They treated us great. Eric Holley and I were always tight. Eric comes over to visit quite a bit."

You still hold the original course record at the middle school kiddo. I changed the course on purpose, just so your record could never be broken. "Appreciate that. Manes.".

So what else you have going on?

"In June, I'm getting six bands together at the Lake County Fairgrounds. We're going to have a benefit concert to raise funds needed to finance volunteers for the National Bone Marrow Registry. Just a positive get-together, play some music, have fun. I'm calling it Scream to Dream xMiraclex. I'm not playing in it, but I really dig all the bands that are going to participate.

"Coming out of that hospital gave me a much more positive outlook. I don't have any enemies. I have a lot better attitude. A life threatening experience just kind of does that to you. There's no other way of explaining it. I just listen to positive music. Listen to what you like, and what you like, is what you are. I like a lot of straight edge hard core music. Are you familiar with it?"

Straight edge... hard core... Oh, yeah, straight core... sure... Groovy.

"When I was in the hospital in Indianapolis, I was fortunate that my grandparents lived there. My best friend Bob Basso also was living in Indy at the time. And my girl friend, Kelly Brown, is from nearby Shelbyville. My family and I were overwhelmed by all the support, cards, and prayers from relatives, friends, and the Lowell Community. It was a difficult time. If I do start to get a little down, I break out those pictures of myself, when I was really sick. I take a look at them. They're my motivator to make the most of every moment.

"I'm really excited about going back to school fulltime next year. I'll have a room of my own. Doctor's orders for first semester since my immune system won't be completely back to normal. St. Joe offers academic support and if I need extra time, I can get it."

It's been great talking to you, Nick.

"Coach?"

Yeah?

"What doesn't kill me, only makes me stronger."

* * *

It was humbling to see my interview with Nick displayed upon an easel at Burdan Funeral Home in Cedar Lake.

Miss you, kiddo.

Nanci Mazzaro-Sanders *(Nov. 2013)*

*"I see trees of green...red roses too
I see 'em bloom... for me and for you
And I think to myself...what a wonderful world.
I see skies of blue...clouds of white
Bright blessed days... dark sacred nights
And I think to myself... what a wonderful world."*
– *Weiss, Douglas, Thiele (performed by Louis Armstrong)*

On Mother's Day, with her children at her side, Nanci Mazzaro-Sanders was diagnosed with pancreatic cancer. The oncologist gave her less than a year. The tumor is lodged against her aorta.

Nanci is a good friend of mine. Being as November is Pancreatic Cancer Awareness Month, this brave woman decided it would be a good time to be interviewed.

Mazzaro-Sanders, 61, lives in Lowell with her husband Brian Sanders. She has raised two adult children from a previous marriage.

Mazzaro-Sanders graduated from Lew Wallace High School and Indiana University, Bloomington.

* * *

"My mom was Polish and my dad was Italian," Mazzaro-Sanders began. *Must have been some good eats at family reunions.*

"Good eating, but a very stubborn home – nobody would give in."
Life after college?

"I became a special education teacher at Jane Ball Elementary School in Cedar Lake. After five years, I quit because I had my daughter. I never went back to teaching."

I didn't know that about you. I just knew you from the Lowell Tribune.

"Because of my illness, I had to quit the newspaper. In late March of this year, I started feeling fatigued all the time. At work, I told Jackie Smith: 'I could go home and take a nap right now.'"

That's not you.

"I told myself it was age. In early May, my urine starting turning colors. Then, it turned reddish-brown. Again, I tried to brush it off: "Do I have a red robe and it's reflecting into the toilet water? Is this my imagination?' And then it really started turning darker and darker. Finally, I decided that I'd better see the doctor."

Then what?

"The doctor did some blood work on me. I had been to the doctor three months earlier for something else and my blood work came out great. Anyway, this was on a Friday and the doctor told me I'd hear from him on Monday."

And?

"I received a phone call at 11:30 that night. He told me that I needed to go to the hospital immediately. He told me that my liver was not functioning."

Lord.

"My husband is a long distance truck driver and was in California, so I had my daughter pick me up. I noticed that she had tears in her eyes. I told her: 'I know, this upsetting. We'll just see what it is.' She said: 'Mom, have you looked in the mirror? You're eyes and skin are yellow.'"

Not good.

"On Sunday morning, May 12, with my kids at my side, an oncologist told me that I had a tumor on my pancreas. I told him: 'Please don't tell me pancreas. I know what that means. I've had friends die from pancreatic cancer. Out of 365 days of the year, DON'T TELL ME PANCREAS ON MOTHER'S DAY!'"

Go ahead and cry, Nanci. Get it out.

"He told me they couldn't do anything more for me. I had to decide whether to go to Chicago or Indianapolis. I chose the University of Chicago.

"On May 16, I told the doctor in Chicago: 'I'm a realist. I don't want anything sugarcoated. I need to know what we're talking here.'"

The doctor's reply?

"Eleven months."

Damn.

"Every time I turn the page of a calendar.... Well, it's a hard thing to do. How did that month go by so fast?"

Some pancreatic cancers are curable.

"Yes, but mine is terminal because the tumor is wrapped around my aorta. My surgeon told me he could never remove the tumor. He told me to pray for a miracle."

Chemotherapy.

"They put me on chemo treatments that are very toxic. I go 12 rounds. I take it every two weeks. I'm on round 10 right now. After 12 rounds, they halt it. A person's body can't take more than that.

"Jeff, I don't feel this tumor whatsoever. The only thing I feel is side effects from the chemo. I can't taste my wonderful pasta fagioli. Everything tastes like metal. I've lost my hair. I didn't think I'd ever wear a wig because of my sweet Aunt Josephine. She was a 4-feet, six-inch Italian lady. I don't know how she kept her head up with that huge wig she wore. It was sooo fake-looking. I told myself, 'I'm not going to look like Auntie Jo.' But wigs have come a long way."

You've been keeping a daily journal on facebook.

"I started it for my children. Then I added my niece, then my girlfriend and it has just grown. I decided to do that because I know how I feel when someone I know is diagnosed with a terminal disease. You don't know how to approach them. You don't know what to say. It can be uncomfortable. Should I say something? Should I just move my cart to aisle five and pretend I don't see her? I don't want any of my friends or family to feel that way.

"If I have to go through this thing, I have to have a purpose. And my purpose is to get the word out about pancreatic cancer. Funds are needed to get research going."

Screening.

"Yes, it's so hard to detect it. They have screening for prostate cancer and breast cancer. Once you get diagnosed with pancreatic, you have a six percent chance of surviving. There are no symptoms. My oncologist said it is on the increase and they don't know why because they don't know what causes it."

Have you made arrangements?

"I told Brian the other day, 'Don't go sticking me in a cornfield.

Some of his family is buried in West Creek out in the middle of nowhere. I need to be right here at Lowell Memorial where I can see what's going on and I can be the first one to know where the fire department is going. I need to be in the mix. I'm a city girl and a reporter. I'm an inquiring mind. You ain't stickin' me in no cornfield! "

That's the Nanci I know. But on a more serious note, I'm sure this situation has changed your outlook on life.

"I call it my ironic blessing. It has given me a new way to live. It has opened my eyes to living life to the fullest. I don't sweat the small stuff. My son and I have gotten so close because of this. Today, I see clouds floating like a tapestry across the sky. I hear birds chirping. I feel a gentle breeze in my face. I smell a delightful rainfall. I crave Farina. It makes me think of my mother every day. Farina is the only thing that tastes good. And it still comes in that same damn box. Mostly, I stop to smell the roses."

* * *

Nanci has quite a support group. She has received sand from the Holy Land, holy water from Fatima, (Italy) and a clutch cross. She posted on facebook that she is a huge Bon Jovi fan and received an 8-by-10 color photograph of the rock group that was signed Jon Bon Jovi. The sender of the photo has remained anonymous. She has received tiny slivers of the rock that Jesus Christ was laid upon after being crucified.

By the end of this month Nanci will have finished all 12 rounds of chemotherapy. Like she said, she comes from a stubborn family and I have no doubt my friend will go the distance in her bout with pancreatic cancer.

And she'll do it with dignity and courage.

Rick Grevenstuk *(Sept. 2014)*

"...If you come down to the river
Bet you gonna find some people who live
You don't have to worry if you got no money
People on the river are happy to give..."
– Creedence Clearwater Revival

I hadn't seen Rick Grevenstuk for 40 years. We both grew up in Lake Village. He was two years behind me in school and took my spot as center fielder for North Newton High School. We were a couple of fast white boys who could run down fly balls.

Soon after high school, Rick moved to neighboring Momence, Illinois. My cousin Tom Hendryx of Cedar Lake rode along with me for the interview. Tommy was in the same graduating class as Rick. They were inseparable while growing up.

Grevenstuk, 55, lives a baseball's toss from the Kankakee River with Kathy, his wife of 35 years, and their son, Grant. They also have a pair of Yorkshire terriers and a solidly built mastiff-rottweiler-pit bull named Diesel. Kathy graduated from Momence High School with my cousin Tony Manes.

Grevenstuk has been gravely ill and is undergoing chemotherapy because of small cell lung cancer in its advanced stages. He refuses to go on disability, and, in fact, works swing shift seven days a week. Our interview was five days before a Sept. 13 fish fry-fundraiser was held to help the family offset medical and living expenses.

* * *

Childhood memories?

"Your cousin Tommy and I would take a blanket and throw it over the clothesline for a makeshift tent," he said. "We'd do that all summer. I wouldn't have wanted to grow up in any other place than Lake Village.

"It was like Gary Niedzwiecki, Tommy and I all had three moms. I could always count on Tom's mom for a plate of lasagna or spaghetti."

Aunt Ann can still put on some pots. She pan-fried a mess of bass for Tommy and me just the other day. Where do you work?

"CSL Behring, it's a pharmaceutical company in Kankakee. I'm a boiler operator. I've been there six years. They've been great. Even my boss, if I do need a day off because of my illness, he says, 'Take a day off.'"

Do you care to talk about your disease?

"I had cancer 17 years ago, when Grant was 5. That was non-small cell cancer. That cancer was in the exact place as my small cell cancer is today, but they're totally different kinds of cancer."

You don't smoke cigarettes.

"Through the years, I've worked at several different places where there were a lot of nasty chemicals. I've had doctors tell me they believed those chemicals had something to do with my cancer. Who's to say? One of my former workmates is dying of cancer as we speak. He's younger than I am."

What companies did you work for?

"I'd rather not mention them by name. At one of those companies, we worked with methanol. That's what they put in Indy cars. Methanol has an invisible flame. As a safety precaution, we used to tie a rag to the end of a pole to see if would catch fire."

Like when miners used caged canaries to tell whether or not deadly gases were present.

"Yeah. I also used to work around toluene. It was taken off the market and replaced by benzene."

Rick, I remember guys working in the by-products section of the coke plant; they would fill their cigarette lighters with benzene. We'd wash off our greasy tools with it. We didn't know. It wasn't until the '80s that the government forced management to issue us respirators and send us to the company clinic twice a year to get checked for cancer.

"I was just glad to have a job in the early '80s."

Because of your condition, you and your immediate family were recently allowed to go out on the field at U.S. Cellular Field and meet some of the Chicago White Sox.

"Yeah, that was something. Harold Baines signed my T-shirt."

Who was the starting pitcher that night?

"Chris Sale."

Did he get the win?

"No, the bullpen imploded."

Rick, we grew up playin' ball on sand lots and goat pastures. Do you remember the first time you walked up those stairs and saw the field at Comiskey Park?

"Like it was yesterday. I miss old Comiskey Park."

In the '70s, it was billed "The World's Largest Outdoor Saloon."

"Bill Veeck. He did some outrageous shit. Remember when the Sox had to wear shorts?"

I try not to. Favorite Sox players?

"Frank Thomas and Mark Buehrle."

Final thoughts?

"I'll tell you what, when I got diagnosed with cancer – it means a lot to me – Gary and Tom were the first ones to call."

* * *

Disability insurance is a great thing for those who really need it, but I know of several guys who take advantage of the system. Guys in their 40s who are on lifetime disability all the while roofing their own houses, chopping firewood and fishing six days a week. They should take a long look at Rick Grevenstuk and then hang their heads in shame.

Like his mother, who also has cancer, Grevenstuk's a worker. I remember "Little Eva" waiting tables at neck-break speed. She took pride in her job and did it well. She still tends bar in Shelby today.

I attended Rick's fundraiser on the 13th. It was held at Sluggers sports bar in Momence. When we were kids, the building was a Ben Franklin dime store.

While at the fundraiser, I talked to a guy from Sumava Resorts by the name of Doug Page. Sumava and Lake Village kids went to elementary school together. Doug told me he remembered the time all his buddies wanted to play baseball one summer day. The Page brothers couldn't play because they had chores to do, including mowing the yard. One by one, every kid who wanted to play ball that day showed up at the Page residence with their own push lawnmower. The work got done. Everybody played ball.

One by one, river folk from Momence, Kankakee, Lake Village, Sumava, Schneider, Pons and Wildwood filled Sluggers on the 13th. Most wore T-shirts with the inscription "Rick's Battle is My Battle." The main course? Smallmouth bass and channel cats caught from our river.

I read a quote by the late Patrick Swayze the other day. He said: "I keep dreaming of a future, a future with a long and healthy life, not lived in the shadow of cancer, but in the light."

I didn't realize it when I took the photograph of Rick and his family in the living room of his home, but later, when I transferred the photo from the camera to the computer, I noticed a light glowing around Rick's head.

I can't explain that.

Bert Pease *(Dec. 2014)*

"My mother watched her loving husband look at her with blankness or contempt and sometimes hatred. And yet dementia is classed as a social condition so that the state is not required to pay for long-term residential care. Calling it what it is – brain damage – is too expensive."
– Rose George, British journalist and author

Bert Pease was born Paniyota Pomonis. She's of Greek ancestry and proud of it. Her soul mate is my buddy Lil' Joe Gutierrez. They've been together for more than 20 years. Bert and Joe went to elementary school together. They are both 74 years of age. Our interview took place at Bert's house in the Woodmar neighborhood of Hammond, where she lives with her adult daughter Cheryl. Lil' Joe did most of the talking and answering of questions for his companion.

Bert Pease suffers from dementia.

* * *

"Bert had always been active and alive in everything she did," Gutierrez began. "She loved to work and make friends. She cooked and baked banana and zucchini bread and gave both away with a smile. And then, things changed."

Talk to me.

"It began four years ago. Her smile appeared less often and she became agitated easily. Her short-term memory became shorter. And, seemingly, for no reason, she would cry. Depression followed. For both of us."

Then what?

"I finally took her to our good friend Dr. Lou Miceli. He ordered a multitude of tests and had to fight city hall for the hospital to do them. Lou is not only a good friend, he's a great doctor who cares.

"When Doc received the results, he called and gave us the news. He told us Bert had vascular dementia. She cried again. I put my arm around her and told her I'd be there at her side. We began to deal with it."

I have no doubt Bert would have done the same for you.

"Doc was up front with her and me. He gave us a compassionate view of the future. He said we had to prepare because when the other foot comes down, it' would come down hard. He suggested making an appointment with a neurologist. We did.

"The first year was rough. As time went on, her condition became more noticeable to friends and family. By the second and third year, taking medicine had become the norm. The other foot is slowly dropping. Fortunately, Bert's daughter Cheryl moved in and became our Mother Teresa. She's worth her weight in gold. Cheryl is not only a loving daughter, but also a companion and friend."

The situation has to be hard on everyone.

"With the bad comes the good. Bert has found solace in attending Mass and singing in church. It's almost as it used to be. She has a quiet dignity and carries herself well. We help each other."

Joe, I can't think of a better person to watch Bert's back. You've watched mine in the past.

'Those afflicted with dementia need love and understanding. Just imagine the frustration in losing the ability to speak your mind, to express your thoughts, to vocalize those simplest of words screaming around in your head fighting to be free. That's the pain of dementia.

"Those not aware of someone's condition may take umbrage or be offended by a seemingly affront with no answer to a question or no response to a greeting. That's where I come in. My eagerness to protect her intensifies. There's an irony in the process of losing awareness. We've become closer."

You break my heart, Joe.

"Bert's condition is deteriorating; confusion has increased. Forming a complete sentence is extremely difficult for her. Trying to understand her simplest request becomes a guessing game, but when we discover her wish, her eyes light up like the sun. God is good.

"We've learned to talk to Him quite often and prayer has become increasingly more important in our life. Bert has difficulty speaking, but there is one sentence she remembers and constantly says."

What's that, mi amigo?

"I love you."

* * *

Sometimes, each other is all we have.

NAME INDEX

Ben-Daniel, Cullen	147
Bohl, Lloyd and Regina	341
Bower, Joy	322
Brigid, Sister	241
Bryant, John	308
Byrne, Maggie	352
Camblin, Ed	177
Campbell, Fuzz	159
Capek, Charlie	292
Carlson, Marcia	38
Catterlin, Mary	311
Coffin, Merritt	180
Cole, Brenda L.	299
Cole, Trilly	280
Collins, Rev. William	2
Cotton, Steve	97
Dalkilic, Mike	213
D'Apice, Dante	183
Darnell, Gina	338
Debois, Paula	21
Del Toro, Victor	42
Dickson, Mary Jane	255
Dummich, Wiley	276
Fisher, Christy	263
Flowers, Yolanta	127
Folmer, Kristy	13
Foster, Nell	244
Frampton, Emonn	123
Frank, Thomas	355
Fullerton, Aubrey	205
Gamez, Rosa	35
Gard, Dave	25
Gard, Rosemary	296
Gardner, Tevin	237
Georgian, Andrea	84

Gorniak, Fred	50
Grady, Lydia	166
Grevenstuk, Rick	376
Grimmer, Butch	76
Gustafson, Ed	326
Hagelburg, Corey	284
Hargrove, Tom	113
Harris, Kimberly Joy	57
Haskell, Neal	221
Hegan, Chuck	190
Howard, R.J.	72
Ivans, Father Joseph	136
Jackson, Willie	46
Johnson, Floyd	163
Johnson, Tom	201
Kanne, Judy	173
Karen	364
Kelly	364
Kersting, Jim	151
Kittle, Ron	217
Klein, Larry	248
Knapp, Ralph	209
Koeppen, Bud	319
Lambert, Eric	271
Lange, Peter	233
Lucas, Marty	330
Lukas, Amy	311
McCloskey, Terry	304
McGee, Mary	9
Millander, Dolly	155
Mille, Don & Gail	60
Moreland, Harold	28
Mueller, Dave	300
Muhhamed, Ish	267
Murchek, Dan	80

Nunemaker, Jessica	53
O'Brien, Sandy	315
Parente, Nick	368
Patterson, Sharon	92
Pease, Bert	380
Petrov, Nick	101
Poore, Mike	288
Roby, Joe	194
Rucker, Bill	68
Sadlowski, Ed	64
Sanders, Nancy Mazzaro	372
Sautter, Edith	140
Schreiner, Jane	5
Schutz, John	197
Sister Brigid	241
Smart, Rasi Sanuchit	120
Smart, Rod	359
Smolke, George	348
Speichert, Sharon	109
Stevens, Rabbi Michael	17
Stoner, Terry	170
Swarner, Bonnie	345
Taylor, John	32
Thiery, Nick	186
Tuohy, Gloria	132
Tidwell, Daisy	259
Utroske, Fred	86
Uselac, Dr. Bilajn	117
Weinberg, Jack	334
Williams, Mayre	225
Wilson, David	105
Wilson, Jonathan	251
Wornhoff, Barney	141

www.ingramcontent.com/pod-product-compliance
Lightning Source LLC
Chambersburg PA
CBHW050100170426
43198CB00014B/2408